Excel® Data Analysis

Analysis

4th Edition

by Paul McFedries

for
dummies®

A Wiley Brand

Excel® Data Analysis For Dummies®, 4th Edition

Published by: **John Wiley & Sons, Inc.,** 111 River Street, Hoboken, NJ 07030-5774, www.wiley.com

Copyright © 2019 by John Wiley & Sons, Inc., Hoboken, New Jersey

Media and software compilation copyright © 2019 by John Wiley & Sons, Inc. All rights reserved.

Published simultaneously in Canada

For general information on our other products and services, please contact our Customer Care Department within the U.S. at 877-762-2974, outside the U.S. at 317-572-3993, or fax 317-572-4002. For technical support, please visit https://hub.wiley.com/community/support/dummies.

Wiley publishes in a variety of print and electronic formats and by print-on-demand. Some material included with standard print versions of this book may not be included in e-books or in print-on-demand. If this book refers to media such as a CD or DVD that is not included in the version you purchased, you may download this material at http://booksupport.wiley.com. For more information about Wiley products, visit www.wiley.com.

Library of Congress Control Number: 2018959384

ISBN 978-1-119-51816-7 (pbk); ISBN 978-1-119-51822-8 (ebk); ISBN 978-1-119-51820-4 (ebk)

Manufactured in the United States of America

C10004980_100318

Contents at a Glance

Table of Contents

Introduction

The world is bursting at the seams with data. It's on our computers, it's in our networks, it's on the web. Some days, it seems to be in the very air itself, borne on the wind. But here's the thing: no one actually cares about data. A collection of data — whether it resides on your PC or some giant server somewhere — is really just a bunch of numbers and text, dates and times. No one cares about data because data doesn't *mean* anything. Data isn't cool. You know what's cool? *Knowledge* is cool. *Insight* is cool.

So how do you turn data into knowledge? How do you tweak data to generate insight? You need to organize that data, and then you need to clean it, sort it, filter it, run calculations on it, and summarize it. In a word, you need to *analyze* the data.

Now for the good news: If you have (or can get) that data into Excel, you have a giant basket of data analysis tools at your disposal. Excel really seems to have been made with data analysis in mind, because it offers such a wide variety of features and techniques for organizing, manipulating, and summarizing just about anything that resides in a worksheet. If you can get your data into Excel, Excel will help you turn that data into knowledge and insight.

This book takes you on a tour of Excel's data-analysis tools. You learn everything you need to know to make your data spill its secrets and to uncover your data's hidden-in-plain-sight wisdom. Best of all, if you already know how to perform the basic Excel chores, you don't need to learn any other fancy-schmancy Excel techniques to get started in data analysis. Sweet? You bet.

About This Book

This book contains 16 chapters (and a bonus appendix), but that doesn't mean that you have to, as the King says gravely in *Alice's Adventures in Wonderland*, "Begin at the beginning and go on till you come to the end: then stop." If you've done a bit of data-analysis work in the past, please feel free to dip into the book wherever it strikes your fancy. The chapters all present their data analysis info and techniques in readily digestible, bite-sized chunks, so you can certainly graze your way through this book.

However, if you're brand-spanking new to data analysis — particularly if you're not even sure what data analysis even *is* — no problem: I'm here to help. To get your data analysis education off to a solid start, I highly recommend reading the book's first three chapters to get some of the basics down cold. From there, you can travel to more advanced territory, safe in the knowledge that you've got some survival skills to fall back on.

What You Can Safely Ignore

This book consists of several hundred pages. Do I expect you to read **every** word on **every** page? Yes, I do. Just kidding! No, of course I don't. Entire sections — heck, maybe even entire *chapters* — might contain information that's not relevant to what you do. That's fine and my feelings won't be hurt if you skim through (or — who's kidding whom? — skip over) those parts of the book.

If time (or attention) is short, what else might you want to ignore? Okay, in many places throughout the book I provide step-by-step instructions to complete some task. Each of those steps includes some bold type that gives you the basic instruction. In many cases, however, below that bold text I offer supplementary information to flesh out or extend or explain the bold instruction. Am I just showing off how much I know about all this stuff? Yes, sometimes. Do you have to read these extended instructions? Nope. Read the bold stuff, for sure, but feel free to skip the details if they seem unnecessary or unimportant.

This book also contains a few sidebars that are marked with the Technical Stuff icon. These sidebars contain extra information that's either a bit on the advanced side or goes into heroic, often obscure, detail about the topic at hand. Do you need to read these sidebars? Not at all. Does that make them a waste of page real estate? I don't think so, because they're useful for folks interested in delving into the minutiae of data analysis. If that's not you, ignore away.

If your time is very limited (or you're just aching to get tonight's binge-watching started), you can also ignore the information contained in this book's Tip sidebars. Yes, these tidbits offer easier and faster ways to get things done, so skipping them to save time now might cost you more time in the long run, but, hey, it's a judgment call.

Foolish Assumptions

This book is for people who are new (or relatively new) to Excel data analysis. That doesn't mean, however, that the book is suitable to people who have never used a PC, Microsoft Windows, or even Excel. So first I assume not only that you have a PC running Microsoft Windows but also that you've had some experience with both. (For the purposes of this book, that just means you know how to start and switch between programs.) I also assume that your PC has a recent version of Excel installed. What does "recent" mean? Well, this book is based on Excel 2019, but you should be fine if you're running Excel 2016 or even Excel 2013.

As I said before, I do *not* assume that you're an Excel expert, but I do assume that you know at least the following Excel basics:

>> Creating, saving, opening, and switching between workbooks.

>> Creating and switching between worksheets.

>> Finding and running commands on the Ribbon.

>> Entering numbers, text, dates, times, and formulas into worksheet cells.

>> Working with Excel's basic worksheet functions.

Icons Used in This Book

Like other books in the *For Dummies* series, this book uses icons, or little margin pictures, to flag things that don't quite fit into the flow of the chapter discussion. Here are the icons that I use:

REMEMBER

This icon marks text that contains some things that useful or important enough that you'd do well to store the text somewhere safe in your memory for later recall.

TECHNICAL STUFF

This icon marks text that contains some for-nerds-only technical details or explanations that you're free to skip.

TIP

This icon marks text that contains a shortcut or easier way to do things, which I hope will make your life — or, at least, the data analysis portion of your life — more efficient.

WARNING

This icon marks text that contains a friendly but unusually insistent reminder to avoid doing something. You have been warned.

Beyond the Book

>> **Examples:** This book's sample Excel workbooks can be found by searching the book's title online at www.dummies.com or at my website: https://www.mcfedries.com/.

>> **Cheat Sheet:** To locate this book's Cheat Sheet, go to www.dummies.com and, again, search for *Excel Data Analysis For Dummies*. See the Cheat Sheet for info on Excel database functions, Boolean expressions, and important statistical terms.

>> **Updates:** If this book has any updates after printing, they will be posted to this book's page at www.dummies.com.

Where to Go from Here

If you're just getting your feet wet with Excel data analysis, flip the page and start perusing the first chapter.

If you have some experience with Excel data analysis or you have a special problem or question, use the Table of Contents or the index to find out where I cover that topic and then turn to that page.

Either way, happy analyzing!

1

Getting Started with Data Analysis

» **Analyzing data by applying conditional formatting**

» **Adding subtotals to summarize data**

» **Grouping related data**

» **Combining data from multiple worksheets**

Chapter **1**

Learning Basic Data-Analysis Techniques

You are awash in data. Information multiplies around you so fast that you wonder how to make sense of it all. I know, you say, I can paste the data into Excel. That way, you've at least got the data nicely arranged in the worksheet cells, and you can add a little formatting to make things somewhat palatable. That's a fine start, but you're often called upon to do more with your data than make it merely presentable. Your boss, your customer, or perhaps just your curiosity requires you to divine some inner meaning from the jumble of numbers and text that litter your workbooks. In other words, you need to *analyze* your data to see what nuggets of understanding you can unearth.

This chapter gets you started down that data-analysis path by exploring a few straightforward but very useful analytic techniques. After discovering what data analysis entails, you investigate a number of Excel data-analysis techniques, including conditional formatting, data bars, color scales, and icon sets. From there, you dive into some useful methods for summarizing your data, including subtotals, grouping, and consolidation. Before you know it, that untamed wilderness of a worksheet will be nicely groomed and landscaped.

What Is Data Analysis, Anyway?

That's an excellent question! Here's an answer that I unpack for you as I go along: *Data analysis* is the application of tools and techniques to organize, study, reach conclusions and sometimes also make predictions about a specific collection of information.

For example, a sales manager might use data analysis to study the sales history of a product, determine the overall trend, and produce a forecast of future sales. A scientist might use data analysis to study experimental findings and determine the statistical significance of the results. A family might use data analysis to find the maximum mortgage it can afford or how much it must put aside each month to finance retirement or the kids' education.

Cooking raw data

The point of data analysis is to understand information on some deeper, more meaningful level. By definition, *raw data* is a mere collection of facts that by themselves tell you little or nothing of any importance. To gain some understanding of the data, you must manipulate the data in some meaningful way. The purpose of manipulating data can be something as simple as finding the sum or average of a column of numbers or as complex as employing a full-scale regression analysis to determine the underlying trend of a range of values. Both are examples of data analysis, and Excel offers a number of tools — from the straightforward to the sophisticated — to meet even the most demanding needs.

Dealing with data

The "data" part of data analysis is a collection of numbers, dates, and text that represents the raw information you have to work with. In Excel, this data resides inside a worksheet, which makes the data available for you to apply Excel's satisfyingly large array of data-analysis tools.

Most data-analysis projects involve large amounts of data, and the fastest and most accurate way to get that data onto a worksheet is to import it from a non-Excel data source. In the simplest scenario, you can copy the data — from a text file, a Word table, or an Access datasheet — and then paste it into a worksheet. However, most business and scientific data is stored in large databases, and Excel offers tools to import the data you need into your worksheet. I talk about all this in more detail later in the book.

After you have your data in the worksheet, you can leave it as a regular range and still apply many data-analysis techniques to the data. However, if you convert the range into a *table*, Excel treats the data as a simple database and enables you to apply a number of database-specific analysis techniques to the table.

Building data models

In many cases, you perform data analysis on worksheet values by organizing those values into a *data model*, a collection of cells designed as a worksheet version of some real-world concept or scenario. The model includes not only the raw data but also one or more cells that represent some analysis of the data. For example, a mortgage amortization model would have the mortgage data — interest rate, principal, and term — and cells that calculate the payment, principal, and interest over the term. For such calculations, you use formulas and Excel's built-in worksheet functions.

Performing what-if analysis

One of the most common data-analysis techniques is *what-if analysis*, for which you set up worksheet models to analyze hypothetical situations. The "what-if" part means that these situations usually come in the form of a question: "What happens to the monthly payment if the interest rate goes up by 2 percent?" "What will the sales be if you increase the advertising budget by 10 percent?" Excel offers four what-if analysis tools: data tables, Goal Seek, Solver, and scenarios, all of which I cover in this book.

Analyzing Data with Conditional Formatting

Many Excel worksheets contain hundreds of data values. You could try to make sense of such largish sets of data by creating complex formulas and wielding Excel's powerful data-analysis tools. However, just as you wouldn't use a steamroller to crush a tin can, sometimes these sophisticated techniques are too much tool for the job. For example, what if all you want are answers to simple questions such as the following:

>> Which cell values are less than 0?

>> What are the top 10 values?

>> Which cell values are above average, and which are below average?

These simple questions aren't easy to answer just by glancing at the worksheet, and the more numbers you're dealing with, the harder it gets. To help you "eyeball" your worksheets and answer these and similar questions, Excel lets you apply *conditional formatting* to the cells. This is a special format that Excel applies only to cells that satisfy some condition, which Excel calls a *rule*. For example, you could apply formatting to show all the negative values in a red font, or you could apply a filter to show only the top 10 values.

Highlighting cells that meet some criteria

A *conditional format* is formatting that Excel applies only to cells that meet the criteria you specify. For example, you can tell Excel to apply the formatting only if a cell's value is greater or less than some specified amount, between two specified values, or equal to some value. You can also look for cells that contain specified text, dates that occur during a specified time frame, and more.

When you set up your conditional format, you can specify the font, border, and background pattern. This formatting helps to ensure that the cells that meet your criteria stand out from the other cells in the range. Here are the steps to follow:

1. **Select the range you want to work with.**

   Just select the data values you want to format. You don't have to (in fact, you shouldn't) select any surrounding data.

2. **Choose Home ⇨ Conditional Formatting.**

3. **Choose Highlight Cells Rules and then select the rule you want to use for the condition.**

   You have six rules to play around with:

   - **Greater than:** Applies the conditional format to cells that have a value larger than a value that you specify.

   - **Less than:** Applies the conditional format to cells that have a value smaller than a value that you specify.

   - **Between:** Applies the conditional format to cells that have a value that is greater than or equal to a minimum value that you specify and less than or equal to a maximum value that you specify.

   - **Equal To:** Applies the conditional format to cells that have a value that is the same as a value that you specify.

   - **Text that Contains:** Applies the conditional format to cells that include the text that you specify.

A **Date Occurring:** Applies the conditional format to cells that have a date value that meets the condition that you specify (such as Yesterday, Last Week, or Next Month).

(There's a seventh rule here — Duplicate Values — that I cover later in this chapter.) A dialog box appears, the name of which depends on the rule you click in Step 3. For example, Figure 1-1 shows the dialog box for the Greater Than rule.

	A	B	C	D	E	F	G	H	I	J	K
1	GDP — % Annual Growth Rates (Source: The World Bank)										
2	Country Name	2007	2008	2009	2010	2011	2012	2013	2014	2015	2016
3	Afghanistan	13.7	3.6	21.0	8.4	6.1	14.4	3.9	2.7	1.3	2.4
4	Albania	5.9	3.8	3.4	3.7	2.6	1.4	1.0	1.8	2.2	3.4
5	Algeria	3.4	2.4	1.6	3.6	2.9	3.4	2.8	3.8	3.8	3.3
6	American Samoa	2.0	-2.6	-4.2	0.4	0.3	-4.4	-2.8	0.9	1.2	-2.6
7	Andorra	0.0	-8.6	-3.7	-5.4	-4.6	-1.6	0.4	2.3	0.8	1.2
8	Angola	22.6	13.8	2.4	3.4	3.9	5.2	6.8	4.8	3.0	-0.7
9	Antigua and Barbuda	9.3	0.0								5.3
10	Arab World	4.6	5.8								3.2
11	Argentina	9.0	4.1								-2.2
12	Armenia	13.7	6.9								0.2
13	Australia	3.7	3.7								2.8
14	Austria	3.6	1.5								1.5
15	Azerbaijan	25.0	10.8	9.4	4.9	0.1	2.2	5.8	2.0	1.1	-3.1
16	Bahamas, The	1.4	-2.3	-4.2	1.5	0.6	3.1	-0.6	-1.2	-3.1	0.2

Dialog box overlay:

Greater Than ? ×

Format cells that are GREATER THAN:

5 ⬆ with Light Red Fill with Dark Red Text ▾

OK   Cancel

FIGURE 1-1: The Greater Than dialog box with some highlighted values.

4. **Type the value to use for the condition.**

   You can also click the button that appears to the right of the text box and then select a worksheet cell that contains the value. Also, depending on the operator, you might need to specify two values.

5. **Use the drop-down list to select the formatting to apply to cells that match your condition.**

   If you're feeling creative, you can make up your own format by selecting the Custom Format command.

6. **Click OK.**

   Excel applies the formatting to cells that meet the condition you specified.

TIP

Excel enables you to specify multiple conditional formats. For example, you can set up one condition for cells that are greater than some value, and a separate condition for cells that are less than some other value. You can apply unique formats to each condition. Follow the same steps to configure the new condition.

Showing pesky duplicate values

You use conditional formatting mostly to highlight numbers greater than or less than some value, or dates occurring within some range. However, you can also use conditional formatting to look for duplicate values in a range. Why would you want to do that? The main reason is that many range or table columns require unique values. For example, a column of student IDs or part numbers shouldn't have duplicates.

Unfortunately, scanning such numbers and picking out the repeat values is hard. Not to worry! With conditional formatting, you can specify a font, border, and background pattern that ensures that any duplicate cells in a range or table stand out from the other cells. Here's what you do:

1. **Select the range that you want to check for duplicates.**

2. **Choose Home ⇨ Conditional Formatting.**

3. **Choose Highlight Cells Rules ⇨ Duplicate Values.**

The Duplicate Values dialog box appears. The left drop-down list has Duplicates selected by default, as shown in Figure 1-2. However, if you want to highlight all the unique values instead of the duplicates, select Unique from this list.

4. **Use the right drop-down list to select the formatting to apply to the cells with duplicate values.**

You can create your own format by choosing the Custom Format command.

5. **Click OK.**

Excel applies the formatting to any cells that have duplicate values in the range.

FIGURE 1-2:
Use the Duplicate Values rule to highlight worksheet duplicates.

Highlighting the top or bottom values in a range

When analyzing worksheet data, looking for items that stand out from the norm is often useful. For example, you might want to know which sales reps sold the most last year, or which departments had the lowest gross margins. To quickly and easily view the extreme values in a range, you can apply a conditional format to the top or bottom values of that range.

You can apply such a format by setting up a *top/bottom rule,* in which Excel applies a conditional format to those items that are at the top or bottom of a range of values. For the top or bottom values, you can specify a number, such as the top 5 or 10, or a percentage, such as the bottom 20 percent. Here's how it works:

1. **Select the range you want to work with.**

2. **Choose Home ⇨ Conditional Formatting.**

3. **Choose Top/Bottom Rules and then select the type of rule you want to create.**

   You have six rules to mess with:

   - **Top 10 Items:** Applies the conditional format to cells that rank in the top *X*, where *X* is a number that you specify (the default is 10).

   - **Top 10 %:** Applies the conditional format to cells that rank in the top *X* %, where *X* is a number that you specify (the default is 10).

   - **Bottom 10 Items:** Applies the conditional format to cells that rank in the bottom *X*, where *X* is a number that you specify (the default is 10).

   - **Bottom 10 %:** Applies the conditional format to cells that rank in the bottom *X* %, where *X* is a number that you specify (the default is 10).

   - **Above Average:** Applies the conditional format to cells that rank above the average value of the range.

   - **Below Average:** Applies the conditional format to cells that rank below the average value of the range.

   A dialog box appears, the name of which depends on the rule that you selected in Step 3. For example, Figure 1-3 shows the dialog box for the Top Ten Items rule.

4. **Type the value to use for the condition.**

   You can also click the button that appears to the right of the text box and then select a worksheet cell that contains the value. Note that you don't need to enter a value for the Above Average and Below Average rules.

5. Use the drop-down list to select the formatting to apply to cells that match your condition.

6. Click OK.

Excel applies the formatting to cells that meet the condition you specified.

	A	B	C	D
1		Sales Rep	2017 Sales	2018 Sales
2		Nancy Freehafer	$996,336	$960,492
3		Andrew Cencini	$606,731	$577,983
4		Jan Kotas	$622,781	$967,580
5		Mariya Sergienko	$765,327	$771,399
6		Steven Thorpe	$863,589	$827,213
7		Michael Neipper	$795,518	$669,394
8		Robert Zare	$722,740	$626,945
9			59	$574,472
10			80	$827,932
11			23	$569,609
12			77	$558,601
13			91	$692,182
14		Andrea Granek	$540,484	$693,762
15		Charles Aster	$650,733	$823,034
16		Karen Reilly	$509,863	$511,569
17		Karen Munson	$503,699	$975,455
18		Vince Voyatzis	$630,263	$599,514
19		Paul Sellars	$779,722	$596,353

Dialog box overlapping rows 9–13:

Top 10 Items   **? ✕**

Format cells that rank in the TOP:

[5 ⏶⏷] with [Light Red Fill with Dark Red Text ⌄]

[OK] [Cancel]

Sheet tabs: GDP Growth Rates | Product Inventory | **Sales Rep Sales** | Tax

FIGURE 1-3:
The Top 10 Items dialog box with the top 5 values highlighted.

REMEMBER

When you set up your top/bottom rule, select a format that ensures that the cells that meet your criteria stand out from the other cells in the range. If none of the predefined formats suits your needs, you can always choose Custom Format and then use the Format Cells dialog box to create a suitable formatting combination. Use the Font, Border, and Fill tabs to specify the formatting you want to apply, and then click OK.

Analyzing cell values with data bars

In some data-analysis scenarios, you might be interested more in the relative values within a range than the absolute values. For example, if you have a table of products that includes a column showing unit sales, you might want to compare the relative sales of all the products.

Comparing relative values is often easiest if you visualize the values, and one of the easiest ways to visualize data in Excel is to use *data bars*, a data visualization feature that applies colored, horizontal bars to each cell in a range of values; these bars appear "behind" (that is, in the background of) the values in the range. The length of the data bar that appears in each cell depends on the value in that cell: the larger the value, the longer the data bar.

Follow these steps to apply data bars to a range:

1. **Select the range you want to work with.**

2. **Choose Home ⇨ Conditional Formatting.**

3. **Choose Data Bars and then select the fill type of data bars you want to create.**

You can apply two type of data bars:

- **Gradient fill:** The data bars begin with a solid color and then gradually fade to a lighter color.

- **Solid fill:** The data bars are a solid color.

Excel applies the data bars to each cell in the range. Figure 1-4 shows an example in the Units column.

	A	B	C
1	Product Name	Units	$ Total
2	Northwind Traders Almonds	20	$ 200
3	Northwind Traders Beer	487	$ 6,818
4	Northwind Traders Boysenberry Spread	100	$ 2,500
5	Northwind Traders Cajun Seasoning	40	$ 880
6	Northwind Traders Chai	40	$ 720
7	Northwind Traders Chocolate	200	$ 2,550
8	Northwind Traders Chocolate Biscuits Mix	85	$ 782
9	Northwind Traders Clam Chowder	290	$ 2,799
10	Northwind Traders Coffee	650	$ 29,900
11	Northwind Traders Crab Meat	120	$ 2,208
12	Northwind Traders Curry Sauce	65	$ 2,600
13	Northwind Traders Dried Apples	40	$ 2,120
14	Northwind Traders Dried Pears	40	$ 1,200
15	Northwind Traders Dried Plums	75	$ 263
16	Northwind Traders Fruit Cocktail	40	$ 1,560
17	Northwind Traders Gnocchi	10	$ 380
18	Northwind Traders Green Tea	275	$ 822
19	Northwind Traders Long Grain Rice	40	$ 280

... Product Inventory | Sales Rep Sales | Taxes | **Data Bars** | Sched... ⊕

FIGURE 1-4: The higher the value, the longer the data bar.

TIP

If your range includes right-aligned values, the gradient-fill data bars are a better choice than the solid-fill data bars because even the longest gradient-fill bars fade to white toward the right edge of the cell, so your range values should mostly appear on a white background, making them easier to read.

Analyzing cell values with color scales

Getting some idea about the overall distribution of values in a range is often useful. For example, you might want to know whether a range has many low values and just a few high values. *Color scales* can help you analyze your data in this way. A color scale compares the relative values in a range by applying shading to each cell, where the color reflects each cell's value.

Color scales can also tell you whether your data includes *outliers:* values that are much higher or lower than the others. Similarly, color scales can help you make value judgments about your data. For example, high sales and low numbers of product defects are good, whereas low margins and high employee turnover rates are bad.

1. Select the range you want to format.

2. Choose Home ⇨ Conditional Formatting.

3. Choose Color Scales and then select the color scale that has the color scheme you want to apply.

The color scales come in two varieties: three-color scales and two-color scales. If your goal is to look for outliers, go with a three-color scale because it helps the outliers stand out more. A three-color scale is also useful if you want to make value judgments about your data, because you can assign your own values to the colors (such as positive, neutral, and negative). Use a two-color scale when you want to look for patterns in the data, because a two-color scale offers less contrast.

Excel applies the color scale to each cell in your selected range.

Analyzing cell values with icon sets

Symbols that have common or well-known associations are often useful for analyzing large amounts of data. For example, a check mark usually means that something is good or finished or acceptable, whereas an *X* means that something is bad or unfinished or unacceptable. Similarly, a green circle is positive, whereas a red circle is negative (think traffic lights). Excel puts these and other symbolic associations to good use with the *icon sets* feature. You use icon sets to visualize the relative values of cells in a range.

REMEMBER

With icon sets, Excel adds a particular icon to each cell in the range, and that icon tells you something about the cell's value relative to the rest of the range. For example, the highest values might be assigned an upward-pointing arrow, the lowest values a downward-pointing arrow, and the values in between a horizontal arrow.

Here's how you apply an icon set to a range:

1. **Select the range you want to format with an icon set.**

2. **Choose Home ⇨ Conditional Formatting.**

3. **Choose Icon Sets and then select the type of icon set you want to apply.**

   The icon sets come in four categories:

   - **Directional:** Indicate trends and data movement

   - **Shapes:** Point out the high (green) and low (red) values in the range

   - **Indicators:** Add value judgments

   - **Ratings:** Show where each cell resides in the overall range of data values

   Excel applies the icons to each cell in the range, as shown in Figure 1-5.

	A	B
1	Student ID	Grade
2	64947	✔ 82
3	69630	▌ 66
4	18324	✖ 52
5	89826	✔ 94
6	63600	✖ 40
7	25089	▌ 62
8	89923	✔ 88
9	13000	▌ 75
10	16895	▌ 66
11	24918	▌ 62
12	45107	▌ 71
13	64090	✖ 53
14	94395	▌ 74
15	58749	▌ 65

FIGURE 1-5:
Excel applies an icon based on the each cell's value.

Creating a custom conditional formatting rule

The conditional formatting rules in Excel — highlight cells rules, top/bottom rules, data bars, color scales, and icon sets — offer an easy way to analyze data through visualization. However, you can also tailor your formatting–based data analysis by creating a custom conditional formatting rule that suits how you want to analyze and present the data.

REMEMBER

Custom conditional formatting rules are ideal for situations in which the normal value judgments — that is, that higher values are good and lower values are bad — don't apply. For example, although the icon sets assume that higher values are more positive than lower values, that's not always true. In a database of product defects, for example, lower values are better than higher ones. Similarly, data bars are based on the relative numeric values in a range, but you might prefer to base them on the relative percentages or on percentile rankings.

To get the type of data analysis you prefer, follow these steps to create a custom conditional formatting rule and apply it to your range:

1. **Select the range you want to analyze with a custom conditional formatting rule.**

2. **Choose Home ⇨ Conditional Formatting ⇨ New Rule.**

The New Formatting Rule dialog box appears.

3. **In the Select a Rule Type box, select the type of rule you want to create.**

4. **Use the controls in the Edit the Rule Description box to edit the rule's style and formatting.**

The controls you see depend on the rule type you selected in Step 3. For example, if you select Icon Sets, you see the controls shown in Figure 1-6.

TIP

With Icon Sets, select Reverse Icon Order if you want to reverse the normal icon assignments, as shown in Figure 1-6.

5. **Click OK.**

Excel applies the conditional formatting to each cell in the range.

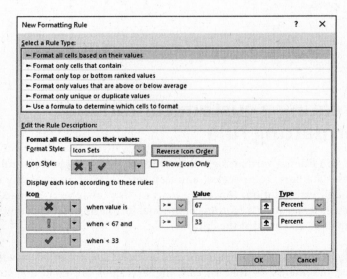

FIGURE 1-6:
Use the New Formatting Rule dialog box to create a custom rule.

TECHNICAL STUFF

HIGHLIGHT CELLS BASED ON A FORMULA

You can apply conditional formatting based on the results of a formula. That is, you set up a logical formula as the conditional formatting criteria. For each cell in which that formula returns TRUE, Excel applies the formatting you specify; for all the other cells, Excel doesn't apply the formatting.

In most cases, you use a comparison formula, or you use an IF function, often combined with another logical function such as AND or OR. In each case, your formula's comparison value must reference only the first value in the range. For example, if the range you are working with is a set of dates in A2:A100, the comparison formula =WEEKDAY(A2)=6 would apply conditional formatting to every cell in the range that occurs on a Friday.

The following steps show you how to apply conditional formatting based on the results of a formula:

1. **Select the range you want to work with.**

2. **Choose Home ⇨ Conditional Formatting ⇨ New Rule.**

   The New Formatting Rule dialog box appears.

3. **Select Use a Formula to Determine Which Cells to Format.**

4. **In the Format Values Where This Formula Is True text box, type the logical formula.**

   The following figure shows an example of using a formula to apply conditional formatting.

(continued)

(continued)

5. **Choose Format, use the Format Cells dialog box to define the rule's style and formatting, and then click OK.**

6. **Click OK.**

   Excel applies the conditional formatting to each cell in the range in which the logical formula returns TRUE.

When you're messing around with formula-based rules, one useful technique is to apply a conditional format based on a formula that compares all the cells in a range to one value in that range. The simplest case is a formula that applies conditional formatting to those range cells that are equal to a cell value in the range. Here's the logical formula to use for such a comparison:

=range=cell

Here, *range* is an absolute reference to the range of cells you want to work with, and *cell* is a relative reference to the comparison cell. For example, to apply a conditional format to those cells in the range A1:A50 that are equal to the value in cell A1, you would use the following logical formula:

=$A$1 : $A$50=A1

Editing a conditional formatting rule

Conditional formatting rules are excellent data visualization tools that can make analyzing your data easier and faster. Whether you're highlighting cells based on criteria, showing cells that are in the top or bottom of the range, or using features such as data bars, color scales, and icon sets, conditional formatting enables you to interpret your data quickly.

But it doesn't follow that all your conditional formatting experiments will be successful ones. For example, you might find that the conditional formatting you used just isn't working out because it doesn't let you visualize your data the way you'd hoped. Similarly, a change in data might require a change in the condition you used. Whatever the reason, you can edit your conditional formatting rules to ensure that you get the best visualization for your data. Here's how:

1. **Select a cell in the range that includes the conditional formatting rule you want to edit.**

   You can select a single cell, multiple cells, or the entire range.

2. Choose Home ⇨ Conditional Formatting ⇨ Manage Rules.

The Conditional Formatting Rules Manager dialog box appears, as shown in Figure 1-7.

FIGURE 1-7:
Use the
Conditional
Formatting Rules
Manager to edit
your rules.

3. Select the rule you want to modify.

If you don't see the rule, click the Show Formatting Rules For drop-down list and then select This Worksheet. The list that appears shows you every conditional formatting rule that you've applied in the current worksheet.

4. Choose Edit Rule.

The Edit Formatting Rule dialog box appears.

5. Make your changes to the rule.

6. Click OK.

Excel returns you to the Conditional Formatting Rules Manager dialog box.

7. Select OK.

Excel updates the conditional formatting.

WARNING

If you have multiple conditional formatting rules applied to a range, the visualization is affected by the order in which Excel applies the rules. Specifically, if a cell already has a conditional format applied, Excel does not overwrite that format with a new one. For example, suppose that you have two conditional formatting rules applied to a list of student grades: one for grades over 90 and one for grades over 80. If you apply the over-80 conditional format first, Excel will never apply the over-90 format because those values are already covered by the over-80 format. The solution is to change the order of the rule. In the Conditional Formatting Rules Manager dialog box, select the rule that you want to modify and then click the Move Up and Move Down button to set the order you want. If you want Excel to stop processing the rest of the rules after it has applied a particular rule, select that rule's Stop If True check box.

Removing conditional formatting rules

Conditional formatting rules are useful critters, but they don't work in all scenarios. For example, if your data is essentially random, conditional formatting rules won't magically produce patterns in that data. You might also find that conditional formatting isn't helpful for certain collections of data or certain types of data. Or, you might find conditional formatting useful for getting a handle on your data set but then prefer to remove the formatting.

Similarly, although the data visualization aspect of conditional formatting rules is part of the appeal of this Excel feature, as with all things visual, you can overdo it. That is, you might end up with a worksheet that has multiple conditional formatting rules and therefore some unattractive and confusing combinations of highlighted cells, data bars, color scales, and icon sets.

If, for whatever reason, you find that a range's conditional formatting isn't helpful or no longer required, you can remove the conditional formatting from that range by following these steps:

1. **Select a cell in the range that includes the conditional formatting rule you want to trash.**

    You can select a single cell, multiple cells, or the entire range.

2. **Choose Home ⇨ Conditional Formatting ⇨ Manage Rules.**

    The Conditional Formatting Rules Manager dialog box appears.

3. **Select the rule you want to remove.**

    If you don't see the rule, use the Show Formatting Rules For list to select This Worksheet, which tells Excel to display every conditional formatting rule that you've applied in the current worksheet.

4. **Choose Delete Rule.**

    Excel removes the rule from the range.

5. **Click OK.**

If you have multiple rules defined and want to remove them all, click the Home tab, choose Conditional Formatting, choose Clear Rules, and then select either Clear Rules from Selected Cells or Clear Rules from Entire Sheet.

Summarizing Data with Subtotals

Although you can use formulas and worksheet functions to summarize your data in various ways — including sums, averages, counts, maximums, and minimums — if you're in a hurry, or if you just need a quick summary of your data, you can get Excel to do the work for you. The secret here is a feature called *automatic subtotals*, which are formulas that Excel adds to a worksheet automatically.

REMEMBER

Excel sets up automatic subtotals based on data groupings in a selected field. For example, if you ask for subtotals based on the Customer field, Excel runs down the Customer column and creates a new subtotal each time the name changes. To get useful summaries, you should sort the range on the field containing the data groupings you're interested in.

Follow these steps to summarize your data with subtotals:

1. **Select a cell within the range you want to subtotal.**

2. **Choose Data ⇨ Subtotal.**

    If you don't see the Subtotal command, choose Outline ⇨ Subtotal. The Subtotal dialog box appears.

3. **Use the At Each Change In list to select the column you want to use to group the subtotals.**

4. **In the Use Function list, select Sum.**

5. **In the Add Subtotal To list, select the check box for the column you want to summarize.**

    Figure 1-8 shows an example where at each change in the Customer field, the sum of that customer's Total cells is displayed.

6. **Click OK.**

    Excel calculates the subtotals and adds them into the range. Note, too, that Excel also adds outline symbols to the range. I talk about outlining in a bit more detail in the next section.

Figure 1-9 shows some subtotals applied to a range.

REMEMBER

Note that in the phrase, *automatic subtotals,* the word *subtotals* is misleading because it implies that you can only summarize your data with totals. Not even close! Using "subtotals," you can also count the values (all the values or just the numeric values), calculate the average of the values, determine the maximum or minimum value, and calculate the product of the values. For statistical analysis, you can also calculate the standard deviation and variance, both of a sample and of a population. To change the summary calculation, follow Steps 1 to 3, open the Use Function drop-down list, and then select the function you want to use for the summary.

FIGURE 1-8:
Use the Subtotal dialog box to apply subtotals to a range.

1 2 3		A	B	C	E	F	G	H
	1	Customer	Country	Region	Unit Price	Quantity	Discount	Total
	2	Cactus Comidas para llevar	Argentina		$ 46.00	7	0%	$ 322.00
	3	Cactus Comidas para llevar	Argentina		$ 7.75	20	0%	$ 155.00
	4	Cactus Comidas para llevar	Argentina		$ 15.00	10	0%	$ 150.00
	5	Cactus Comidas para llevar	Argentina		$ 45.60	8	0%	$ 364.80
	6	Cactus Comidas para llevar	Argentina		$ 14.00	20	0%	$ 280.00
	7	**Cactus Comidas para llevar Total**						$ 1,271.80
	8	Océano Atlántico Ltda.	Argentina		$ 6.00	5	0%	$ 30.00
	9	Océano Atlántico Ltda.	Argentina		$ 21.35	20	0%	$ 427.00
	10	Océano Atlántico Ltda.	Argentina		$ 30.00	6	0%	$ 180.00
	11	Océano Atlántico Ltda.	Argentina		$ 34.80	5	0%	$ 174.00
	12	Océano Atlántico Ltda.	Argentina		$ 21.00	30	0%	$ 630.00
	13	Océano Atlántico Ltda.	Argentina		$ 81.00	15	0%	$ 1,215.00
	14	Océano Atlántico Ltda.	Argentina		$ 18.00	10	0%	$ 180.00
	15	Océano Atlántico Ltda.	Argentina		$ 13.00	15	0%	$ 195.00
	16	**Océano Atlántico Ltda. Total**						$ 3,031.00
	17	Rancho grande	Argentina		$ 81.00	5	0%	$ 405.00
	18	Rancho grande	Argentina		$263.50	2	0%	$ 527.00
	19	Rancho grande	Argentina		$ 17.45	6	0%	$ 104.70
	20	Rancho grande	Argentina		$ 32.00	6	0%	$ 192.00

Product Defects | Schedule | Invoices | Consolidated Sales | Co ...

FIGURE 1-9:
Some subtotals applied to the Total column for each customer.

Grouping Related Data

To help you analyze a worksheet, you can control a worksheet range display by grouping the data based on the worksheet formulas and data. Grouping the data creates a worksheet outline, which works similarly to the outline feature in

Microsoft Word. In a worksheet outline, you can *collapse* sections of the sheet to display only summary cells (such as quarterly or regional totals), or *expand* hidden sections to show the underlying detail. Note that when you add subtotals to a range, as I describe in the previous section, Excel automatically groups the data and displays the outline tools.

REMEMBER

Not all worksheets can be grouped, so you need to make sure that your worksheet is a candidate for outlining:

» The worksheet must contain formulas that reference cells or ranges directly adjacent to the formula cell. Worksheets with SUM functions that subtotal cells above or to the left are particularly good candidates for outlining.

» There must be a consistent pattern to the direction of the formula references. For example, a worksheet with formulas that always reference cells above or to the left can be outlined. Excel won't outline a worksheet with, say, SUM functions where some of the range references are above the formula cell and some are below.

Here are the steps to follow group-related data:

1. **Display the worksheet you want to outline.**

2. **Choose Data ⇨ Group ⇨ Auto Outline.**

If you don't see the Group command, choose Outline ⇨ Group. Excel outlines the worksheet data.

As pointed out in Figure 1-10, Excel uses *level bars* to indicate the grouped ranges and *level numbers* to indicate the various levels of the underlying data available in the outline.

Here are some ways you can use the outline to control the range display:

» Click a Collapse button to hide the range indicated by the level bar.

» Select a level number to collapse multiple ranges that are on the same outline level.

» Click an Expand button to view a collapsed range again.

» Select a level number to show multiple collapsed ranges that are on the same outline level.

Level numbers   Collapse button   Expand button

	A	B	C	D	E	I	M	Q	R
1		Jan	Feb	Mar	1st Quarter	2nd Quarter	3rd Quarter	4th Quarter	TOTAL
2	*Sales*								
3	Division I	23,500	23,000	24,000	70,500	75,500	74,000	74,000	294,000
4	Division II	28,750	27,800	29,500	86,050	91,500	90,000	91,000	358,550
5	Division III	24,400	24,000	25,250	73,650	80,350	77,500	78,500	310,000
6	SALES TOTAL	76,650	74,800	78,750	230,200	247,350	241,500	243,500	962,550
7	*Expenses*								
8	Cost of Goods	6,132	5,984	6,700	18,816	19,788	19,320	19,480	77,404
9	Advertising	4,600	4,200	5,200	14,000	15,750	15,900	14,900	60,550
10	Rent	2,100	2,100	2,100	6,300	6,300	6,300	6,300	25,200
11	Supplies	1,300	1,200	1,400	3,900	3,950	4,100	4,000	15,950
12	Salaries	16,000	16,000	16,500	48,500	50,000	51,000	52,000	201,500
13	Shipping	14,250	13,750	14,500	42,500	44,250	44,000	46,500	177,250
14	Utilities	500	600	600	1,700	1,800	1,850	1,925	7,275
15	EXPENSES TOTAL	44,882	43,834	47,000	135,716	141,838	142,470	145,105	565,129
16	GROSS PROFIT	31,768	30,966	31,750	94,484	105,512	99,030	98,395	397,421
17									

FIGURE 1-10:
When you group a range, Excel displays its outlining tools.   Level bar

Consolidating Data from Multiple Worksheets

Companies often distribute similar worksheets to multiple departments to capture budget numbers, inventory values, survey data, and so on. Those worksheets must then be combined into a summary report showing company-wide totals. Combining multiple worksheets into a summary report is called *consolidating* the data.

Sounds like a lot of work, right? It sure is, if you do it manually, so forget that. Instead, Excel can consolidate your data automatically. You can use the Consolidate feature to consolidate the data in either of two ways:

>> **By position:** Excel consolidates the data from two or more worksheets, using the same range coordinates on each sheet. This is the method to use if the worksheets you're consolidating have an identical layout.

>> **By category:** Excel consolidates the data from two or more worksheets by looking for identical row and column labels in each sheet. This is the method to reach for if the worksheets you're consolidating have different layouts but common labels.

In both cases, you specify one or more *source ranges* (the ranges that contain the data you want to consolidate) and a *destination range* (the range where the consolidated data will appear).

Consolidating by position

Here are the steps to trudge through if you want to consolidate multiple work-sheets by position:

1. **Create a new worksheet that uses the same layout — including row and column labels — as the sheets you want to consolidate.**

   The identical layout in this new worksheet is your destination range.

2. **If necessary, open the workbooks that contain the worksheets you want to consolidate.**

   If the worksheets you want to consolidate are in the current workbook, you can skip this step.

3. **In the new worksheet from Step 1, select the upper-left corner of the destination range.**

4. **Choose Data ⇨ Consolidate.**

   The Consolidate dialog box appears.

5. **Use the Function list to select the summary function you want to use.**

6. **In the Reference text box, select one of the ranges you want to consolidate.**

7. **Click Add.**

   Excel adds the range to the All References list, as shown in Figure 1-11.

8. **Repeat Steps 6 and 7 to add all the consolidation ranges.**

9. **Click OK.**

   Excel consolidates the data from the source ranges and displays the summary in the destination range.

FIGURE 1-11: Consolidate multiple worksheets by adding a range from each one.

TIP

If the source data changes, you probably want to reflect those changes in the consolidation worksheet. Rather than run the entire consolidation over again, a much easier solution is to select the Create Links to Source Data check box in the Consolidate dialog box. You can then update the consolidation worksheet by choosing Data⇨Refresh All.

Consolidating by category

Here are the steps to follow to consolidate multiple worksheets by category:

1. **Create a new worksheet for the consolidation.**

You use this worksheet to specify your destination range.

2. **If necessary, open the workbooks that contain the worksheets you want to consolidate.**

If the worksheets you want to consolidate are in the current workbook, you can skip this step.

3. **In the new worksheet from Step 1, select the upper-left corner of the destination range.**

4. **Choose Data⇨Consolidate.**

The Consolidate dialog box appears.

5. **In the Function list, select the summary function you want to use.**

6. **In the Reference text box, select one of the ranges you want to consolidate.**

When you're selecting the range, be sure to include the row and column labels in the range.

7. **Click Add.**

Excel adds the range to the All References list.

8. **Repeat Steps 6 and 7 to add all the consolidation ranges.**

9. **If you have labels in the top row of each range, select the Top Row check box.**

10. **If you have labels in the left-column row of each range, select the Left Column check box.**

Figure 1-12 shows a completed version of the Consolidate dialog box.

11. **Click OK.**

Excel consolidates the data from the source ranges and displays the summary in the destination range.

FIGURE 1-12:
When consolidating by category, tell Excel where your labels are located.

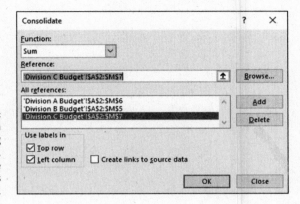

» **Analyzing your data using the Goal Seek tool**

» **Creating and running scenarios**

» **Optimizing your data with the Solver tool**

Chapter **2**

Working with Data-Analysis Tools

W hen it comes to data analysis, you're best off getting Excel to perform most — or, ideally, all — of the work. After all, Excel is a complex, powerful, and expensive piece of software, so why shouldn't it take on the lion's share of the data-analysis chores? Sure, you still have to get your data into the worksheet (although a bit later in the book, I talk about ways to get Excel to help with that chore, too), but after you've done that, it's time for Excel to get busy.

In this chapter, you investigate some built-in Excel tools that will handle most of the data analysis dirty work. I show you how to build two different types of data tables; give you the details on using the very cool Goal Seek tool; delve into scenarios and how to use them for fun and profit; and take you on a tour of the powerful Solver add-in.

Working with Data Tables

If you want to study the effect that different input values have on a formula, one solution is to set up the worksheet model and then manually change the formula's input cells. For example, if you're calculating a loan payment, you can enter different interest rate values to see what effect changing the value has on the payment.

The problem with modifying the values of a formula input is that you see only a single result at one time. A better solution is to set up a *data table*, which is a range that consists of the formula you're using and multiple input values for that formula. Excel automatically creates a solution to the formula for each different input value.

REMEMBER

Data tables are an example of *what-if analysis*, which is perhaps the most basic method for analyzing worksheet data. With what-if analysis, you first calculate a formula D, based on the input from variables A, B, and C. You then say, "What happens to the result if I change the value of variable A?" "What happens if I change B or C?" and so on.

WARNING

Don't confuse data tables with the Excel tables that I talk about in Chapter 3. Remember that a data table is a special range that Excel uses to calculate multiple solutions to a formula.

Creating a basic data table

The most basic type of data table is one that varies only one of the formula's input cells. Not even remotely surprisingly, this basic version is known far and wide as a *one-input data table*. Here are the steps to follow to create a one-input data table:

1. **Type the input values.**

   - To enter the values in a column, start the column one cell down and one cell to the left of the cell containing the formula, as shown in Figure 2-1.

   - To enter the values in a row, start the row one cell up and one cell to the right of the cell containing the formula.

2. **Select the range that includes the input values and the formula.**

3. **Choose Data ⇨ What-If Analysis ⇨ Data Table to open the Data Table dialog box.**

4. **Enter the address of the *input cell,* which is the cell referenced by the formula that you want the data table to vary.**

   That is, for whatever cell you specify, the data table will substitute each of its input values into that cell and calculate the formula result. You have two choices:

Formula

FIGURE 2-1:
This data table
has the input
values in a
column.

Input values

- If the input values are in a column, enter the input cell's address in the Column Input Cell text box. In the example shown in Figure 2-1, the data table's input values are annual interest rates, so the column input cell is C2, as shown in Figure 2-2.

- If you entered the input values in a row, enter the input cell's address in the Row Input Cell text box.

FIGURE 2-2:
Enter the address
of the input cell.

5. Click OK.

Excel fills the input table with the results. Figure 2-3 shows the results of the example data table.

WARNING

When you see the data table results, you might find that all the calculated values are identical. What gives? The problem most likely is Excel's current calculation mode. Choose Formulas⇨Calculation Options⇨Automatic, and the data table results should recalculate to the correct values.

FIGURE 2-3:
The data table results.

Creating a two-input data table

Rather than vary a single formula input at a time — as in the one-input data table I discuss in the previous section — Excel also lets you kick things up a notch by enabling you to set up a *two-input* data table. As you might have guessed, a two-input data table is one that varies two formula inputs at the same time. For example, in a loan payment worksheet, you could set up a two-input data table that varies both the interest rate and the term.

To set up a two-input data table, you must set up two ranges of input cells. One range must appear in a column directly below the formula, and the other range must appear in a row directly to the right of the formula. Here are the steps to follow:

1. **Type the input values:**

   - To enter the column values, start the column one cell down and one cell to the left of the cell containing the formula.

   - To enter the row values, start the row one cell up and one cell to the right of the cell containing the formula.

   Figure 2-4 shows an example.

2. **Select the range that includes the input values and the formula.**

3. **Choose Data ⇨ What-If Analysis ⇨ Data Table to open the Data Table dialog box.**

4. **In the Row Input Cell text box, enter the cell address of the input cell that corresponds to the row values you entered.**

   In the example shown in Figure 2-4, the row values are term inputs, so the input cell is C3 (see Figure 2-5).

B7	▼	:	×	✓	fx	=PMT(C2 / 12, C3 * 12, C4)

⊿	A	B	C	D	E	F
1	Loan Payment Analysis					
2		Interest Rate (Annual)	3.0%			
3		Term (Years)	25			
4		Principal	$100,000			
5						
6		Monthly Payment			Term	
7		($474.21)	15	20	25	30
8		1.0%				
9		1.5%				
10		2.0%				
11	Interest Rate	2.5%				
12		3.0%				
13		3.5%				
14		4.0%				
15		5.5%				
16						

◄ ► | Basic Data Table | Two-Input Data Table | ⊕ | : | ◄

FIGURE 2-4:
For a two-input data table, enter one set of values in a column and the other in a row.

5. **In the Column Input Cell text box, enter the cell address of the input cell you want to use for the column values.**

In the example shown in Figure 2-4, the column values are interest rate inputs, so the input cell is C2 (see Figure 2-5).

Data Table   ?   ✕

Row input cell: C3   ⬆

Column input cell: C2   ⬆

OK   Cancel

FIGURE 2-5:
Enter the addresses of the input cells.

6. **Click OK.**

Excel displays the results. Figure 2-6 shows the results of the example two-input data table.

TECHNICAL STUFF

When you run the Data Table command, Excel enters an array formula in the interior of the data table. The formula is a TABLE function (a special function available only by using the Data Table command) with the following syntax:

```
{=TABLE(row_input_ref, column_input_ref)}
```

Here, *row_input_ref* and *column_input_ref* are the cell references you entered in the Data Table dialog box. The braces ({ }) indicate an array, which means that you can't change or delete individual elements within the results. If you want to change the results, you need to select the entire data table and then run the Data Table command again. If you want to delete the results, you must select the entire array and then delete it.

The following figure caption appears in the left margin:

FIGURE 2-6:
The two-input
data table results.

The spreadsheet figure shows:

Formula bar: C8 | {=TABLE(C3,C2)}

	A	B	C	D	E	F
1	Loan Payment Analysis					
2		Interest Rate (Annual)	3.0%			
3		Term (Years)	25			
4		Principal	$100,000			
5						
6		Monthly Payment		Term		
7		($474.21)	15	20	25	30
8		1.0%	($598.49)	($459.89)	($376.87)	($321.64)
9		1.5%	($620.74)	($482.55)	($399.94)	($345.12)
10		2.0%	($643.51)	($505.88)	($423.85)	($369.62)
11	Interest Rate	2.5%	($666.79)	($529.90)	($448.62)	($395.12)
12		3.0%	($690.58)	($554.60)	($474.21)	($421.60)
13		3.5%	($714.88)	($579.96)	($500.62)	($449.04)
14		4.0%	($739.69)	($605.98)	($527.84)	($477.42)
15		5.5%	($817.08)	($687.89)	($614.09)	($567.79)
16						

Sheet tabs: Basic Data Table | **Two-Input Data Table**

Skipping data tables when calculating workbooks

Because a data table is an array, Excel treats it as a unit, so a worksheet recalculation means that the entire data table is always recalculated. Such a recalculation is not a big problem for a small data table that has just a few dozen formulas. However, it's not uncommon to have data tables with hundreds or even thousands of formulas, and these larger data tables can really slow down worksheet recalculation.

If you're working with a large data table, you can reduce the time it takes for Excel to recalculate the workbook if you configure Excel to bypass data tables when it's running the recalculation. Here are the two methods you can use:

» Choose Formulas ➪ Calculation Options ➪ Automatic Except for Data Tables.

» Choose File ➪ Options to open the Excel Options dialog box, choose Formulas, select the Automatic Except for Data Tables option, and then click OK.

The next time you calculate a workbook, Excel bypasses the data tables.

TIP

When you want to recalculate a data table, you can repeat either of the preceding procedures and then choose the Automatic option. On the other hand, if you prefer to leave the Automatic Except for Data Tables option selected, you can still recalculate the data table by selecting any cell inside the data table and either choosing Formulas ➪ Calculate Now or pressing F9.

Analyzing Data with Goal Seek

What if you already know the formula result you need and you want to produce that result by tweaking one of the formula's input values? For example, suppose that you know that you need to have $100,000 saved for your children's college education. In other words, you want to start an investment now that will be worth $100,000 at some point in the future.

This is called a *future value* calculation, and it requires three parameters:

>> The term of the investment

>> The interest rate you earn on the investment

>> The amount of money you invest each year

Assume that you need that money 18 years from now and that you can make a four percent annual return on your investment. Here's the question that remains: How much should you invest each year to make your goal?

Sure, you could waste large chunks of your life guessing the answer. Fortunately, you don't have to, because you can put Excel's Goal Seek tool to work. Goal Seek works by trying dozens of possibilities — called *iterations* — that enable it to get closer and closer to a solution. When Goal Seek finds a solution (or finds a solution that's as close as it can get), it stops and shows you the result.

You must do three things to set up your worksheet for Goal Seek:

>> Set up one cell as the *changing cell,* which is the formula input cell value that Goal Seek will manipulate to reach the goal. In the college fund example, the formula cell that holds the annual deposit is the changing cell.

>> Set up the other input values for the formula and give them proper initial values. In the college fund example, you enter four percent for the interest rate and 18 years for the term.

>> Create a formula for Goal Seek to use to reach the goal. In the college fund example, you use the FV() function, which calculates the future value of an investment given an interest rate, term, and regular deposit.

When your worksheet is ready for action, here are the steps to follow to get Goal Seek on the job:

1. **Select Data ⇨ What-If Analysis ⇨ Goal Seek.**

   The Goal Seek dialog box appears.

2. **In the Set Cell box, enter the address of the cell that contains the formula you want Goal Seek to work with.**

3. **In the To Value text box, enter the value that you want Goal Seek to find.**

4. **In the By Changing Cell box, enter the address of the cell that you want Goal Seek to modify.**

Figure 2-7 shows an example model for the college fund calculation as well as the completed Goal Seek dialog box.

FIGURE 2-7:
Using Goal Seek
to calculate the
annual deposit
required to
end up with
$100,000 in a
college fund.

5. **Click OK.**

Goal Seek adjusts the changing cell value until it reaches a solution. When it's done, the formula shows the value you entered in Step 3, as shown in Figure 2-8.

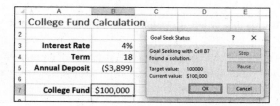

FIGURE 2-8:
Goal Seek took all
of a second or
two to find a
solution.

6. **Click OK to accept the solution.**

TECHNICAL
STUFF

In some cases, Goal Seek might not find an exact solution to your model. Failing to find a solution can happen if Goal Seek takes a relatively long time to find a solution, because Goal Seek stops either after 100 iterations or if the current result is within 0.001 of the desired result.

You can get a more accurate solution by increasing the number of iterations that Goal Seek can use, by reducing the value that Goal Seek uses to mark a solution as "close enough," or both. Choose File ⇨ Options and then choose Formulas. Increase the value of the Maximum Iterations spin button, decrease the value in the Maximum Change text box, or both, and then click OK.

Analyzing Data with Scenarios

Many formulas require a number of input values to produce a result. Earlier in this chapter, in the "Working with Data Tables" section, I talk about using data tables to quickly see the results of varying one or two of those input values. Handy stuff, for sure, but when you're analyzing a formula's results, manipulating three or more input values at a time and performing this manipulation in some systematic way often help. For example, one set of values might represent a best-case approach, whereas another might represent a worst-case approach.

In Excel, each of these coherent sets of input values — known as *changing cells* — is called a *scenario.* By creating multiple scenarios, you can quickly apply these different value sets to analyze how the result of a formula changes under different conditions.

Excel scenarios are a powerful data-analysis tool for a number of reasons. First, Excel enables you to enter up to 32 changing cells in a single scenario, so you can create models that are as elaborate as you need. Second, no matter how many changing cells you have in a scenario, Excel enables you to show the scenario's result with just a few taps or clicks. Third, because the number of scenarios you can define is limited only by the available memory on your computer, you can effectively use as many scenarios as you need to analyze your data model.

REMEMBER

When building a worksheet model, you can use a couple of techniques to make the model more suited to scenarios:

>> Group all your changing cells in one place and label them.

>> Make sure that each changing cell is a constant value. If you use a formula for a changing cell, another cell could change the formula result and throw off your scenarios.

Create a scenario

If scenarios sound like your kind of data-analysis tool, here are the steps to follow to create a scenario for a worksheet model that you've set up:

1. Choose Data ⇨ What-If Analysis ⇨ Scenario Manager.

The Scenario Manager dialog box appears.

2. Click Add.

The Add Scenario dialog box appears.

3. **In the Scenario Name box, type a name for the scenario.**

4. **In the Changing Cells box, enter the cells you want to change in the scenario.**

   You can type the address of each cell or range, separating each by a comma, or you can select the changing cells directly in the worksheet.

5. **In the Comment box, enter a description for the scenario.**

TIP

Your scenarios appear in the Scenario Manager, and for each scenario, you see its changing cells and its description. The description is often very useful, particularly if you have several scenarios defined, so be sure to write a detailed description to help you differentiate your scenarios later on.

Figure 2-9 shows a worksheet model for a mortgage analysis and a filled-in Add Scenario dialog box.

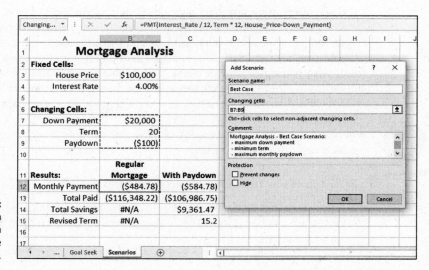

FIGURE 2-9: Creating a scenario for a mortgage analysis.

6. **Click OK.**

   The Scenario Values dialog box appears.

7. **In the text boxes, enter a value for each changing cell.**

   Figure 2-10 shows some example values for a scenario.

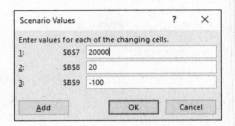

FIGURE 2-10:
Example values
for a scenario's
changing cells.

8. **To add more scenarios, click Add and then repeat Steps 3 through 7.**

9. **Click OK.**

   The Scenario Values dialog box closes and then Scenario Manager dialog box returns, showing the scenarios you've added.

10. **Click Close.**

Apply a scenario

The real value of a scenario is that no matter how many changing cells you've defined or how complicated the formula is, you can apply any scenario with just a few straightforward steps. Don't believe me? Here, I'll prove it:

1. **Choose Data ⇨ What-If Analysis ⇨ Scenario Manager.**

   The Scenario Manager dialog box appears.

2. **Select the scenario you want to display.**

3. **Click Show.**

   Without even a moment's hesitation, Excel enters the scenario values into the changing cells and displays the formula result.

4. **Feel free to repeat Steps 2 and 3 to display other scenarios. When it's this easy, why not?**

5. **When you've completed your analysis, click Close.**

Edit a scenario

If you need to make changes to a scenario, you can edit the name, the changing cells, the description, and the scenario's input values. Here are the steps to follow:

1. **Choose Data ⇨ What-If Analysis ⇨ Scenario Manager.**

   The Scenario Manager dialog box appears.

2. **Select the scenario you want to modify.**

3. **Click Edit.**

   The Edit Scenario dialog box appears.

4. **Modify the scenario name, changing cells, and comment, as needed.**

5. **Click OK.**

   The Scenario Values dialog box appears.

6. **Modify the scenario values, as needed.**

7. **Click OK.**

8. **Click Close.**

Delete a scenario

If you have a scenario that has worn out its welcome, you should delete it to reduce clutter in the Scenario Manager. Here are the steps required:

1. **Choose Data ⇨ What-If Analysis ⇨ Scenario Manager.**

   The Scenario Manager dialog box appears.

2. **Select the scenario you want to remove.**

   Excel does not ask you to confirm the deletion, so double- (perhaps even triple-) check that you've selected the correct scenario.

   WARNING

3. **Click Delete.**

   The Scenario Manager gets rids of the scenario.

4. **Click Close.**

Optimizing Data with Solver

Spreadsheet tools such as Goal Seek that change a single variable are useful, but unfortunately most problems in business are not so easy. You'll usually face formulas with at least two and sometimes dozens of variables. Often, a problem will have more than one solution, and your challenge will be to find the *optimal* solution (that is, the one that maximizes profit, or minimizes costs, or matches other criteria). For these bigger challenges, you need a more muscular tool. Excel has just the answer: Solver. Solver is a sophisticated optimization program that enables you to find the solutions to complex problems that would otherwise require high-level mathematical analysis.

Understanding Solver

Solver, like Goal Seek, uses an iterative method to perform its calculations. Using iteration means that Solver tries a solution, analyzes the results, tries another solution, and so on. However, this cyclic iteration isn't just guesswork on Solver's part. That would be silly. No, Solver examines how the results change with each new iteration and, through some sophisticated mathematical processes (which, thankfully, happen way in the background and can be ignored), can usually tell in what direction it should head for the solution.

The advantages of Solver

Yes, Goal Seek and Solver are both iterative, but that doesn't make them equal. In fact, Solver brings a number of advantages to the table:

>> **Solver enables you to specify multiple adjustable cells.** You can use up to 200 adjustable cells in all.

>> **Solver enables you to set up constraints on the adjustable cells.** For example, you can tell Solver to find a solution that not only maximizes profit, but also satisfies certain conditions, such as achieving a gross margin between 20 and 30 percent, or keeping expenses less than $100,000. These conditions are said to be *constraints* on the solution.

>> **Solver seeks not only a desired result (the "goal" in Goal Seek) but also the optimal one.** For example, looking for an optimal result might mean that you can find a solution that's the maximum or minimum possible.

>> **For complex problems, Solver can generate multiple solutions.** You can then save these different solutions under different scenarios.

When should you use Solver?

Okay, I'll be straight with you: Solver is a powerful tool that most Excel users don't need. It would be overkill, for example, to use Solver to compute net profit given fixed revenue and cost figures. Many problems, however, require nothing less than the Solver approach. These problems cover many different fields and situations, but they all have the following characteristics in common:

>> **They have a single *objective cell* (also called the *target cell*) that contains a formula you want to maximize, minimize, or set to a specific value.** This formula could be a calculation such as total transportation expenses or net profit.

>> **The objective cell formula contains references to one or more *variable cells* (also called *unknowns* or *changing cells*).** Solver adjusts these cells to find the optimal solution for the objective cell formula. These variable cells might include items such as units sold, shipping costs, or advertising expenses.

>> **Optionally, there are one or more *constraint cells* that must satisfy certain criteria.** For example, you might require that advertising be less than 10 percent of total expenses, or that the discount to customers be an amount between 40 and 60 percent.

For example, Figure 2-11 shows a worksheet data model that's all set up for Solver. The model shows revenue (price times units sold) and costs for two products, the profit produced by each products, and the total profit. The question to be answered here is this: How many units of each product must be sold to get a total profit of $0? This is known in business as a *break-even analysis.*

FIGURE 2-11: The goal for this data model is to find the break-even point (where total profit is $0).

| B8 | | ⋮ | × ✓ | f_x | =B7 * B4 - C4 |

⊿	A	B	C	D
1				
2		**Inflatable Dartboard**	**Dog Polisher**	
3	**Price**	$24.95	$19.95	
4	**Units**	1	1	
5	**Revenue**	$25	$20	
6				
7	**Unit Cost**	$12.50	$9.50	
8	**Variable Costs**	$12	$9	
9	**Fixed Costs**	$100,000	$75,000	
10	**Total Costs**	$100,012	$75,009	
11				
12	**Product Profit**	-$99,987	-$74,989	
13				
14	**Total Profit**	-$174,975		
15				

◂ ▸ ... Goal Seek | Scenarios | **Solver** ⊕

That sounds like a straightforward Goal Seek task, but this model has a tricky aspect: the variable costs. Normally, the variable costs of a product are its unit cost times the number of units sold. If it costs $10 to produce product A, and you sell 10,000 units, the variable costs for that product are $100,000. However, in the real world, such costs are often mixed up among multiple products. For example, if you run a joint advertising campaign for two products, those costs are borne by both products. Therefore, this model assumes that the costs of one product are related to the units sold of the other. Here, for example, is the formula used to calculate the costs of the Inflatable Dartboard (cell B8):

```
=B7 * B4 - C4
```

In other words, the variable costs for the Inflatable Dartboard are reduced by one dollar for every unit sold of the Dog Polisher. The latter's variable costs use a similar formula (in cell C8):

```
=C7 * C4 - B4
```

Having the variable costs related to multiple products puts this data model outside of what Goal Seek can do, but Solver is up to the challenge. Here are the special cells in the model that Solver will use:

>> The objective cell is C14; the total profit and the target solution for this formula is 0 (that is, the break-even point).

>> The changing cells are B4 and C4, which hold the number of units sold for each product.

>> For constraints, you might want to add that both the product profit cells (B12 and C12) should also be 0.

Loading the Solver add-in

An *add-in* is software that adds one or more features to Excel. Installing add-ins gives you additional Excel features that aren't available in the Ribbon by default. Bundled add-in software is included with Excel but isn't automatically installed when you install Excel. Several add-ins come standard with Excel, including Solver, which enables you to solve optimization problems.

You install the bundled add-ins by using the Excel Options dialog box; you can find them in the Add-Ins section. After they're installed, add-ins are available right away. They usually appear on a tab related to their function. For example, Solver appears on the Data tab.

Here are the steps to follow to load the Solver add-in:

1. **Choose File ⇨ Options.**

   The Excel Options dialog box appears.

2. **Choose Add-Ins.**

3. **In the Manage list, select Excel Add-Ins and then select Go.**

   Excel displays the Add-Ins dialog box.

4. **Select the Solver Add-In check box**

5. **Click OK.**

   Excel adds a Solver button to the Data tab's Analyze group.

Optimizing a result with Solver

You set up your Solver model by using the Solver Parameters dialog box. You use the Set Objective box to specify the objective cell, and you use the To group to tell Solver what you want from the objective cell: the maximum possible value; the minimum possible value; or a specific value. Finally, you use the By Changing Variable Cells box to specify the cells that Solver can use to plug in values to optimize the result.

When Solver finds a solution, you can choose either Keep Solver Solution or Restore Original Values. If you choose Keep Solver Solution, Excel permanently changes the worksheet. You cannot undo the changes.

With your Solver-ready worksheet model ready to go, here are the steps to follow to find an optimal result for your model using Solver:

1. **Choose Data ⇨ Solver.**

Excel opens the Solver Parameters dialog box.

2. **In the Set Objective box, enter the address of your model's objective cell.**

In the example in the "When should you use Solver?" section, earlier in the chapter (refer to Figure 2-11), the objective cell is B14. Note that if you click the cell to enter it, Solver automatically enters an absolute cell address (for example, $B$14 instead of B14). Solver works fine either way.

3. **In the To group, select an option:**

- **Max:** Returns the maximum possible value.
- **Min:** Returns the minimum possible value.
- **Value Of:** Enter a number to set the objective cell to that number.

For the example model, I select Value Of and enter **0** in the text box.

4. **In the By Changing Variable Cells box, enter the addresses of the cells you want Solver to change while it looks for a solution.**

In the example, the changing cells are B4 and C4. Figure 2-12 shows the completed Solver Parameters dialog box. (What about constraints? I talk about those in the next section.)

5. **Click Solve.**

Solver gets down to business. As Solver works on the problem, you might see the Show Trial Solution dialog boxes show up one or more times.

6. **In any Show Trial Solution dialog box that appears, click Continue to move things along.**

When the optimization is complete, Excel displays the Solver Results dialog box, shown in Figure 2-13.

FIGURE 2-12:
The completed Solver Parameters dialog box.

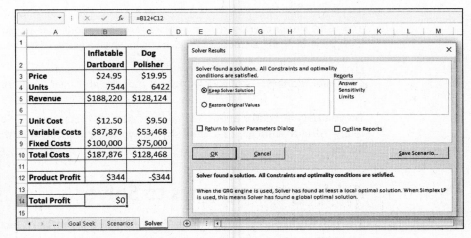

FIGURE 2-13:
The Solver Results dialog box and the solution to the break-even problem.

7. **Select the Keep Solver Solution option.**

   If you don't want to accept the result, select the Restore Original Values option instead.

8. **Click OK.**

You can ask Solver to display one or more reports that give you extra information about the results. In the Solver Results dialog box, use the Reports list to select each report you want to view:

>> **Answer:** Displays information about the model's objective cell, variable cells, and constraints. For the objective cell and variable cells, Solver shows the original and final values.

>> **Sensitivity:** Attempts to show how sensitive a solution is to changes in the model's formulas. The layout of the Sensitivity report depends on the type of model you're using.

>> **Limits:** Displays the objective cell and its value, as well as the variable cells and their addresses, names, and values.

Solver can use one of several solving methods. In the Solver Parameters dialog box, use the Select a Solving Method list to select one of the following:

>> **Simplex LP:** Use if your worksheet model is linear. In the simplest possible terms, a linear model is one in which the variables are not raised to any powers and none of the so-called transcendent functions — such as SIN and COS — are used.

>> **GRG Nonlinear:** Use if your worksheet model is nonlinear and smooth. In general terms, a smooth model is one in which a graph of the equation used doesn't show sharp edges or breaks.

>> **Evolutionary:** Use if your worksheet model is nonlinear and nonsmooth.

Do you have to worry about any of this? Almost certainly not. Solver defaults to using GRG Nonlinear, and that should work for almost anything you do with Solver.

Adding constraints to Solver

The real world puts restrictions and conditions on formulas. A factory might have a maximum capacity of 10,000 units a day, the number of employees in a company can't be a negative number, and your advertising costs might be restricted to 10 percent of total expenses.

Similarly, suppose that you're running a break-even analysis on two products, as I discuss in the previous section. If you run the optimization without any restrictions, Solver might reach a total profit of 0 by setting one product at a slight loss and the other at a slight profit, where the loss and profit cancel each other out. In fact, if you take a close look at Figure 2-13, this is exactly what Solver did. To get a true break-even solution, you might prefer to see both product profit values as 0.

Such restrictions and conditions are examples of what Solver calls *constraints*. Adding constraints tells Solver to find a solution so that these conditions are not violated.

Here's how to run Solver with constraints added to the optimization:

1. **Choose Data ⇨ Solver.**

Excel opens the Solver Parameters dialog box.

2. **Use the Set Objective box, the To group, and the By Changing Variable Cells box to set up Solver as I describe in the previous section, "Optimizing a result with Solver."**

3. **Click Add.**

Excel displays the Add Constraint dialog box.

4. **In the Cell Reference box, enter the address of the cell you want to constrain.**

You can type the address or select the cell on the worksheet.

5. **In the drop-down list, select the operator you want to use.**

Most of the time, you use a comparison operator, such as equal to (=) or greater than (>). Use the int (integer) operator when you need a constraint, such as total employees, to be an integer value instead of a real number (that is, a number with a decimal component; you can't have 10.5 employees!). Use the bin (binary) operator when you have a constraint that must be either TRUE or FALSE (or 1 or 0).

6. **If you chose a comparison operator in Step 5, in the Constraint box, enter the value by which you want to restrict the cell.**

Figure 2-14 shows an example of a completed Add Constraint dialog box. In the example model, this constraint tells Solver to find a solution such that the product profit of the Inflatable Dartboard (cell B12) is equal to 0.

FIGURE 2-14:
The completed
Add Constraint
dialog box.

7. **To specify more constraints, click Add and repeat Steps 4 through 6, as needed.**

For the example, you add a constraint that asks for the Dog Polisher product profit (cell C12) to be 0.

8. **Click OK.**

Excel returns to the Solver Parameters dialog box and displays your constraints in the Subject to the Constraints list box.

9. **Click Solve.**

10. **In any Show Trial Solution dialog box that appears, click Continue to move things along.**

Figure 2-15 shows the example break-even solution with the constraints added. Notice that not only is the Total Profit cell (B14) set to 0, but so are the two Product Profit cells (B12 And C12).

FIGURE 2-15: The Solver Results dialog box and the final solution to the break-even problem.

11. **Select the Keep Solver Solution option.**

If you don't want to accept the result, select the Restore Original Values option instead.

12. **Click OK.**

REMEMBER

You can add a maximum of 100 constraints. Also, if you need to make a change to a constraint before you begin solving, select the constraint in the Subject to the Constraints list box, click Change, and then make your adjustments in the Change Constraint dialog box that appears. If you want to delete a constraint that you no longer need, select the constraint and then click Delete.

Save a Solver solution as a scenario

Whenever you have a spreadsheet model that uses a coherent set of input values — known as *changing cells* — you have what Excel calls a *scenario*. With Solver, these changing cells are its variable cells, so a Solver solution amounts to a kind of scenario. However, Solver does not give you an easy way to save and rerun a particular solution. To work around this problem, you can save a solution as a scenario that you can then later recall using Excel's Scenario Manager feature.

Follow these steps to save a Solver solution as a scenario:

1. **Choose Data ⇨ Solver.**

Excel opens the Solver Parameters dialog box.

2. **Use the Set Objective box, the To group, the By Changing Variable Cells box, and the Subject to the Constraints list to set up Solver as I describe in the "Optimizing a result with Solver" section, earlier in this chapter.**

3. **Click Solve.**

4. **Anytime the Show Trial Solution dialog box appears, choose Continue.**

When the optimization is complete, Excel displays the Solver Results dialog box.

5. **Click Save Scenario.**

Excel displays the Save Scenario dialog box.

6. **In the Scenario Name dialog box, type a name for the scenario and then click OK.**

Excel returns you to the Solver Results dialog box.

7. **Select the Keep Solver Solution option.**

If you don't want to accept the result, select the Restore Original Values option instead.

8. **Click OK.**

Chapter **3**

Introducing Excel Tables

One of the secrets of data-analysis success is being organized. I'm not talking about your desk or your office (insert sigh of relief here), but your data. If you have a worksheet with numbers and text inserted haphazardly, analyzing that data will be next to impossible. Why? Because Excel is the neat freak of the software world. If data is strewn around the worksheet any old way, Excel throws up its hands and says "I can't work under these conditions!"

Fortunately, Excel understands that the rest of us aren't so orderly, so it offer the table — a powerful tool designed not only to get your data lined up like soldiers on parade but also to help you analyze that data and extract useful information. In this chapter, you discover what tables are and why they're so darned useful in the data-analysis world. You also dive in to building, analyzing, sorting, and filtering a table.

What Is a Table and Why Should I Care?

In Excel, a *table* is a rectangular range of cells used to store data; it includes special tools for entering, editing, and analyzing that data. A table is designed to store a collection of related information. For example, one table might store business data such as customers, invoices, or inventory, whereas another might store personal data such as contacts, movies, or household items. You can use Excel tables to create, retrieve, and manage large or small collections of information.

To get the most out of Excel tables, you need to understand a few basic concepts:

>> **A table is a kind of database:** Microsoft Access is a powerful database management tool that lets you work with large, complex databases. If your needs are simpler, however, you can use a table as a database in which the data is organized into columns and rows. In this case, each column is the equivalent of a database field, which contains a single type of information, such as a name, address, or phone number; and each row serves as the equivalent of a database record, which holds a set of associated field values, such as the information for a specific contact.

>> **a table has its advantages:** Because a table is a collection of rows and columns on a worksheet, it looks very much like a regular Excel range. However, a table is actually a special type of range because Excel provides some tools that help you work more easily with the data in the table. These tools enable you to convert existing worksheet data into a table, select the rows and fields you want to work with, add new records and fields to the table, delete existing records and fields, and insert rows to show totals.

>> **A table makes data analysis easier:** Tables are also useful tools for analyzing your data. For example, you can sort the table data, both on a single field and on multiple fields. You can also make the table data easier to manage by filtering the data to show only the subset of records you want to work with. In addition, you can use a table as the basis of a PivotTable, which is a powerful tool for summarizing and analyzing data that I discuss in Part 2 of this book.

Before creating your tables, you should spend some time deciding what type of data each table should contain, which involves thinking about what purpose your tables will serve, which fields you will need in each table, and how you'll differentiate between each record in the table. Each table should have a single, well-defined purpose. For example, a table might store customer contact information, product inventory, or personnel records. Combining multiple purposes in a single table results in needless duplication and increases the chance of data-entry error. If you think you might need to sort or filter the data by a certain type of information, put that information in a separate field. Finally, having at least one field that is unique to each record to differentiate between them is usually a good idea.

To help you work with Excel tables, here's a list of table terms, all of which are pointed out in Figure 3-1:

>> **Table column:** A single type of information, such as names, addresses, or phone numbers. In an Excel table, each column is the equivalent of a database field.

>> **Table row:** A set of associated table cells, such as the data for a single contact. In an Excel table, each row is the equivalent of a database record.

>> **Table cell:** An item in a table column that represents a single instance of that column's data, such as a name, address, or phone number. In an Excel table, each cell is equivalent to a database field value.

>> **Headers:** The unique names you assign to every table column that serve to label the data in each column. These names are always found in the first row of the table.

>> **Sort & Filter buttons:** An Excel feature that gives you access to a set of commands that perform various actions on a column, such as sorting or filtering the column data.

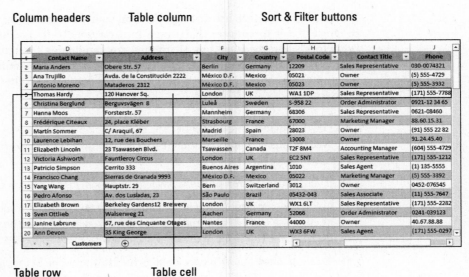

Column headers   Table column   Sort & Filter buttons

FIGURE 3-1:
Some table
terminology you
should know.

Table row   Table cell

Building a Table

You build an Excel table in one of two ways:

>> Get the data from an external source, such as a database.

>> Convert an existing range to a table.

Getting the data from an external source

The usual way to create an Excel table is to import the information from an external source, such as another workbook, an Access database, a text file, or even a web page. Importing data is such an important — and time-saving — method of getting data into Excel that I devote all of Chapter 4 to it. There, I describe the process of getting the external data into a format that Excel can use and then importing the data into Excel so that you can analyze it. Hop over to that chapter for more on creating a table by importing its data.

TIP

Even if you plan on creating your tables by importing data from an external source, read through the next few paragraphs of this chapter anyway. Why? Because they give you a better understanding of the nuts and bolts of building a table, and having that know-how in your brain makes understanding and working with external data easier when you're ready to go down that road.

Converting a range to a table

If the data you want to use already exists on your worksheet, you might be able to convince Excel to convert that range into an honest-to-goodness table. I say "convince" here because not all ranges are candidates for table-hood. Fortunately, getting your data ready doesn't require elaborate planning or modifications, but you should follow a few guidelines for best results. Here are some pointers:

>> Decide whether you want your table to have column headers. This is an excellent idea because it makes your table much easier to read and to analyze, but the headers are optional, if that works for you.

>> If you do use column headers, always place them in the top row of the range.

>> Column headers must be unique and must be text or text formulas. If you need to use numbers, format them as text. (That is, select the headers and then use the Home tab's Number Format list to select Text.)

>> Excel can often automatically identify the size and shape of the range that contains your data. To avoid confusing Excel, make sure that you have no blank rows or columns in your range.

>> If the same worksheet contains data that you don't want to appear in your table, leave at least one blank row or column between the data and the range. The blank row or column helps Excel identify the correct table range without also including the nontable data.

Excel has a command that enables you to filter your table data to show only records that match certain criteria. This command works by hiding rows of data. Therefore, if the same worksheet contains nontable data that you need to see or work with, don't place this data to the left or right of the table.

Note that you don't need to enter all your data before converting the range to a table. After you have the table, you can add new rows and columns as needed. Okay, I think you're ready to find out how to convert a range to a table:

1. **Select a cell within the range that you want to convert to a table.**

2. **Choose Insert ⇨ Tables ⇨ Table or press Ctrl+T.**

The Create Table dialog box appears. As shown in Figure 3-2, Excel makes its best guess about the extent of the range that it will convert to a table.

	A	B	C	D	E	F	G	H
1	Division	Description	Number	Quantity	Unit Cost	Total Cost	Retail	Gross Margin
2	4	Gangley Pliers	D-178	57	$10.47	$596.79	$17.95	71%
3	3	HCAB Washer	A-201	856	$0.12	$102.72	$0.25	108%
4	3	Finley Sprocket	C-098	357	$1.57	$560.49	$2.95	88%
5	2	6" Sonotube	B-111	86	$15.24	$1,310.64	$19.95	31%
6	4	Langstrom 7" Wrench	D-017	75	$18.69	$1,401.75	$27.95	50%
7	3	Thompson Socket	C-321	298	$3.11	$926.78	$5.95	91%
8	1	S-Joint	A-182	155	$6.85	$1,061.75	$9.95	45%
9	2	LAMF Valve	B-047	482	$4.01	$1,932.82	$6.95	73%

Create Table   ?   X

Where is the data for your table?

$A$1:$H$9

☑ My table has headers

OK   Cancel

FIGURE 3-2:
Excel takes a stab at the full range you want to convert.

3. **If Excel got it wrong, drag over the correct range.**

4. **If your range has labels that you want to use as column headers, make sure that the My Table Has Headers check box is selected.**

5. **Click OK.**

Excel converts the range to a table, which, as you can eyeball in Figure 3-3, also means that Excel does the following:

>> Applies a table format to the range.

>> Shoehorns a Sort & Filter button into each column header.

>> Displays the Design tab whenever you select a cell anywhere inside the table. The Design tab is chock-full of useful table tools.

Basic table maintenance

After you've converted your range to a table, the data isn't set in stone. In fact, you can perform all kinds of actions to keep your table up-to-date. Here's a quick summary:

>> **Selecting a row:** Right-click any cell in the row and then choose Select ⇨ Table Row.

>> **Selecting a column:** Right-click any cell in the column and then choose Select ⇨ Table Column Data. If you want the selection to also include the column header, choose Select ⇨ Entire Table Column instead.

>> **Inserting a row:** Right-click the row above which you want the new row to appear; then choose Insert ⇨ Table Rows Above. If you select cells in two or more rows, Excel inserts the same number of new rows.

>> **Inserting a column:** Right-click the column to the left of which you want the new column to appear; then choose Insert ⇨ Table Columns to the Left. If you select cells in two or more columns, Excel inserts the same number of new columns.

>> **Deleting a row:** Right-click the row you want to delete and then choose Delete ⇨ Table Rows. If you select cells in two or more rows, Excel deletes those rows.

>> **Deleting a column:** Right-click the column you want to delete and then choose Delete ⇨ Table Columns. If you select cells in two or more columns, Excel deletes those columns.

>> **Resizing the table:** Select any cell in the table; then choose Design ⇨ Resize Table to open the Resize Table dialog box. Drag over the new range and then click OK.

>> **Converting the table back to a range:** Select any cell in the table; then choose Design ⇨ Convert to Range. When Excel asks you to confirm, click Yes.

Analyzing Table Information

Now that your data is nicely arranged inside a table, a whole new world of data analysis opens right before your eyes. That's because Excel offers quite a few useful data-analysis tools that were designed with tables in mind. In the rest of this chapter, I introduce you to these handy table tools.

Displaying simple statistics

If your table includes a column that contains numeric values or prices, you might want to perform a quick analysis on that column by generating some basic statistics, such as the column's sum or average. Happily, one of Excel's slickest and quickest tools enables you to effortlessly calculate not only the sum or average for a column, but also other stats such as the count, the minimum value, and the maximum value.

To get these stats, you take advantage of the fact that a table is still a range, and Excel automatically displays statistics in the status bar when you select a range. For example, if you select the range D2 to D9 in Figure 3-4 (that is, all the items in the table's Quantity column), Excel calculates the column's average, count, and sum, and then displays this useful information in the status bar:

```
Average: 295.75 Count: 8 Sum: 2366
```

FIGURE 3-4: Select a column's cells, and Excel displays a few stats in the status bar.

Division	Description	Number	Quantity	Unit Co	Total Co	Reta	Gross Margin
4	Gangley Pliers	D-178	57	$10.47	$596.79	$17.95	71%
3	HCAB Washer	A-201	856	$0.12	$102.72	$0.25	108%
3	Finley Sprocket	C-098	357	$1.57	$560.49	$2.95	88%
2	6" Sonotube	B-111	86	$15.24	$1,310.64	$19.95	31%
4	Langstrom 7" Wrench	D-017	75	$18.69	$1,401.75	$27.95	50%
3	Thompson Socket	C-321	298	$3.11	$926.78	$5.95	91%
1	S-Joint	A-182	155	$6.85	$1,061.75	$9.95	45%
2	LAMF Valve	B-047	482	$4.01	$1,932.82	$6.95	73%

Parts Customers Sheet3

Ready   Average: 295.75   Count: 8   Sum: 2366

TIP

If the column you want to analyze contains many items, you might not want to select them all by dragging over the entire column. An easier way to select the entire column is to right-click any item in the column and then choose Choose⇨Table Column Data. Alternatively, select the first item in the column and then press Ctrl+Shift+Down Arrow.

To display some other statistical calculations for the selected table column, right-click the status bar to show the Customize Status Bar menu. Near the bottom of that menu, Excel provides six statistical measures that you can add to or remove from the status bar: Average, Count, Numerical Count, Minimum, Maximum, and Sum. In Table 3-1, I describe each of these statistical measures briefly, but you can probably guess what they do. Note that if a statistical measure is displayed on the status bar, Excel places a check mark in front of the measure on the Customize Status Bar menu. To remove the statistical measure from the status bar, select the measure.

TABLE 3-1

Quick Statistical Measures Available on the Status Bar

Measure	What It Displays
Average	The average of the cells in the selected range.
Count	The number of cells that hold labels, values, or formulas. In other words, use this statistical measure when you want to count the number of cells that are not empty.
Numerical Count	The number of cells in a selected range that hold values or formulas.
Minimum	The smallest value in the selected range.
Maximum	The largest value in the selected range.
Sum	The total of the values in the selected range.

These basic statistical measures are often all you need to gain useful insights into data that you collect and store in an Excel table. True, by using an example parts table that contains just nine items, the power of these quick statistical measures doesn't seem all that earthshaking. But with real data, these measures often produce interesting insights that you can use.

Adding a column subtotal

The quick statistical measures that I talk about in the previous section are handy and useful, but they suffer from two problems:

» Excel displays the status bar statistics when you select any range, so you can get those stats without bothering to convert a range to a table.

» The stats appear in the status bar only when you've selected the data. If you select another cell or range, the stats disappear or change.

Because you've gone to the trouble of converting a regular range to a table, you can take advantage of the data's "table-ness" by summarizing a column with a subtotal that appears full time at the bottom of the column.

Although the word *subtotal* implies that you're summing the numeric values in a column, Excel uses the term more broadly. That is, a subtotal can be not only a numeric sum but also an average, a maximum or minimum, or a count of the values in the field. You can also choose more advanced subtotals such as the standard deviation or the variance.

Follow these steps to add a subtotal to a table column:

1. **Select the data in the column you want to total.**

2. **Click the Quick Analysis smart tag or press Ctrl+Q.**

   The Quick Analysis options appear.

3. **Click the Totals tab.**

4. **Select the type of calculation you want to use.**

   Excel adds a Total row to the bottom of the table and inserts the result of the calculation you selected in Step 4. In Figure 3-5, you can see that I've added a calculation for the average of the Quantity column. Notice that when you select the result, its cell displays a drop-down arrow to the right. You can click the drop-down arrow to choose a different calculation.

FIGURE 3-5:
Excel adds a total row to the bottom of the table and displays the result of the calculation.

	A	B	C	D	
	Division	Description	Number	Quantity	U
2	4	Gangley Pliers	D-178	57	
3	3	HCAB Washer	A-201	856	
4	3	Finley Sprocket	C-098	357	
5	2	6" Sonotube	B-111	86	
6	4	Langstrom 7" Wrench	D-017	75	
7	3	Thompson Socket	C-321	298	
8	1	S-Joint	A-182	155	
9	2	LAMF Valve	B-047	482	
10				295.75	

D10 =SUBTOTAL(101,[Quantity])

TIP

If the column you want to total is the last column in the table, Excel offers a short-cut method to add the total row and display a subtotal for that column. Select any cell within the table and then, on the Design tab, select the Total Row check box. Excel automatically inserts a row named Total at the bottom of the table. Excel also adds a Sum subtotal below the last column. Select the subtotal, click the cell's drop-down arrow, and then choose the type of subtotal you want to use.

Sorting table records

Another way to analyze your table data is to sort the data based on the values in a column, which means arranging that column's numeric values from highest to lowest or from lowest to highest. (You can also sort text values alphabetically and date values from oldest to newest or newest to oldest, but these techniques are less useful for data analysis.) How does sorting help you analyze your data? Here are some ideas:

REMEMBER

>> Sorting enables you to get a feel for how your data is distributed overall. For example, you might notice that most of the values cluster around the low end of the range of values.

>> Sorting enables you to identify certain types of trends in the data. For example, you might notice that records (that is, rows) with low values in the sorted column all come from the same geographic area, or that high values in another table all come from the same division of the company.

>> Sorting enables you to identify *outliers,* which are data points that are significantly outside the norm for your data. For example, if your sort shows that most of your column values lie between 1 and 100, but one row contains the value 250, you'll want to investigate why that value is so much greater than the others.

To sort a table based on the values in a column, follow these steps:

1. **Click the Sort & Filter button for the column you want to sort.**

Excel displays the Sort & Filter menu. Figure 3-6 shows the top part of the Sort & Filter menu that appears when selecting the Sort & Filter button for the Quantity column.

2. **Select the sort option you want:**

- **Sort Smallest to Largest:** Sorts the column values in ascending numeric order.

- **Sort Largest to Smallest:** Sorts the column values in descending numeric order.

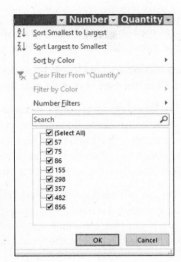

FIGURE 3-6:
Selecting the
Quantity column's
Sort & Filter
button displays
this menu.

When you can't sort table information exactly the way you want by using the Sort Smallest to Largest and Sort Largest to Smallest commands, use the Custom Sort command.

To use the Custom Sort command, follow these steps:

1. **Click any Sort & Filter button in the table.**

   Excel displays the Sort & Filter menu.

2. **Choose Sort by Color ⇨ Custom Sort.**

   Excel displays the Sort dialog box.

3. **Use the Sort By drop-down list to select the field that you want to use for sorting.**

4. **Use the Sort On list to select Cell Values.**

   If you're using conditional formatting, as described in Chapter 1, you can also choose to sort on Cell Color, Font Color, or Conditional Formatting Icon.

5. **Use the Order list to select a sort order.**

   For numeric data, select either Smallest to Largest or Largest to Smallest. If you sort by color or icons, you need to tell Excel how it should sort the colors by using the options that the Order list provides.

   TIP

   Typically, you want the sort to work in ascending or descending order. However, you might want to sort records by using a chronological sequence, such as Sunday, Monday, Tuesday, and so on, or January, February, March, and so forth. To use one of these other sorting options, choose the Order list's Custom List command and then choose one of these other ordering methods from the

Custom Lists dialog box that Excel displays. You can also create your own custom lists if, say, you need to sort your data by department or job title.

6. **(Optional) Specify one or more secondary sort levels by clicking Add Level and then repeating Steps 3 to 5 for the new sort level that appears.**

A secondary sort level means that Excel first sorts the table based on the data in the primary sort level, and it then further sorts the table based on the data in the secondary sort level. For example, in the parts table, you can first sort the table based on the Division column, and then sort based on the Quantity column. Figure 3-7 shows the Sort dialog box set up for such a two-level sort.

If you add a level that you later decide you don't want or need, select the sort level and then click the Delete Level button. You can also duplicate the selected level by clicking Copy Level. Finally, if you create multiple sort levels, you can move the selected sort up or down a level by clicking the Move Up or Move Down button.

Note: The Sort dialog box also provides a My Data Has Headers check box that enables you to indicate whether the worksheet range selection includes the row and field names. If you've already told Excel that a worksheet range is a table, however, this check box is disabled.

7. **Click OK.**

Excel sorts your list.

FIGURE 3-7:
The Sort dialog box set up for a two-level sort.

Filtering table records

When you're generating statistics, adding subtotals, and sorting data, you'll most often want to work with all the table data. However, working with just a subset of the table data can sometimes be beneficial. In the parts database, for example, you might want to see only the records from Division 3 or only those items whose Retail price is greater than ten dollars.

To help you work with subsets of your table data, Excel provides an AutoFilter command that's pretty cool. When you use AutoFilter, you produce a new view of your table that includes only those records that match whatever criteria you spec-ify, such as the Division value being equal to 3 or the Retail value being greater than 10.

To apply an AutoFilter to a table, follow these steps:

1. **Click the Sort & Filter button for the column you want to filter.**

Excel displays the column's Sort & Filter menu. Above the OK and Cancel buttons, you see a list of check boxes, where the name of each check box is a unique value from the column.

2. **Deselect the Select All check box to deselect all the check boxes.**

3. **Select the check box for each column value you want to see in the filtered table.**

Figure 3-8 shows the Sort & Filter menu for the Division column, with only the 3 check box selected.

4. **Click OK.**

Excel filters the table to show only those values you selected in Step 3. Figure 3-9 shows the filtered parts table, which now displays only the records from Division 3. The Sort & Filter button of the Division column header now sports a tiny funnel icon, which gives you a visual heads-up that the column is filtered.

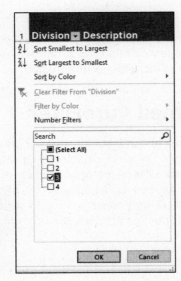

FIGURE 3-8:
Select the check box beside each column value that you want to include in your filtered table.

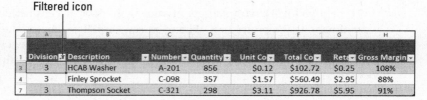

FIGURE 3-9:
The Parts table
filtered to show
only the records
from Division 3.

	A	B	C	D	E	F	G	H
1	Division	Description	Number	Quantity	Unit Co	Total Co	Reta	Gross Margin
3	3	HCAB Washer	A-201	856	$0.12	$102.72	$0.25	108%
4	3	Finley Sprocket	C-098	357	$1.57	$560.49	$2.95	88%
7	3	Thompson Socket	C-321	298	$3.11	$926.78	$5.95	91%

Clearing a filter

To remove an AutoFilter, you have a couple ways to go:

>> To clear a filter from a single column, select the column's Sort & Filter button and then select the Clear Filter From "*Column*" command from the menu (where *Column* is the name of the filtered column).

>> If you have multiple filters applied to the table, you can clear all the filters in one fell swoop by choosing Data ⇨ Clear (look for it in the Sort & Filter group).

Turning off AutoFilter

If you find that you don't use AutoFilter and so those Sort & Filter buttons just cramp your style, no problem: The AutoFilter command is actually a toggle switch. When AutoFilter is turned on, Excel adds the Sort & Filter buttons to each cell in the table's header row; when you turn off AutoFilter, Excel removes the Sort & Filter buttons.

To turn off AutoFilter and remove the Sort & Filter buttons, choose Data ⇨ Filter (or press Ctrl+Shift+L). If you change your mind and decide to reinstate AutoFilter, choose Data ⇨ Filter again (or do the Ctrl+Shift+L thing again).

Applying a predefined AutoFilter

A basic AutoFilter creates a subset of the table by showing only those rows in which the filtered column contains the value or values you selected using the check boxes in the Sort & Filter menu. That's pretty useful, but what if your filtering needs (I bet you didn't even know you had filtering needs) are more complex? For example, you might want to see only those records in which the Quantity column is greater than or equal to 100, or in which the Gross Margin column is above the average for that column.

These more complex filters sound like more work, and I won't lie to you: They do take a few extra steps. Ah, but only a few, I promise you, because Excel comes with quite a few predefined filter operators, including Greater Than Or Equal To and Above Average. Here are the steps to follow to apply one of these predefined filters to a column in your table:

1. **Click the Sort & Filter button for the column you want to filter.**

   Excel displays the column's Sort & Filter menu.

2. **Choose the *X* Filters command, where *X* refers to the type of data in the column.**

   You have three possible commands:

   - **Number Filters:** Appears when the column contains numeric data.

   - **Date Filters:** Appears when the column contains date values, time values, or both.

   - **Text Filters:** Appears when the column contains text data.

3. **Select the filter operator you want to apply.**

   Excel displays a menu of predefined filter operators. The contents of the menu depend on the data type of your column. For example, if your column contains numeric data, you see the following operators:

   - **Equals:** Filters the column to show only those rows whose column value equals a number you specify.

   - **Does Not Equal:** Filters the column to show only those rows whose column value does not equal a number you specify.

   - **Greater Than:** Filters the column to show only those rows whose column value is greater than a number you specify.

   - **Greater Than or Equal To:** Filters the column to show only those rows whose column value is greater than or equal to a number you specify.

   - **Less Than:** Filters the column to show only those rows whose column value is less than a number you specify.

   - **Less Than or Equal To:** Filters the column to show only those rows whose column value is less than or equal to a number you specify.

   - **Between:** Filters the column to show only those rows whose column value lies between (and including) two numbers you specify.

   - **Top 10:** Filters the column to show only those rows whose column value is in the top 10 of all the values in the column. Note that this filter is slightly misnamed because you can pick a number other than 10 (such as 5 or 25), you can show the bottom 10 (or 20 or 30 or whatever), and you can filter based on the percentage (for example, the top 10 percent) instead of the values.

- **Above Average:** Filters the column to show only those rows whose column value is greater than the average value of the column.

- **Below Average:** Filters the column to show only those rows whose column value is less than the average value of the column.

- **Custom Filter:** Displays the Custom AutoFilter dialog box, which enables you to create your own filter condition. In particular, you can specify two separate filter conditions, and you can then select the And option to have Excel filter the table to show only those rows with column values that match both filter conditions, or you can select the Or option to have Excel filter the table to show only those rows with column values that match one or both filter conditions.

In most cases, you see the Custom AutoFilter dialog box with the operator you selected already filled in in the drop-down list. For example, Figure 3-10 shows the Custom AutoFilter dialog box that appears when you select the Greater Than Or Equal operator. Note that some operators — such as Above Average and Below Average — don't require more information from you, so Excel applies the filter right away.

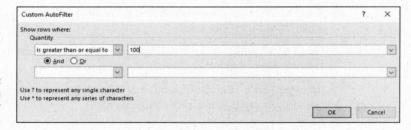

FIGURE 3-10:
The Custom AutoFilter dialog box.

4. **Complete the AutoFilter condition.**

   How you complete the condition depends on the operator you chose. For most numeric filters, you specify a number. For example, in Figure 3-11, you can see that I've entered the number 100 in the text box, which means that this filter will show the subset of the table when the Quantity column value is 100 or more.

5. **Click OK.**

   Excel filters your table according to your custom AutoFilter. Figure 3-11 shows the filter from Figure 3-11 applied to the Parts table.

FIGURE 3-11:
The filter shown
in Figure 3-10
applied to the
Parts table.

	A	B	C	D	E	F	G	H
1	Division	Description	Number	Quantity	Unit Co	Total Co	Reta	Gross Margin
3	3	HCAB Washer	A-201	856	$0.12	$102.72	$0.25	108%
4	3	Finley Sprocket	C-098	357	$1.57	$560.49	$2.95	88%
7	3	Thompson Socket	C-321	298	$3.11	$926.78	$5.95	91%
8	1	S-Joint	A-182	155	$6.85	$1,061.75	$9.95	45%
9	2	LAMF Valve	B-047	482	$4.01	$1,932.82	$6.95	73%

Applying multiple filters

The predefined AutoFilter operators described in the previous section enable you to filter your table based on a condition applied to a single column. What if your filtering needs (there are those needs again) are such that you want to filter the table using multiple columns? In the Parts table, for example, you might want to filter the table to show only those rows where the Quantity field is greater than or equal to 100, and you might want the resulting rows to themselves be filtered to show only those where the Gross Margin column is less than 75%.

The good news is that Excel doesn't mind in the least if you apply an AutoFilter to one column and then apply another AutoFilter to a second column. In fact, you can apply AutoFilters to as many columns as you need. In each case, just follow the same steps as those outlined in the previous section.

REMEMBER

The idea of applying multiple filters might seem unnecessary. Okay, granted, it's most likely an over-the-top technique for small tables. However, when you start dealing with massive tables containing hundreds, nay, thousands, of rows, you'll almost certainly find that applying several sets of filters can reduce a very large and nearly incomprehensible table to a smaller subset of data that provides just the information you need.

Applying advanced filters

Most of the time, you'll be able to filter table records by using the Sort & Filter menu's check boxes or the Filter command. However, in some cases, you might want to gain more control over your filters, and that requires applying Excel's advanced filters.

Before you can create advanced filters in Excel, you need to know how to construct *comparison* expressions, through which you compare the items in a column with a value you specify. To construct a comparison expression, you enter a comparison operator from Table 3-2 and then a value used in the comparison.

TABLE 3-2

Excel's Comparison Operators

Operator	Name
=	Equals
<>	Not equal to
>	Greater than
>=	Greater than or equal to
<	Less than
<=	Less than or equal to

For example, if you want to filter the parts table so that it shows only those items where the Unit Cost is less than $10, you use the following comparison expression:

```
< 10
```

Hmm, okay, I hear you musing, but where does the expression appear?

Surprisingly, it goes on the worksheet itself. To get this set up, first insert three or four blank rows above the table headers. Now copy your table headers and then paste them above your table.

With that done, enter your comparison expression in the cell immediately below the copied header of the column you want to work with. In my example, I want to filter based on the Unit Cost column, so I enter **< 10** in the cell below the copied Unit Cost header. In Figure 3-12, you can see the expression in cell E2.

Comparison expression   Copied headers

	A	B	C	D	E	F	G	H
1	Division	Description	Number	Quantity	Unit Cost	Total Cost	Retail	Gross Margin
2					< 10			
3								
4								
5	Division	Description	Number	Quantity	Unit Cost	Total Cost	Retail	Gross Margin
6	4	Gangley Pliers	D-178	57	$10.47	$596.79	$17.95	71%
7	3	HCAB Washer	A-201	856	$0.12	$102.72	$0.25	108%
8	3	Finley Sprocket	C-098	357	$1.57	$560.49	$2.95	88%
9	2	6" Sonotube	B-111	86	$15.24	$1,310.64	$19.95	31%
10	4	Langstrom 7" Wrench	D-017	75	$18.69	$1,401.75	$27.95	50%
11	3	Thompson Socket	C-321	298	$3.11	$926.78	$5.95	91%
12	1	S-Joint	A-182	155	$6.85	$1,061.75	$9.95	45%
13	2	LAMF Valve	B-047	482	$4.01	$1,932.82	$6.95	73%

FIGURE 3-12:
A table set
up for an
advanced filter.

So far, this "advanced" filtering doesn't seem all that different than using one of Excel's predefined operators. True! But the real power of advanced filters is that you're free to enter as many comparison expressions as you need. There are three ways to go about this:

>> **Enter the comparison expressions on the same row:** This tells Excel to filter the table to show only those rows that match all the comparison expressions you enter. In Figure 3-13, for example, I'm asking Excel to filter the Parts table to show only those rows in which the Unit Cost is less than 10 (cell E2), the Quantity is greater than 300 (cell D2), and the Division equals 3 (cell A2; notice that you don't need to use Equals (=) when you want to match a value exactly).

>> **Enter the comparison expression on separate rows:** This tells Excel to filter the table to show only those rows that match at least one of the comparison expressions you enter. In Figure 3-14, for example, I'm asking Excel to filter the Parts table to show only those rows in which either the Total Cost is greater than 1,000 (cell F2) or the Quantity is greater than 400 (cell D3).

>> **Mix and match the preceding as needed:** Feel free to add as many comparison expressions as you need, and don't be shy about using multiple columns and multiple rows. Hey, it's your filter!

FIGURE 3-13: Put the comparison expressions on one row to match them all.

	Division	Description	Number	Quantity	Unit Cost	Total Cost	Retail	Gross Margin
1	Division	Description	Number	Quantity	Unit Cost	Total Cost	Retail	Gross Margin
2	3			> 300	< 10			
3								
4								
5	Division	Description	Number	Quantity	Unit Cost	Total Cost	Retail	Gross Margin
6	4	Gangley Pliers	D-178	57	$10.47	$596.79	$17.95	71%
7	3	HCAB Washer	A-201	856	$0.12	$102.72	$0.25	108%
8	3	Finley Sprocket	C-098	357	$1.57	$560.49	$2.95	88%
9	2	6" Sonotube	B-111	86	$15.24	$1,310.64	$19.95	31%
10	4	Langstrom 7" Wrench	D-017	75	$18.69	$1,401.75	$27.95	50%
11	3	Thompson Socket	C-321	298	$3.11	$926.78	$5.95	91%
12	1	S-Joint	A-182	155	$6.85	$1,061.75	$9.95	45%
13	2	LAMF Valve	B-047	482	$4.01	$1,932.82	$6.95	73%

FIGURE 3-14: Put the comparison expressions on separate rows to match one or more.

	Division	Description	Number	Quantity	Unit Cost	Total Cost	Retail	Gross Margin
1	Division	Description	Number	Quantity	Unit Cost	Total Cost	Retail	Gross Margin
2						> 1,000		
3				> 400				
4								
5	Division	Description	Number	Quantity	Unit Cost	Total Cost	Retail	Gross Margin
6	4	Gangley Pliers	D-178	57	$10.47	$596.79	$17.95	71%
7	3	HCAB Washer	A-201	856	$0.12	$102.72	$0.25	108%
8	3	Finley Sprocket	C-098	357	$1.57	$560.49	$2.95	88%
9	2	6" Sonotube	B-111	86	$15.24	$1,310.64	$19.95	31%
10	4	Langstrom 7" Wrench	D-017	75	$18.69	$1,401.75	$27.95	50%
11	3	Thompson Socket	C-321	298	$3.11	$926.78	$5.95	91%
12	1	S-Joint	A-182	155	$6.85	$1,061.75	$9.95	45%
13	2	LAMF Valve	B-047	482	$4.01	$1,932.82	$6.95	73%

The extra column headers that you copied and the rows below where you enter your comparison expressions are known as the *criteria range.* Note, however, that just setting up the criteria range doesn't do any filtering. Only after you've set up your criteria range — as was done for Figures 3-13 and 3-14 — are you ready to run the advanced filter operation. Here's how it works:

1. **Select any cell in the table.**

2. **Choose Data ⇨ Advanced.**

   Excel displays the Advanced Filter dialog box.

3. **Tell Excel where to place the filtered table.**

   Use the Action radio buttons to specify where you want the filtered records to appear:

   - **Filter the list, in-place:** Excel hides the records in the table that don't meet the filtering criteria. (Note that "list" is just another word for "table.") This is the most common way to go, because it means that you can work with the filtered data and whatever changes you make will remain when you remove the filter.

   - **Copy to another location:** Excel copies the records that meet the filtering criteria to a new location. Take this route if you want to include the filtered data as part of a report or you want to manipulate the filtered data and don't want those changes to appear in the original table.

4. **Use the List Range box to verify the table range.**

   Because you selected a cell in the table in Step 1, Excel should correctly identify the table and display its range coordinates in the List Range box. If the text box doesn't show the proper worksheet range for your table, either enter or select the correct range.

5. **Use the Criteria Range box to select the criteria range.**

   The criteria range consists of the copied headers plus the row or rows below the copied headers that you're using to enter the comparison expressions. In Figure 3-14, for example, the criteria range is $A$1:$H$3.

6. **(Optional) If you're copying the filtered records, use the Copy To box to specify the destination.**

   Because you don't know in advance how many records will be in the results, you don't need to specify a range in the Copy To box. Instead, enter or select the address of the cell that you want to be the top-left cell of the destination.

   Figure 3-15 shows the completed Advanced Filter dialog box, which I use to apply the advanced filter (refer to in Figure 3-14).

7. Click OK.

Excel filters your table. Figure 3-16 shows what the filtered list looks like. Note that the table now shows only those parts where the Total Cost is greater than $1,000 or the Quantity is greater than 400.

FIGURE 3-15:
An advanced filter all set to go.

	A	B	C	D	E	F	G	H
1	Division	Description	Number	Quantity	Unit Cost	Total Cost	Retail	Gross Margin
2						> 1000		
3				> 400				
4								
5	Division	Description	Number	Quantity	Unit Cost	Total Cost	Retail	Gross Margin
7	3	HCAB Washer	A-201	856	$0.12	$102.72	$0.25	108%
9	2	6" Sonotube	B-111	86	$15.24	$1,310.64	$19.95	31%
10	4	Langstrom 7" Wrench	D-017	75	$18.69	$1,401.75	$27.95	50%
12	1	S-Joint	A-182	155	$6.85	$1,061.75	$9.95	45%
13	2	LAMF Valve	B-047	482	$4.01	$1,932.82	$6.95	73%
14								

FIGURE 3-16:
The results of the advanced filter from Figure 3-15.

If you filtered your table in-place, you can remove the advanced filter and restore the Sort & Filter buttons by selecting any cell in the filtered results and then choosing Data ⇨ Filter in the Sort & Filter group.

Yep, advanced filters take a bit of work to set up, but after you have your criteria range in place, you can entertain yourself for hours by adding comparison expressions to different columns and different rows. Before you know it, that once ornery table data will be like putty in your hands.

» **Exporting data from other programs**

» **Importing data into Excel**

» **Grabbing data from the web**

» **Querying an external database**

Chapter **4**

Grabbing Data from External Sources

I n many cases, the data that you want to analyze resides outside Excel. That data could be in a text file or a Word document, on a web page, in a database file, in a database program, such as a corporate accounting system, or on a special database server. Alas, you can't analyze anything that's hunkered down "out there" in a file, a program, or a server. Instead, you've got to figure out a way to get that data "in here," by which I mean that you import that data into an Excel workbook and in the form of an Excel table. Importing can be quite a challenge, but fortunately, Excel offers many powerful tools for importing outside data.

You can use two basic approaches to grabbing the external data that you want to analyze. You can export data from another program and then import that data into Excel, or you can query a database directly from Excel. I describe both approaches in this chapter.

What's All This About External Data?

A vast amount of data exists in the world, and most of it resides in some kind of nonworkbook format. Some data exists in simple text files, perhaps as comma-separated lists of items. Other data resides in tables, either in Word documents or, more likely, Access databases. Also, an increasing amount of data is available on web pages. *External data* is data that resides outside Excel in a file, database, server, or website.

By definition, external data is not directly available to you via Excel. However, Excel offers a number of tools that enable you to import external data into the program, and from there you can break out Excel's data-analysis tools to extract useful information from that data.

The world's data exists in a seemingly endless variety of files and formats. Here are some of the external data types you're most likely to come across:

- » **Access table:** Microsoft Access is the Office suite's relational database management system. It's often used to store and manage the bulk of the data used by a person, team, department, or company. You can connect to Access tables either via Excel's Query Wizard or by importing table data directly into Excel.

- » **Word table:** Simple collections of data are often stored in a table embedded in a Word document. You can perform only so much analysis on that data within Word, so importing the data from the Word table into an Excel worksheet is often useful.

- » **Text file:** Text files often contain useful data. If that data is formatted properly — for example, each line has the same number of items, all separated by spaces, commas, or tabs — you can import that data into Excel for further analysis.

- » **Web page:** People and companies often make useful data available on web pages that reside either on the Internet or on company networks. This data is often a combination of text and tables, but you can't analyze web-based data in any meaningful way in your web browser. Fortunately, Excel enables you to create a web query that lets you import text and tables from a web page.

- » **XML file:** XML (Extensible Markup Language) is a special text format for storing data in a machine-readable format.

- » **External programs and services:** Many programs store data: accounting and finance systems; contact management programs; inventory control software; and on and on. The bad news is that for the vast majority of such programs, Excel has no way to import the program's data directly. The good news is that Excel is so popular that many programs that store data also include a feature that lets you export the data as an Excel workbook. Even those programs that don't offer a way to save data as a workbook do offer techniques for exporting the data to other formats that Excel can work with, such as text or XML files.

Exporting Data from Other Programs

Before getting to the techniques for importing data into Excel, take a minute to consider how you might export data from an external program into a format that Excel can use. Fortunately, most programs that store data also offer a (usually) straightforward way to export data. Even better, because Excel is the dominant data-analysis tool available to business, you can almost always tweak a program's export routine to produce data in an Excel-friendly format.

What does it mean for exported data to be Excel friendly? It means that the resulting data is in one of the following two formats:

>> **Excel workbook:** This is the gold standard of exporting, because it means that you don't even need to import the data into Excel. Instead, you just open the workbook and start analyzing the data (although you might need to convert the data into a table as a first step).

>> **An external file that Excel can import:** In most cases, this means a text file or an XML file.

Therefore, when exporting data from some other program, your first step is to do a little bit of digging to see whether you have a way to easily and automatically export data to Excel. This fact-finding shouldn't take much time if you use the program's Help system. Next, you need to find the program's Export feature. You can usually find the Export command on the File menu, although you might first need to open a submenu with a name such as Import/Export, Save As, or Utilities. After you've launched the export process, look for an option to save the data directly to an Excel workbook. If you don't see an Excel option, say "Aw, too bad!" and look for a way to export the data as a text file or XML file. If you go the text file route, be sure to export the data using one of the following two formats:

>> **Delimited text file:** Uses a structure in which each item on a line of text is separated by a character called a *delimiter*. The most common text delimiter is the comma (,) and such a file is known as a *comma-separated values* (*CSV*) file. When Excel imports a delimited text file, it treats each line of text as a record and each item between the delimiter as a field.

>> **Fixed-width text file:** Uses a structure in which all the items use a set amount of space — for example, one item might always use 10 characters, whereas another might always use 20 characters — and these fixed widths are the same on every line of text. Excel imports a fixed-width text file by treating each line of text as a record and each fixed-width item as a field.

With your external data in a format that Excel can work with, you're ready to get that data imported into Excel.

Importing External Data into Excel

After you have access to the data, your next step is to import it into an Excel worksheet for analysis and manipulation. Depending on the amount of data, this can make your worksheet quite large. However, having direct access to the data gives you maximum flexibility when it comes to analyzing the data. Not only can you use Excel's main data-analysis tools — tables, scenarios, and what-if analysis — but you can also create a PivotTable from the imported data. I talk about powerful PivotTables in Part 2, "Analyzing Data with PivotTables and PivotCharts."

The next few sections take you through the specifics of importing various data types into Excel.

Importing data from an Access table

If you want to use Excel to analyze data from a table or query within an Access database, you can import the table or query into an Excel worksheet. You can use the Query Wizard (described later in this chapter) to perform this task. However, if you don't need to filter or sort the data before importing it, you can import the table or query directly from the Access database, which is usually a bit faster. Here are the steps to follow to import a table or query directly from Access:

1. **(Optional) If you want the imported data to appear in an existing worksheet, select the cell that you want Excel to use as the upper-left corner of the destination range.**

2. **Choose Data ⇨ Get Data ⇨ From Database ⇨ From Microsoft Access Database.**

   The Import Data dialog box appears.

3. **Open the folder that contains the database, select the Access database file, and then click Import.**

   Excel analyzes the Access database and then displays a window that lists the tables and queries that are available to import.

   Alternatively, you might see message similar to `The database has been place in a state by user 'Whoever' on machine 'Whatever' that prevents it from being opened or locked`. Yikes! This means that someone else is using the database right now, so you should try again later.

4. **Use the Navigator pane to select the table or query you want to import.**

   A preview of the data appears, as shown in Figure 4-1.

FIGURE 4-1:
Select a table
or query in the
Navigator pane to
see a preview of
the data.

5. **Tell Excel where you want the imported data to appear by choosing Load ⇨ Load To and then selecting one of the following:**

- **Existing Worksheet:** Imports the data starting at the cell you selected in Step 1. If you decide that you prefer a different cell, use the range box below this option to select where you want the imported data to begin.

- **New Worksheet:** Imports the data into a new worksheet. Note that this is the default import, so you can import the data directly to a new worksheet by selecting the Load button instead of dropping down the Load list.

6. **Select OK.**

Excel imports the Access data into the worksheet.

Importing data from a Word table

A Microsoft Word *table* is a collection of rows, columns, and cells, which means that it looks something like an Excel range. Moreover, you can insert fields into Word table cells to perform calculations. These fields support cell references, built-in functions, and operators. Cell references designate specific cells; for example, a reference such as B1 refers to the cell in the second column and first row of the table. You can use cell references with built-in functions such as SUM and AVERAGE, and operators such as addition (+), multiplication (*), and greater than (>), to build formulas that calculate results based on the table data.

However, Excel still offers far more sophisticated data-analysis tools. Therefore, to analyze your Word table data properly, you should import the table into an Excel worksheet. Here are the steps to trudge through:

1. **Launch Microsoft Word and open the document that contains the table.**

2. **Select a cell inside the table you want to import.**

   Excel adds the Table Tools contextual tab to the ribbon.

3. **Under the Table Tools contextual tab, choose Layout ⇨ Select ⇨ Select Table.**

   You can also select the table by selecting the table selection handle, which appears in the upper-left corner of the table.

4. **Choose Home ⇨ Copy or press Ctrl+C.**

5. **Switch to the Excel workbook into which you want to import the table.**

6. **Select the cell where you want the table to appear.**

7. **Paste the table data.**

   How you paste the table depends on whether you want Excel to create a link with the original Word table:

   - If you don't want any connection between Excel and the original Word table, choose Home ⇨ Paste or press Ctrl+V. This means that if you make changes to the Word data, those changes aren't reflected in the Excel data (and vice versa).

   - If you want any changes made to the original Word table to be reflected in the pasted Excel range, choose Home ⇨ Paste ⇨ Paste Special. In the Paste Special dialog box, select the Paste Link radio button, select HTML in the As list, and then click OK. The resulting Excel range is linked to the original Word data, which means that any changes you make to the data in Word automatically appear in the Excel range. Sweet! However, you can't change the data in Excel.

Introducing text file importing

Nowadays, most data reside in some kind of special format: an Excel workbook, an Access database, a server database, a web page, and so on. However, finding data stored in simple text files is still relatively common because text is a universal format that users can work with on any system and in a wide variety of programs. You can analyze the data contained in certain text files by importing the data into an Excel worksheet. Note, however, that you cannot import just any text file into Excel; the file needs to use either the *delimited* or *fixed-width* format.

Importing a delimited text file

A *delimited* text file uses a structure in which each item on a line of text is separated by a character called a *delimiter*. The most common text delimiter is the comma (,), and the resulting file is called a *comma-separated values* (or CSV) file. When Excel imports a delimited text file, it treats each line of text as a row (record) and each item between the delimiter as a column (field).

Follow these steps to import a delimited text file into Excel:

1. **(Optional) To import the data to a specific location in an existing worksheet, select the cell that you want to use as the upper-left corner of the destination range.**

2. **Choose Data ⇨ From Text/CSV (or, if you want the workout, choose Data ⇨ Get Data ⇨ From File ⇨ From Text/CSV).**

   The Import Data dialog box appears.

3. **Open the folder that contains the text file, select the file, and then click Import.**

   Excel analyzes the file and then opens a window that displays a preview of the data in the file.

4. **In the Delimiter list, select the delimiter character that your text data uses.**

   How do you know which delimiter character to choose? The comma is by far the most common delimiter, so start with that. You'll know you've hit the delimiter jackpot when the previewed data appears in separate columns, as shown in Figure 4-2.

FIGURE 4-2: Select the delimiter that gets the data into nice, neat columns.

5. **Either choose Load to import the data into a new worksheet or choose Load ⇨ Load To ⇨ Existing Worksheet ⇨ OK to import the data starting at the cell you selected in Step 1.**

Excel imports the delimited text data into the worksheet.

Importing a fixed-width text file

A *fixed-width* text file uses a structure in which all the items use a set amount of space. The first item might always be, say, 10 characters wide (including spaces); the second item might always be 8 characters wide; and so on. Crucially, these fixed widths are the same on every line of text, which gives the entire file a predictable and regular structure that Excel can work with. Excel imports a fixed-width text file by treating each line of text as a row (record) and each fixed-width item as a column (field).

If you're importing data that uses the fixed-width structure, you need to tell Excel where the separation between each field occurs. In a fixed-width text file, each column of data is a constant width, and Excel is usually quite good at determining these widths. So in most cases, Excel automatically sets up *column break lines*, which are vertical lines that separate one field from the next. However, titles or introductory text at the beginning of the file can impair the wizard's calculations, so you should check carefully that the proposed break lines are accurate.

Follow these steps to import a fixed-width text file into Excel:

1. **(Optional) To load the data into a specific worksheet location, select the cell that you want to use as the upper-left corner of the destination range.**

2. **Choose Data ⇨ From Text/CSV (or, if you have extra time to kill, choose Data ⇨ Get Data ⇨ From File ⇨ From Text/CSV).**

The Import Data dialog box appears.

3. **Open the folder that contains the text file, select the file, and then click Import.**

Excel analyzes the file and then opens a window that displays a preview of the data in the file.

4. **In the Delimiter list, make sure that the Fixed Width item is selected.**

Below the Delimiter list, Excel displays a series of numbers, each of which represents the starting point of a column in the text file. The first column always starts at 0, and each subsequent value depends on the width of each column. Figure 4-3 shows these values as 0, 30, 45.

5. If your columns look incorrect — for example, one or more columns are too large or too small — edit the column starting-point values until the columns are correct, as shown in Figure 4-3.

Starting-point values

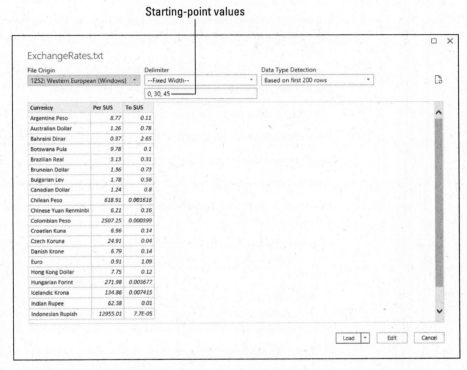

FIGURE 4-3:
If needed, edit the column starting points until your columns are correct.

6. Either choose Load to import the data into a new worksheet or choose Load ⇨ Load To ⇨ Existing Worksheet ⇨ OK to import the data starting at the cell you selected in Step 1.

Excel imports the fixed-width text data into the worksheet.

Importing data from a web page

You already know that the web is home to more information than you can ever use, but did you know that some of that data is available to import into Excel? I talk about a more sophisticated web-based data format in the next section, but here I want to introduce you to web data that comes in the form of a table. A web page *table* is a rectangular array of rows and columns, with data values in the cells created by the intersection of the rows and columns. Why, that sounds just like an Excel table, doesn't it? It sure does, and that similarity means that if you know the address of the page that contains the table, Excel offers a tool that lets you import that data into a worksheet for more data-analysis fun.

Here are the steps to follow to import a web page table into Excel:

1. **(Optional) To load the data into a specific worksheet location, select the cell that you want to use as the upper-left corner of the destination range.**

2. **Choose Data ⇨ From Web (or, if you prefer the scenic route, choose Data ⇨ Get Data ⇨ From Other Sources ⇨ From Web).**

   The From Web window appears.

3. **Enter the address of the web page in the URL text box and then click OK.**

   Excel displays the Access Web Content dialog box.

4. **Specify how you want to access the web page and then click Connect.**

   As shown in Figure 4-4, Excel offers five methods that you can use to access the web content:

   - **Anonymous:** Accesses the content directly, without authentication (such as a username and password). This is the method to use for most web pages.

   - **Windows:** Accesses the content by logging in using the credentials (that is, the username and password) of your Windows account. This is the method to use if the content resides on your company's network.

   - **Basic:** Accesses the content by logging in with a username and password that you provide. This is the method to use if you have an account on the website that hosts the content.

   - **Web API:** Accesses the content by using a unique value — called a *key* — to authenticate your request. This is the method to use if content is made available through a web application programming interface (API). The instructions for using the web API tell you how to obtain a key.

   - **Organizational Account:** Accesses the content by having you sign in to your organization's Office 365 or OneDrive for Business account.

   Excel connects to the web content, analyzes the web page, and then opens the Navigator dialog box, which displays a list of the tables found on the page. One of these objects is always named Document, and it contains a table of data related to the entire web page (so you can safely ignore it).

FIGURE 4-4:
Choose the
method you
want to use to
access the
web data.

5. **Select the table you want to import.**

Excel displays a preview of the table, as shown in Figure 4-5. If you want to see what the table looks like on the web page, click the Web View tab.

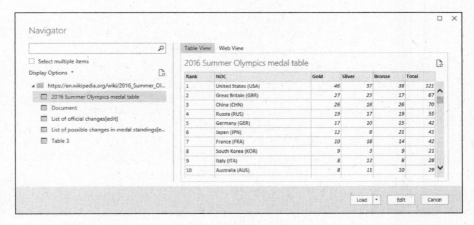

FIGURE 4-5:
Select a table to
preview its data.

6. **(Optional) If you want to import multiple tables, select the Select Multiple Items check box and then select the check box beside each table you want to import.**

7. **Either choose Load to import the data into a new worksheet or choose Load ⇨ Load To ⇨ Existing Worksheet ⇨ OK to import the data starting at the cell you selected in Step 1.**

Excel imports the web table data into the worksheet.

Importing an XML file

XML (Extensible Markup Language) is a standard that enables the management and sharing of structured data using simple text files. These XML files organize data using *tags*, among other elements, that specify the equivalent of a table name and field names. Here's an example that shows the first few records in an XML table of book info:

```xml
<?xml version="1.0"?>
<catalog>
   <book>
      <author>Gambardella, Matthew</author>
      <title>XML Developer's Guide</title>
      <genre>Computer</genre>
      <price>44.95</price>
      <publish_date>2000-10-01</publish_date>
      <description>An in-depth look at creating applications
      with XML.</description>
   </book>
   <book>
      <author>Ralls, Kim</author>
      <title>Midnight Rain</title>
      <genre>Fantasy</genre>
      <price>5.95</price>
      <publish_date>2000-12-16</publish_date>
      <description>A former architect battles corporate zombies,
      an evil sorceress, and her own childhood to become queen
      of the world.</description>
   </book>
   <book>
      <author>Corets, Eva</author>
      <title>Maeve Ascendant</title>
      <genre>Fantasy</genre>
      <price>5.95</price>
      <publish_date>2000-11-17</publish_date>
      <description>After the collapse of a nanotechnology
      society in England, the young survivors lay the
      foundation for a new society.</description>
   </book>
   etc.
</catalog>
```

Because XML is just text, if you want to perform data analysis on the XML file, you must import the file into an Excel worksheet. Excel stores imported XML data in an Excel table.

Here are the steps to follow to import an XML file into an Excel worksheet:

1. **(Optional) To import the data to a specific location in an existing worksheet, select the cell that you want to use as the upper-left corner of the destination range.**

2. **Choose Data ⇨ Get Data ⇨ From File ⇨ From XML.**

The Import Data dialog box appears.

3. **Open the folder that contains the XML file, select the file, and then click Import.**

Excel analyzes the XML file and then opens the Navigator dialog box, which displays a list of the tables found in the file.

4. **Select the table you want to import.**

Excel displays a preview of the table, as shown in Figure 4-6.

5. **(Optional) If you want to import multiple XML tables, select the Select Multiple Items check box and then select the check box beside each table you want to import.**

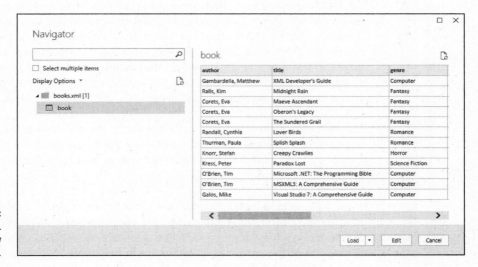

FIGURE 4-6:
Select an XML table to preview its data.

6. **Either choose Load to import the data into a new worksheet or choose Load ⇨ Load To ⇨ Existing Worksheet ⇨ OK to import the data starting at the cell you selected in Step 1.**

Excel imports the XML data into the worksheet.

Querying External Databases

If you want to analyze data using a sorted, filtered subset of an external data source, Excel offers the Query Wizard tool, which enables you to specify the sorting and filtering options and the subset of the source data that you want to work with. Why bother doing all that work? Because databases such as those used in Microsoft Access and SQL Server are often very large indeed and contain a wide variety of data scattered over many different tables.

With data analysis, you rarely use an entire database as the source. Instead, you extract a subset of the database: a table, or perhaps two or three related tables. You might also require the data to be sorted in a certain way, and perhaps need to filter the data so that you work with only certain records. The specifics of these three operations — extracting a subset, sorting, and filtering — constitute the *criteria* for the data you want to work with, and all together they make up what's known in the trade as a database *query*.

Defining a data source

All database queries require two things at the very beginning: access to a database and an *Open Database Connectivity*, or *ODBC*, data source for the database. ODBC is a database standard that enables a program to connect to and manipulate a data source. An ODBC data source contains three things: a pointer to the file or server where the database resides; a driver that enables the Query Wizard to connect to, manipulate, and return data from the database; and optional login information that you require to access the database.

Before you can do any work with the Query Wizard, you must select the data source that you want to use. If you have a particular database that you want to query, you can define a new data source that points to the appropriate file or server.

Most data sources point to database files. For example, the relational database management program Microsoft Access uses file-based databases. You can also create data sources based on text files and Excel workbooks. However, some data sources point to server-based databases. For example, SQL Server and Oracle run their databases on special servers. As part of the data source definition, you need to include the software driver that the Query Wizard uses to communicate with the database, as well as any information that you require to access the database.

Follow these steps to define a data source for your query:

1. **Choose Data ➪ Get Data ➪ From Other Sources ➪ From Microsoft Query.**

The Choose Data Source dialog box appears, as shown in Figure 4-7.

Your computer probably comes with a few predefined data sources that you can use instead of creating new ones. In the Choose Data Source dialog box, any predefined data sources appear in the Databases tab. For example, Microsoft Office creates two default data sources: Excel Files and MS Access

Database. These incomplete data sources don't point to a specific file. Instead, when you select one of these data sources and then click OK, Excel prompts you for the name and location of the file. These data sources are useful if you often switch the files that you're using. However, if you want a data source that always points to a specific file, you need to follow the steps in this section.

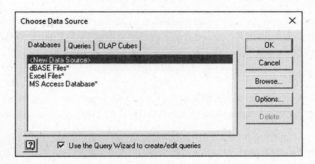

2. **Choose <New Data Source>, deselect the Use the Query Wizard to Create/Edit Queries check box, and then click OK.**

   The Create New Data Source dialog box appears.

3. **In the What Name Do You Want to Give Your Data Source? text box, enter a name for your data source.**

   This name appears in the Databases tab of the Choose Data Source dialog box, so enter a name that helps you remember which data source you're working with.

4. **From the Select a Driver for the Type of Database You Want to Access list, select the database driver that your data source requires.**

   For example, for an Access database, select `Microsoft Access Driver (*.mdb, *.accdb)`.

TECHNICAL STUFF

   Many businesses store their data in Microsoft SQL Server databases (SQL is usually pronounced *ess-kew-ell*). This is a powerful server-based system that can handle the largest databases and thousands of users. To define an SQL Server data source, select SQL Server. Click Connect to display the SQL Server Login dialog box. Ask your SQL Server database administrator for the information you require to complete this dialog box. Type the name or remote address of the SQL Server in the Server text box, type your SQL Server login ID and password, and then click OK. Perform Steps 9 and 10 later in this section to complete the data source.

5. **Click Connect.**

   The dialog box for the database driver appears. The steps that follow show you how to set up a data source for a Microsoft Access database.

6. **Click the Select button.**

The Select Database dialog box appears.

7. **Open the folder that contains the database, select the database file, and then click OK.**

Excel returns you to the database driver's dialog box.

If you use a login name and password to access the database, click Advanced to display the Set Advanced Options dialog box. Type the login name and password and then click OK.

8. **Click OK.**

Excel returns you to the Create New Data Source dialog box. Figure 4-8 shows the completed dialog box for the Northwind Access database that I'm using.

TIP

You can use the Select a Default Table for Your Data Source list to select a table from the database. When you do this, each time you start a new query based on this data source, the Query Wizard automatically adds the default table to the query, thus saving you several steps.

If you specified a login name and password as part of the data source, you can select the Save My User ID and Password in the Data Source Definition check box to save the login data.

Create New Data Source   ✕

What name do you want to give your data source?

1. Northwind

Select a driver for the type of database you want to access:

2. Microsoft Access Driver (*.mdb, *.accdb) ▼

Click Connect and enter any information requested by the driver:

3. [Connect...]   C:\Users\Paul\Documents\Northwind.accdb

Select a default table for your data source (optional):

4. ▼

☐ Save my user ID and password in the data source definition

[?]   [OK]   [Cancel]

FIGURE 4-8:
The completed
Create New Data
Source dialog box
for the Northwind
database.

---

9. **Click OK.**

Excel returns to the Choose Data Source dialog box, which now displays your shiny, new data source.

10. **Click Cancel to bypass the steps for importing the data.**

You can now use the data source in the Query Wizard, which I talk about in the next section.

Querying a data source

To run a database query and import the query results, follow these steps:

1. **Choose Data ⇨ Get Data ⇨ From Other Sources ⇨ From Microsoft Query.**

Excel displays the Choose Data Source dialog box. In Figure 4-9, you can see that the Northwind data source I created in the previous section now appears in the Databases tab.

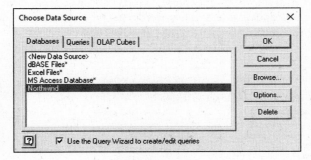

FIGURE 4-9:
Any data sources that you've created appear in the Databases tab.

2. **Select the Use the Query Wizard to Create/Edit Queries check box.**

If you didn't define a new data source as described in the previous section, this check box should already be selected for you.

3. **On the Databases tab, select the database you want to query and then click OK.**

If you choose one of the predefined database types, Excel displays the Select Database dialog box. In this dialog box, select the database that you want to query and then click OK.

Excel displays the Query Wizard - Choose Columns dialog box.

You use the Query Wizard - Choose Columns dialog box to pick which tables and which table columns (fields) you want to appear in your query results. In the Available Tables and Columns box, Excel lists tables and columns. Initially, this list shows only tables, but you can see the columns within a table by clicking the + icon next to the table name.

4. **Populate the Columns in Your Query list with the columns you want to work with.**

You have three techniques to use:

- To add an entire table to the list, click the table name and then click the right-facing arrow button that points to the Columns in Your Query list box.

- To add a single column from a table to the list, click the + icon beside the table name, select the column, and then click the right-facing arrow button that points to the Columns in Your Query list box.

- To remove a column, select the column in the Columns in Your Query list box and then click the left-facing arrow button that points to the Available Tables and Columns list box.

This all sounds very complicated, but it really isn't. Essentially, all you do is identify the columns of information that you want in your Excel table. Figure 4-10 shows how the Query Wizard - Choose Columns dialog box looks after adding several columns from the Products table and one column (CategoryName) from the Categories table.

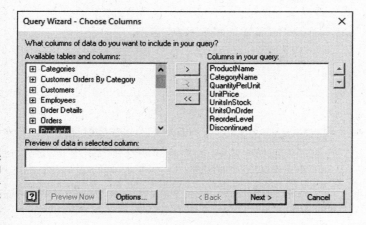

FIGURE 4-10:
The completed
Query Wizard –
Choose Columns
dialog box.

5. **After you identify which columns you want in your query, click the Next button to filter the query data.**

   Excel displays the Query Wizard - Filter Data dialog box.

   You can filter the data returned as part of your query by using the Only Include Rows Where text boxes. For example, to include only rows in which the CategoryName column equals Beverages, click the CategoryName column in the Column to Filter list box. Then select the Equals filtering operation from the first drop-down list and enter the value Beverages into the second drop-down list (or select it); you can see this filter in action in Figure 4-11.

TIP

   The Query Wizard - Filter Data dialog box performs the same sorts of filtering that you can perform with the AutoFilter command and the Advanced Filter command. Because I discuss these tools in Chapter 3, I don't repeat that discussion here. However, note that you can perform quite sophisticated filtering as part of your query.

FIGURE 4-11:
The Query
Wizard – Filter
Data dialog box
with a filter
added.

6. **(Optional) Filter your data based on multiple filters by selecting the And or Or radio buttons.**

- **And:** A row is included in the query only if it matches all the filter conditions.

- **Or:** A row is included in the query if it matches one or more of the filter conditions.

7. **Click Next.**

Excel displays the Query Wizard - Sort Order dialog box.

8. **Choose a sort order for the query result data from the Query Wizard - Sort Order dialog box.**

Select the column that you want to use for sorting from the Sort By drop-down list and then select one of the following radio buttons (see Figure 4-12):

- **Ascending:** The column values are sorted in increasing order: A to Z if the column contains text, 0 to 9 for numbers, earlier to later for dates or times.

- **Descending:** The column values are sorted in decreasing order: Z to A for text, 9 to 0 for numbers, later to earlier for dates or times.

You can also use additional sort keys by selecting fields in one or more of the Then By drop-down lists that appear in the Query Wizard – Sort Order dialog box. The wizard displays enough drop-down lists for every field in your query.

TIP

You sort query results the same way that you sort rows in an Excel table. If you have more questions about how to sort rows, refer to Chapter 3. Sorting works the same whether you're talking about query results or rows in a table.

9. **Click Next.**

Excel displays the Query Wizard - Finish dialog box.

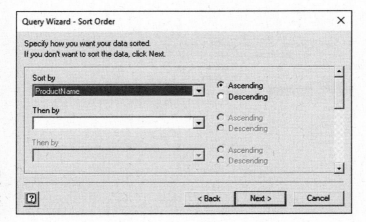

FIGURE 4-12:
The Query
Wizard – Sort
Order dialog box.

10. **In the Query Wizard - Finish dialog box, specify where Excel should place the query results.**

For most types of data, you have two choices:

- **Return Data to Microsoft Excel:** Sends the data to Excel without further review on your part.

- **View Data or Edit Query on Microsoft Query:** Opens the query in a separate Office program called Microsoft Query. This is a sophisticated database query program, the workings of which are beyond the scope of this book. If you decide to try this program, when you're finished with it, choose File ⇨ Return Data to Microsoft Excel and then continue with Step 12.

11. **Click the Finish button.**

After you click the Finish button to complete the Query Wizard, Excel displays the Import Data dialog box.

12. **In the Import Data dialog box, choose the worksheet location for the query result data.**

Use this dialog box to specify where query-result data should be placed.

- To place the query-result data in an existing worksheet, select the Existing Worksheet radio button. Then identify the cell in the top-left corner of the worksheet range and enter its location in the Existing Worksheet text box.

- Alternatively, to place the data into a new worksheet, select the New Worksheet radio button.

13. **Click OK.**

Excel places the data at the location that you chose.

It's Sometimes a Raw Deal

By using the instructions that I describe in this chapter to retrieve data from some external source, you can probably get the data rather quickly into an Excel workbook. But you may have also found that the data is rather raw and are saying to yourself (as I would be, in your shoes), "Wow, this stuff is pretty raw."

But don't worry: You are where you need to be. Having your information be raw at this point is okay. In Chapter 5, I discuss how you clean up the workbook by eliminating rows and columns and information that are not part of your data. I also cover how you scrub and rearrange the actual data in your workbook so that it appears in a format and structure that's useful to you in your upcoming analysis.

The bottom line is this: Don't worry that your data seems a bit ugly right now. Getting your data into a workbook accomplishes an important step. Now you need to spend a little time on your housekeeping. Read through the next chapter for the lowdown on how to do that.

By the way, if the process of importing data from some external source has resulted in very clean and pristine data — and this might be the case if you've grabbed data from a well-designed database or with help from the corporate database administrator — that's great. You can jump right into the data-analysis techniques that I start describing in Chapter 6.

Chapter **5**

Scrub-a-Dub-Dub: Cleaning Data

N o matter how hard you work to get data into Excel, the hard truth of the data analysis business is that in almost every case, the data that you start with — especially external data that you import from other programs — will be, at best, disorganized and, at worst, inconsistent and inaccurate. When data is messy, erratic, and wrong, data mavens describe it as *dirty*. Your job, should you decide to accept it, is to scrub that dirty data until it shines. Why? Because getting your data into a clean form makes it easier to work with, easier to organize, and easier to analyze. Best of all, Excel's data-cleaning cup runneth over with tools and techniques that can help take the drudgery out of a necessary chore.

Editing Your Imported Workbook

I start this discussion with some basic workbook editing techniques. If you take a look at the workbook shown in Figure 5-1, you see that the data, although somewhat neatly formatted, suffers from quite a few problems:

» The data is a regular range, not an Excel table.

» The workbook has several blank rows and a blank column.

» The "numbers" you see in columns B, C, and F are actually text values. How can you tell? They're left-aligned within their cells instead of being right-aligned, as is usual for numbers. Also, you see an error indicator in each cell, and when you click the error icon, Excel tells you that the cell contains a number formatted as text.

» The column are poorly sized for the data they contain. For example, columns A, B, C, and F are too wide, whereas column E is too narrow (which is why those pound signs (#) appear in some cells).

	A	B	C	D	E	F
1	Nuclear Power By Country (2016)					
2	Country	Reactors	Megawatts		Gigaw	Energy Share
3						
4	Argentina	3	1633		5716	4.5%
5	Armenia	1	375		2411	32.5%
6	Belgium	7	5918		####	49.9%
7	Brazil	2	1884		####	2.7%
8	Bulgaria	2	1926		####	34.3%
9	Canada	19	13554		####	14.6%
10	China	39	34514		####	3.9%
11	Czech Republic	6	3930		####	33.1%
12						
13	Finland	4	2769		####	33.2%
14	France	58	63130		####	71.6%
15	Germany	8	10799		####	11.6%
16	Hungary	4	1889		####	50.0%
17	India	22	6255		####	3.2%
18	Iran	1	915		6366	2.2%
19	Japan	42	39752		####	3.6%
20						
21	Korea, Republic of	25	23070		####	27.1%
22	Mexico	2	1552		####	6.0%

FIGURE 5-1: This worksheet needs a good scrubbing.

Alas, a dirty worksheet like the one shown in Figure 5-1 isn't unusual. Fortunately, you can use several workbook-editing techniques to clean up a workbook. In the following sections, I give you a rundown of the most useful ones.

Deleting unnecessary columns

To delete unnecessary columns (these might be blank columns or columns that store data that you don't need), either click the column header to select the entire column and then choose Home ⇨ Delete, or right-click the column header and then click Delete.

TIP

You can also select a column by clicking any cell in the column and then pressing Ctrl+spacebar. You can select multiple columns for multiple deletions by holding down the Ctrl key and then individually selecting column headers.

Deleting unnecessary rows

To delete unnecessary rows (for example, blank rows or rows that contain unneeded data), either click the row header to select the entire row and then choose Home ⇨ Delete, or right-click the row header and then click Delete.

TIP

You can also select a row by clicking any cell in the row and then pressing Shift+spacebar. To select multiple rows for deletion, hold down the Ctrl key and then select the row header for each of the rows that you want to delete.

Resizing columns

To resize (that is, change the width of) a column so that its contents display clearly, you have four choices:

>> Double-click the column header's right edge to size the column so that it's just wide enough to fit its widest item. Handily, this also works if you select multiple columns and then double-click any one of their right edges.

>> Select any cell in the column and then choose Home ⇨ Format ⇨ AutoFit Column Width. Excel widens the column just enough to fit its widest item.

>> Select any cell in the column and then choose Home ⇨ Format ⇨ Column Width. In the Column Width dialog box that appears, enter the width you want to use and then click OK.

>> Drag the right edge of the column header: Drag to the left for a narrower column, or drag to the right for a wider column.

Resizing rows

To resize (that is, change the height of) a row so that its contents appear fully without too much extra space above the content, you have four choices:

>> Double-click the row header's bottom edge to size the row so that it's just high enough to fit its tallest item. This also works if you select multiple rows and then double-click any one of their bottom edges.

>> Select any cell in the row and then choose Home ⇨ Format ⇨ AutoFit Row Height. Excel resizes the row height just enough to fit its tallest item.

>> Select any cell in the row and then choose Home ⇨ Format ⇨ Row Height. In the Row Height dialog box that appears, enter the height you want to use and then click OK.

>> Drag the bottom edge of the row header: Drag down for a shorter row, or drag up for a taller row.

Erasing unneeded contents in a cell or range

To erase the contents of a cell or range that contains data you don't need, select the worksheet cell or range and then choose Home ⇨ Clear ⇨ Clear All. Excel erases both the contents of the cells in the selected range and any formatting assigned to those cells.

Formatting numeric values

If you find that some of your data is in the wrong format (such as numbers displayed with text formatting), you have three techniques to use to apply the correct format for the data:

>> Select the range you want to format, click the Number Format drop-down list on the Home tab, and then select the format you want to apply.

>> Select the range you want to format and then select a predefined format in the Home tab's Number group.

>> Select the range you want to format, click the Number Format drop-down list on the Home tab, and then select More Number Formats. Excel displays the Format Cells dialog box with the Number tab displayed, as shown in Figure 5-2. Select a category and then select among the options (such as Decimal Places in the Number category) to specify the format you want to use. While you're here. you can use the other tabs in this dialog box to change the formatting of the selected range. For example, select among the options from the Alignment tab to change the way the text and values are positioned in the cell; go to the Font tab to choose the font used for values and labels in the selected range; and go to the Border tab to assign cell borders to the selected range.

FIGURE 5-2:
Format your
numeric
values here.

Copying worksheet data

To copy worksheet data, you have two choices:

>> Select the data that you want to duplicate (which could be a single cell or range of cells) and then select Home ➪ Copy (or press Ctrl+C). Select the cell that you want to use as the upper-left corner of the destination range and then select Home ➪ Paste (or press Ctrl+V).

>> Select the worksheet range that you want to copy, hold down the Ctrl key, and then drag the range border to the destination range where you want the copy to appear.

Moving worksheet data

To move worksheet data, you have two techniques to choose from:

>> Select the range you want to move (a single cell or range of cells) and then choose Home ➪ Cut (or press Ctrl+X). Select the cell that you want to use as the upper-left corner of the destination range and then choose Home ➪ Paste (or press Ctrl+V).

>> Select the worksheet range that you want to move and then drag the range border to the new position where you want the data to appear.

Replacing data in fields

Here are some common causes of crud in an imported worksheet:

>> Extraneous characters

>> Repeated characters

>> Misspelled words

>> Inconsistent spellings of certain words

>> Abbreviations or acronyms instead of full words

Sure, you could trudge through the entire worksheet and manually fix all these annoying glitches, but who has time for that? Instead, let Excel do the heavy lifting with its irreplaceable Replace command. With Replace, you tell it what text you don't want, tell it what text to use instead, and then let it rip. The result? Cleaner data without so much as a scrub brush in sight.

To use Replace, choose Home ⇨ Find & Select ⇨ Replace to open the Find and Replace dialog box with the Replace tab displayed, as shown in Figure 5-3. Enter the incorrect text that you want to find in the Find What text box and then enter the correct text in the Replace With text box. Now you have two ways to proceed:

>> Click Find Next to find the next instance of the Find What text. If you want to change this instance, click Replace; otherwise, click Find Next. Repeat until you've run through all the instances.

>> If you're absolutely certain that you want to replace every last instance of the Find What text with the Replace With text, click the Replace All button to make all the changes at one time.

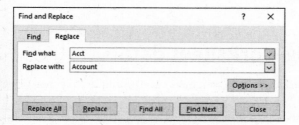

FIGURE 5-3:
Fix funky data with Excel's Replace feature.

Cleaning Data with Text Functions

One of the common problems with data that you import is that your text labels aren't quite right. For example, you might find yourself with the city, state, and ZIP code information that's part of an address stored in a single cell rather than in three separate cells. Or you might find that same information stored in three separate cells when you want the data stored in a single cell. You might also find that pieces of information that you want stored as labels instead are stored as values, and vice versa.

I mentioned in the previous section that you can use Excel's Replace feature to handle some data-cleaning chores, but Excel also offers lots of useful worksheet functions that can give you much more control over how you scrub your data. The next few sections take you through these functions and explain how they can make your data-cleaning chores go much faster and easier.

REMEMBER

For each of the text functions that follow, I've set up an example worksheet in the Chapter05.xlsx file that accompanies this chapter. See the Introduction to learn how to access this file. Also, the functions that follow all require one or more *text* arguments. Rather than repeat what *text* means each time, I summarize the possibilities here:

>> A string literal — that is, some text surrounded by double quotation marks (such as `"Hello World!"`)

>> A reference to a cell that contains text

>> A function that returns a text result

The CLEAN function

You use the CLEAN function to remove nonprintable characters from the text. For example, if the text in a column is displaying characters that appear as solid blocks or weird symbols, it means that Excel doesn't recognize those characters.

A more common scenario is imported data where one or more cells contain multiple lines of text, which means that the text includes one or more line feeds or carriage returns. CLEAN can expunge the line feeds and carriage returns, making the data display on a single line.

You can apply the CLEAN function to each cell in the column, which enables you to store the cleaned-up text in a new column that you can work with instead of the original.

The CLEAN function uses the following syntax:

```
CLEAN(text)
```

For example, to clean the text stored in cell A2, use the following syntax:

```
CLEAN(A2)
```

The CONCAT function

The CONCAT function joins two or more chunks of text into a single string. This is extremely useful if a particular bit of data (such as a name) is split over multiple columns (such as separate first name and last name columns).

The CONCAT function uses the following syntax:

```
CONCAT(text1, text2, text3,...)
```

The *text1*, *text2*, *text3*, and so on arguments are the chunks of text that you want to combine into a single string. For example, if your data displays first names in column A and last names in column B, you can add a new column named Full Name and use CONCAT to populate the new column with each first name and last name joined together, separated by a space. Here's an example:

```
CONCAT(A1, " ", B1)
```

This tells Excel to take the text from cell A1, tack on a space, and then add the text from cell B1. If A1 contains "Paul" and B1 contains "McFedries," the CONCAT function returns the following string:

```
Paul McFedries
```

REMEMBER

Having said all that, I'm also duty-bound to point out that no one ever uses the CONCAT function. Why not? Because Excel offers an easier method to join strings: the concatenation operator (&). When you insert this operator between two strings, Excel joins them together, like so:

```
A1 & " " & B1
```

I talk about an even more powerful way to join strings in "The TEXTJOIN function" section, later in this chapter, which covers Excel's new TEXTJOIN function.

The EXACT function

The EXACT function compares two strings. If the two strings are exactly the same, the EXACT function returns the logical value TRUE. If the two strings differ in any way, the EXACT function returns the logical value FALSE. The EXACT function is case sensitive. For example, *Redmond* spelled with a capital *R* differs from *redmond* spelled with a lowercase *r*.

The EXACT function uses the following syntax:

```
EXACT(text1,text2)
```

The *text1* and *text2* arguments are the strings that you want to compare. For example, to check whether the two strings "Redmond" and "redmond" are the same, use the following:

```
EXACT("Redmond","redmond")
```

This function returns the logical value FALSE because these two strings don't match exactly. One begins with an uppercase *R* and the other begins with a lowercase *r*.

The FIND function

The FIND function finds the starting character position of one string within another string. For example, if you have a column of full names (first and last), you might want to know where the space occurs in each name (which would be handy when you want to write a formula that splits the names). The FIND function handles that chore with no problem.

The FIND function uses the following syntax:

```
FIND(find_text,within_text,[start_num])
```

The *find_text* argument is the text that you're looking for. The *within_text* argument identifies where or for what you're searching. The optional *start_num* argument tells Excel at what point within the string it should begin its search. For example, to find at what point the two-letter state abbreviation WA begins in the string Redmond WA 98052, use the following:

```
FIND("WA","Redmond WA 98052",1)
```

The function returns the value 9 because WA begins at the ninth position (because spaces are counted).

As another example, suppose you have the text "Paul McFedries" in cell A2. Here's an expression that returns the location of the space (5, in this case):

```
FIND(" ", A2)
```

The *start_num* function argument is optional. If you omit this argument, Excel begins searching at the beginning of the string.

FIND runs a case-sensitive search, meaning that FIND("Sales ", A2) will return a number if A2 contains "Annual Sales" or "Sales Representative", but it will return a #VALUE! error if A2 contains "The sales team" or "salesperson." To locate text within a string without having to worry about case, use the SEARCH function that I describe later in this chapter (see the section "The SEARCH function").

The LEFT function

The LEFT function returns a specified number of characters from the left end of a string. The function uses the following syntax:

```
LEFT(text,num_chars)
```

The *text* argument either supplies the string or references the cell holding the string. The optional *num_chars* argument tells Excel how many characters to grab.

For example, to grab the leftmost seven characters from the string Redmond WA, use the following formula:

```
LEFT("Redmond WA",7)
```

The function returns the text Redmond.

On a more practical note, suppose you have a column of full names and you want to extract the first name. To do this, first use the FIND function to locate the space in the full name; then use the LEFT function to extract up to, but not including, the location of the space. For example, suppose you have the text "Paul McFedries" in cell A2. Here's an expression that extracts the first name from this text:

```
LEFT(A2, FIND(" ", A2) - 1)
```

The LEN function

The LEN function counts the number of characters in a string. The function uses the following syntax:

```
LEN(text)
```

The *text* argument either supplies the string that you want to measure or references the cell holding the string. For example, to measure the length of the string in cell I81, use the following formula:

```
LEN(I81)
```

If cell I81 holds the string Semper fidelis, the function returns the value 14. Spaces are counted as characters, too.

The LOWER function

Many external databases return all-uppercase data, which is a pain. If an all-uppercase column should really be all-lowercase, use the LOWER function, which returns an all-lowercase version of a string. The function uses the following syntax:

```
LOWER(text)
```

The *text* argument either supplies the string that you want to convert or references the cell holding the string. For example, to convert the string PROFESSIONAL to professional, use the following formula:

```
LOWER("PROFESSIONAL")
```

The function returns professional.

The MID function

The MID function returns a chunk of text from inside (that is, not necessarily from the beginning or the end) of a string. The function uses the following syntax:

```
MID(text, start_num, num_char)
```

The *start_num* argument tells Excel where the text fragment starts that you want to grab. The *num_char* argument tells Excel how many characters long the text fragment is. For example, to grab the text fragment `tac` from the string `tic tac toe`, use the following formula:

```
=MID("tic tac toe",5,3)
```

In many cases, you don't know the starting point of the string that you want to extract because the text prior to that point isn't a fixed length. For example, here are some part numbers that you might have imported from a database:

```
LDW-2125-X52
MP-9790-C78
PNH-7793-W40
SA-8703-I16
RB-3024-Z87
N-4191-W23
```

Suppose you want to extract the four digits that appear between the hyphens (-). How do you do that when the string before the first hyphen is anywhere from one to three characters long?

For starters, use the FIND function to locate the first hyphen, and then add 1 to get the starting point of the four-digit numeric value. Here's expression to use if the text is in cell A2:

```
FIND("-", A2) + 1
```

You can then plug this expression into your MID function:

```
MID(A2, FIND("-", A2) + 1, 4)
```

For the first example string, this expression return 2125.

The NUMBERVALUE function

The NUMBERVALUE function converts digits formatted as a string to a true numeric value. Here's the syntax:

```
NUMBERVALUE(text, decimal_separator, group_separator)
```

Here, *decimal_separator* is the character used in the string to separate the decimal portion of the number, and *group_separator* is the character used in the string to separate the groups (that is, thousands, millions, and so on) of the number.

For example, the formula I use in the previous section to extract four digits from within a string returns those digits as a string instead of a number. Assuming that one such string resides in cell B2, you use the following expression to convert it to a number:

```
NUMBERVALUE(B2)
```

As another example, suppose your imported data includes the following values as strings:

```
71.970,53
3.479,39
68.774,80
9.205,36
88.852,73
```

To convert these strings to numbers, you use the following version of NUMBER-VALUE (assuming that the first string is in B2):

```
NUMBERVALUE(B2, ",", ".")
```

This tells Excel to treat the comma (,) as the decimal separator and the period (.) as the group separator . For the first string, this function returns the numeric value 71970.53.

The PROPER function

The PROPER function capitalizes the first letter of every word in a string. The function uses the following syntax:

```
PROPER(text)
```

For example, to capitalize the initial letters in the string SALES REPRESENTATIVE , use the following formula:

```
PROPER("SALES REPRESENTATIVE")
```

The function returns the string Sales Representative.

The REPLACE function

The REPLACE function replaces a portion of a string with new text. The function uses the following syntax:

```
REPLACE(old_text, start_num, num_chars, new_text)
```

The *old_text* argument, which is case sensitive, either supplies the string from which you grab some text fragment or references the cell holding the string. The *start_num* argument, which is the starting position, tells Excel where the text starts that you want to replace. The *num_chars* argument tells Excel the length of the text fragment (how many characters) that you want to replace. The *new_text* argument tells Excel what new text you want to use to replace the old text.

For example, to replace the string man with the string Representative in the string Salesman, use the following expression:

```
REPLACE("Salesman",6,3," Representative")
```

The function returns the string Sales Representative.

The RIGHT function

The RIGHT function returns a specified number of characters from the end of a string. The function uses the following syntax:

```
RIGHT(text,num_chars)
```

The *num_chars* argument tells Excel how many characters to grab from the end of *text*.

For example, to get the rightmost two characters from the string Redmond WA, use the following expression:

```
RIGHT("Redmond WA",2)
```

The function returns the text WA.

As another example, suppose you have a column of full names — that is, a first name and last name separated by a space — and you want to extract the last name. Okay, begin by using FIND to locate the space in the full name, and then use the RIGHT function to extract everything after the location of the space. Hmm, how many characters is that? It's the total length of the string (as given by the LEN function) minus the location of the space:

```
LEN(text) — FIND(" ", text)
```

Now you plug this expression into the RIGHT function as the *num_chars* argument. For example, suppose you have the text "Paul McFedries" in cell A2. Here's an expression that extracts the last name from this text:

```
RIGHT(A2, LEN(A2) — FIND(" ", A2))
```

The SEARCH function

The SEARCH function performs a case-insensitive search to return the starting position of a specified string within a larger string. The function uses the following syntax:

```
SEARCH(find_text,within_text,start_num)
```

The *find_text* argument tells Excel what string fragment you're looking for. The *within_text* argument tells Excel what string you want to search. The optional *start_num* argument tells Excel where to start its search. (If you omit *start_num*, Excel starts the search at the beginning of *within_text*.)

For example, to identify the position at which the text fragment Churchill starts in the string Mr. Churchill, use the following formula:

```
SEARCH("Churchill","Mr. Churchill",1)
```

The function returns the value 5.

The SUBSTITUTE function

The SUBSTITUTE function replaces occurrences of text in a string. The function uses the following syntax:

```
SUBSTITUTE(text,old_text,new_text,instance_num)
```

The *old_text* argument identifies the to-be-replaced text fragment; *new_text* supplies the new replacement text; and the optional *instance_num* argument specifies which instance of *old_text* you want replaced. (If you omit this argument, Excel replaces all the instances.)

As an example of how the SUBSTITUTE function works, suppose your imported data comes with a phone number column in which the numbers use the following format:

```
123 555 6789
```

Assuming that one such string is in cell A2, here's a SUBSTITUTE expression that replaces all the spaces with dashes:

```
SUBSTITUTE(A2, " ", "-")
```

The TEXT function

The TEXT function formats a value and then returns the value as text. The function uses the following syntax:

```
TEXT(value,format_text)
```

The `value` argument is the value that you want formatted and returned as text. The `format_text` argument is a string that shows the currency symbol and placement, commas, and decimal places that you want. For example, the formula

```
=TEXT(1234.5678,"$##,###.00")
```

returns the text $1,234.57.

The TEXTJOIN function

The TEXTJOIN function combines two or more strings into a single string with a specified character — called the *delimiter* — between each of the original strings. The function uses the following syntax:

```
TEXTJOIN(delimiter,ignore_empty, text1, text2,...))
```

The `delimiter` argument is the character you want placed between the concatenated strings (or, if you want everything smashed together without anything in between, using ""). The `ignore_empty` argument tells Excel whether it should ignore empty cells when joining the string; the default is TRUE; `text1`, `text2`, and so on are the strings you want to join.

For example, suppose you imported some data that includes separate fields for three types of code: Manufacturer, Category, and Location. Suppose further that you can generate the values of a Part Number field by combining these three codes into a single string, with the codes separated by hyphens (-). If the three codes are in cells A2, B2, and C2, here's a TEXTJOIN expression that generates a part number

```
=TEXTJOIN("-", TRUE, A2, B2, C2)
```

Figure 5-4 shows an example of this expression in action.

The TRIM function

Some of the biggest causes of untidiness in imported data are extra characters added to some or all of the cells. For example, many cells come with extra spaces before, after, and even within the cell value. Other cells might have line breaks (caused by extraneous line feed or carriage return characters) or tabs.

FIGURE 5-4:
The TEXTJOIN function doing its thing.

The aptly named TRIM function removes extra spaces, line feeds, carriage returns, and tabs from a string. The function uses the following syntax:

```
TRIM(text)
```

For example, to trim the text stored in cell A2, use the following syntax:

```
TRIM(A2)
```

The UPPER function

The UPPER function returns an all-uppercase version of a string. The function uses the following syntax:

```
UPPER(text)
```

For example, to convert the string professional to PROFESSIONAL, you can use the following formula:

```
UPPER("professional")
```

The function returns the string PROFESSIONAL.

The VALUE function

The VALUE function converts a string that looks like a numeric value to an actual number. The function uses the following syntax:

```
VALUE(text)
```

For example, to convert the string $123,456.78 — assume that this isn't a numeric value but a string — you use the following expression:

```
VALUE("$123,456.78")
```

The function returns the numeric value 123456.78.

Converting text function formulas to text

When you're using text functions to clean up imported data, the most common technique is to start a new column beside the data and then create a formula that uses a text function to convert the first cell of the imported data into the format you want. You then fill that formula down the column to get cleaned-up versions of all the cells.

The aforementioned technique works like a charm, except for one inconvenient fact: Your cleaned-up versions appear as formula results instead of plain text or numbers. That won't be inconvenient for long because you can convert those formulas to the strings and numbers that they return. Here's how:

1. Select the worksheet range that holds the formulas.

2. Choose Home ⇨ Copy.

3. Choose Home ⇨ Paste ⇨ Paste Values.

   Because you left the formula range selected, the paste replaces the formulas with the values they returned.

Using Validation to Keep Data Clean

One useful command related to this business of keeping your data clean is the Data Validation command. Use this command to describe what information can be entered into a cell. The command also enables you to supply messages that give data input information and error messages that attempt to help someone correct data-entry errors.

To use Data Validation, follow these steps:

1. **Select the worksheet range where the to-be-validated data will go.**

   You can do this by dragging your mouse or by using the navigation keys.

2. **Choose Data ➪ Data Validation.**

   Excel displays the Data Validation dialog box, as shown in Figure 5-5.

3. **On the Settings tab of the Data Validation dialog box, use the controls in the Validation Criteria area to describe what is valid data.**

   Select options from the Allow drop-down list box, for example, to supply what types of information can go into the range: whole numbers, decimal numbers, values from the list, valid dates, valid times, text of a particular length, and so on.

   Select options from the Data drop-down list box to further define your validation criteria. The Data drop-down list box provides several comparisons that can be made as part of the validation: between, not between, equal to, not equal to, greater than, and so on.

   Refine the validation criteria, if necessary, by selecting from any of the other drop-down list boxes available. ***Note:*** The other validation criteria options depend on what you enter into the Allow and Data drop-down list boxes. For example, as shown in Figure 5-5, if you indicate that you want to allow only whole numbers between a particular range of minimum and maximum values, Excel provides Minimum and Maximum text boxes for you to enter or define the range. However, if you select other entries from the Allow or Data drop-down list boxes, you see other text boxes appearing on the Settings tab. In other words, Excel customizes the Settings tab depending on the kind of validation criteria that you define.

FIGURE 5-5:
Keep data clean with the Data Validation dialog box.

4. **Fine-tune the validation.**

   After you describe the validation criteria, either select or deselect (clear) the Ignore Blank check box to indicate whether blank cells are allowed.

5. (Optional) Consider expanding the scope of the data validation.

Select the Apply These Changes to All Other Cells with the Same Settings check box to indicate whether the validation criteria should be expanded to other similar cells.

TIP

Click the Clear All button, and Excel clears (removes) the validation criteria.

6. Provide an input message from the Input Message tab of the Data Validation dialog box.

The Input Message tab, as shown in Figure 5-6, enables you to tell Excel to display a small message when a cell with specified data validation is selected. To create the input message, you enter a title for the message into the Title text box and message text into the Input Message text box. Make sure that the Show Input Message When Cell Is Selected check box is selected. Look at Figure 5-7 to see how the Input Message entered in Figure 5-6 looks in the workbook.

FIGURE 5-6:
Create a data entry instruction message.

FIGURE 5-7:
When the user selects the cell, Excel displays the message.

7. Provide an error message from the Error Alert tab of the Data Validation dialog box (see Figure 5-8).

You can also supply an error message that Excel displays when someone attempts to enter invalid data. To create an error message, first verify that the

Show Error Alert After Invalid Data Is Entered check box is selected. Then use the Style drop-down list box to select what Excel should do when it encounters invalid data: Stop the data entry on the user without the incorrect data entry, or simply display an informational message after the data has been entered.

Just as you do when creating an input message, enter the error message title into the Title text box. Then enter the full text of the error message into the Error Message text box. In Figure 5-8, you can see a completed Error Alert tab. Check out Figure 5-9 for how the error message appears after a user enters invalid data.

TIP

Curious about the options in the Style drop-down list box (as shown in Figure 5-8)? The style of the error alert determines what icon and command buttons the error message presents when someone attempts to enter bad data. If the error style is Stop, the error message box displays Retry and Cancel command buttons. If the error style is Warning, the error message box displays Yes, No, and Cancel command buttons. If the error style is Informational, the error message box displays OK and Cancel command buttons.

FIGURE 5-8:
Create an annoying data-entry error message.

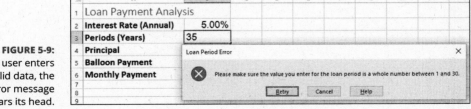

FIGURE 5-9:
If the user enters invalid data, the error message rears its head.

Chapter **6**

Analyzing Table Data with Functions

After you've imported your data, cleaned it up as best you can, and converted it to an Excel range, you might find yourself asking a most unmusical question: Now what? The what-do-I-do-next? conundrum is particularly relevant to tables that contain a vast sea of numbers. You're sure that those numbers must contain some important information for you to glean, but how do you get at it? You're sure that the data has something useful to say about your business, but how do you hear it?

The answer to all these questions is to put Excel to work analyzing the table. Excel handily provides a special set of functions — called *database functions* — especially for the statistical analysis of information that's stored in Excel tables. In this chapter, you learn about the database functions and see how to take advantage of them to get your table to spill its secrets.

The Database Functions: Some General Remarks

You might be wondering right off the bat why Excel calls these "database" functions, which seems a touch grand. However, Excel is using the word *database* as a synonym for *table*, so I follow suit and use the terms interchangeably in the pages that follow. Why not just call them table functions and avoid confusion? Because technically, these functions don't require a table: any old range will do in a pinch.

The database functions all use the same three arguments, so I describe those arguments here to save some wear and tear on my typing fingers:

>> *database*: The range of cells that make up the table you want to work with. You can use either the table name or the table range address. If you go with the table name, be sure to reference the entire table by using the syntax `Table[#All]` (where `Table` is the name of your table).

>> *field*: A reference to the table column on which you want to perform the operation. You can use either the column header or the column number (where the leftmost column is 1, the next column is 2, and so on). If you use the column name, enclose it in quotation marks (for example, "Unit Price").

>> *criteria*: The range of cells that hold the criteria you want to work with. You can use either a range name, if one is defined, or the range address.

I talk about making a criteria range for advanced filter work in Chapter 3, and setting up a criteria range for the database functions is very similar. That is, you insert three or four blank rows above your table headers, copy your table headers, and paste them above your table. For example, Figure 6-1 shows two ranges: the bigger range beginning in cell A7 is a table named Inventory, whereas the smaller range in A4:G5 is the criteria range.

Now you can enter your criteria, which consists of one or more comparison expressions that you enter into the cells below the copied header of each column you want to work with:

>> **Enter the comparison expressions on the same row:** This tells Excel to apply the database function to those *field* rows that match all the comparison expressions you enter.

>> **Enter the comparison expressions on separate rows:** This tells Excel to apply the database function to those *field* rows that match at least one of the comparison expressions you enter.

	A	B	C	D	E	F	G
3							
4	**Product Name**	**Category**	**On Hold**	**On Hand**	**Unit Cost**	**List Price**	**Value**
5							
6							
7	**Product Name** ▾	**Category** ▾	**On Hold** ▾	**On Hand** ▾	**Unit Cost** ▾	**List Price** ▾	**Value** ▾
8	Chai	Beverages	25	25	$13.50	$18.00	$337.50
9	Syrup	Confections	0	50	$7.50	$10.00	$375.00
10	Cajun Seasoning	Confections	0	0	$16.50	$22.00	$0.00
11	Olive Oil	Condiments	0	15	$16.01	$21.35	$240.19
12	Boysenberry Spread	Condiments	0	0	$18.75	$25.00	$0.00
13	Dried Pears	Fruits	0	0	$22.50	$30.00	$0.00
14	Curry Sauce	Sauces/Soups	0	0	$30.00	$40.00	$0.00
15	Walnuts	Produce	0	40	$17.44	$23.25	$697.50
16	Fruit Cocktail	Produce	0	0	$29.25	$39.00	$0.00
17	Chocolate Biscuits Mix	Confections	0	0	$6.90	$9.20	$0.00
18	Marmalade	Condiments	0	0	$60.75	$81.00	$0.00
19	Scones	Grains/Cereals	0	0	$7.50	$10.00	$0.00
20	Beer	Beverages	23	23	$10.50	$14.00	$241.50
21	Crab Meat	Seafood	0	0	$13.80	$18.40	$0.00

FIGURE 6-1:
A table and its
criteria range.

Retrieving a Value from a Table

As part of your data analysis, retrieving a single value from a table to use in a formula is often useful. For example, if you have a table that lists the inventory of all your products, you might want to check how much of a particular product is on hand now to decide whether now's the time to reorder that product. Similarly, you might want to calculate a product's gross margin given its list price and unit cost:

```
(List Price - Unit Cost) / List Price
```

Whenever you need a value from the table to use in a formula, use the DGET function. DGET retrieves a value from a table according to the criteria you specify. The function uses the following syntax:

```
DGET(database, field, criteria)
```

For example, consider the Inventory table shown earlier in Figure 6-1. Suppose you want to know how many units are on hand of the product named Beer. To set up the criteria range, you enter Beer below the Product Name field, as shown in Figure 6-2. With that done, you can build your DGET function, which is in cell B1 in Figure 6-2:

```
DGET(Inventory[#All], "On Hand", A4:G5)
```

This DGET function is saying to Excel, in effect, "Take a look at the entire table named Inventory, locate the row that has "Beer" in the Product Name column, and then retrieve the value in the On Hand column. Thanks in advance." Sure enough, DGET returns the value 23 because that's the On Hand value of the Beer product.

| B1 | | : | × | ✓ | fx | =DGET(Inventory[#All], "On Hand", A4:G5) |

▲	A	B	C	D	
1	Beer on hand:	23			
2	Gross margin:	33%			
3					
4	**Product Name**	**Category**	**On Hold**	**On Hand**	U
5	Beer				
6					
7	**Product Name** ▽	**Category** ▽	**On Hold** ▽	**On Hand** ▽	U
8	Chai	Beverages	25	25	
9	Syrup	Confections	0	50	
10	Cajun Seasoning	Confections	0	0	
11	Olive Oil	Condiments	0	15	
12	Boysenberry Spread	Condiments	0	0	
13	Dried Pears	Fruits	0	0	
14	Curry Sauce	Sauces/Soups	0	0	
15	Walnuts	Produce	0	40	
16	Fruit Cocktail	Produce	0	0	
17	Chocolate Biscuits Mix	Confections	0	0	
18	Marmalade	Condiments	0	0	
19	Scones	Grains/Cereals	0	0	
20	Beer	Beverages	23	23	

‹ › | DGET | DSUM | ⊕

FIGURE 6-2:
Use DGET to retrieve a value from a table based on your criteria.

TIP

By the way, if no record in your list matches your selection criteria, DGET returns the #VALUE error message. For example, if you construct selection criteria that look for Northwind Traders Lager, DGET returns #VALUE because that product doesn't exist. Also, if multiple records in your list match your selection criteria, DGET returns the #NUM error message. For example, if you enter *Chocolate* in the Product Name field of the criteria range, that string matches all the products that have Chocolate in the name. Two such products exist, so DGET returns the #NUM error message.

Summing a Column's Values

In Chapter 3, "Introducing Excel Tables," I talk about two ways to display simple table sums: by selecting some column cells and viewing the sum in Excel's status bar, and by adding subtotals to the table. Those techniques are fine if all you want to do is view the sum, but what if you want to use the sum in a formula or as part of a table summary? Yep, Excel's SUM function would work, but what if you want the sum of only those items that meet some criteria? For example, in an inventory table, what if you want to know the total value of just the items in the Beverages category?

Ah, for that you need the DSUM function, which adds values from a table based on the criteria you specify. The function uses the standard database function syntax:

```
DSUM(database, field, criteria)
```

For example, to get the total value of just the products in the Beverages category, you set up your criteria range with the string Beverages under the Category header (see Figure 6-3). With that value in place, you build your DSUM function (as shown in cell B1 in Figure 6-3):

```
DSUM(Inventory2[#All], "Value", A3:G4)
```

B1		×	✓	fx	=DSUM(Inventory2[#All], "Value", A3:G4)		
	A	B	C	D	E	F	G
1	Total value of Beverages:	$12,041.50					
2							
3	Product Name	Category	On Hold	On Hand	Unit Cost	List Price	Value
4		Beverages					
5							
6	Product Name	Category	On Hold	On Hand	Unit Cost	List Price	Value
7	Chai	Beverages	25	25	$13.50	$18.00	$337.50
8	Syrup	Confections	0	50	$7.50	$10.00	$375.00
9	Cajun Seasoning	Confections	0	0	$16.50	$22.00	$0.00
10	Olive Oil	Condiments	0	15	$16.01	$21.35	$240.19
11	Boysenberry Spread	Condiments	0	0	$18.75	$25.00	$0.00
12	Dried Pears	Fruits	0	0	$22.50	$30.00	$0.00
13	Curry Sauce	Sauces/Soups	0	0	$30.00	$40.00	$0.00
14	Walnuts	Produce	0	40	$17.44	$23.25	$697.50
15	Fruit Cocktail	Produce	0	0	$29.25	$39.00	$0.00
16	Chocolate Biscuits Mix	Confections	0	0	$6.90	$9.20	$0.00
17	Marmalade	Condiments	0	0	$60.75	$81.00	$0.00
18	Scones	Grains/Cereals	0	0	$7.50	$10.00	$0.00
19	Beer	Beverages	23	23	$10.50	$14.00	$241.50
20	Crab Meat	Seafood	0	0	$13.80	$18.40	$0.00

DGET **DSUM** ⊕

FIGURE 6-3:
Use DSUM to add a column's values based on your criteria.

You might be wondering why the table name changed from Inventory in the DGET example to Inventory2 in the DSUM example. That's because in my example workbook for this chapter, I use a separate worksheet for each database function, so when I copy the inventory table to a new worksheet, I need to give the table a new name (because table names must be unique in a workbook).

TIP

DSUM isn't the only way to total stuff based on criteria. Excel also offers the SUMIF and SUMIFS functions, which I talk about in Chapter 11, "Analyzing Data with Statistics."

Counting a Column's Values

If you select some values in a table column, Excel's status bar will gladly display a Count item, which tells you how many cells you selected. Fine and dandy, but data analysis is usually a bit more sophisticated than that. For example, in an inventory table, suppose you want to know many products are low in stock (that is, have fewer than 10 in the On Hand column)?

That kind of calculation falls under the bailiwick of both the DCOUNT and DCOUNTA functions, which count records in a table that match criteria you specify:

```
DCOUNT(database, field, criteria)
DCOUNTA(database, field, criteria)
```

What's the diff? DCOUNT counts the numeric values in `field`, whereas DCOUNTA counts all the nonblank items in `field`.

For example, to get the count of the products that have low stock, you set up your criteria range with the expression < 10 under the On Hand header (see Figure 6-4) and then add the DCOUNT function (as shown in cell B1 in Figure 6-4):

```
DCOUNT(Inventory3[#All], "On Hand", A3:G4)
```

B1	▼ : × ✓ fx	=DCOUNT(Inventory3[#All], "On Hand", A3:G4)					
	A	B	C	D	E	F	G
1	Count of out of stock:	25					
2							
3	Product Name	Category	On Hold	On Hand	Unit Cost	List Price	Value
4				<10			
5							
6	Product Name	Category	On Hold	On Hand	Unit Cost	List Price	Value
7	Chai	Beverages	25	25	$13.50	$18.00	$337.50
8	Syrup	Confections	0	50	$7.50	$10.00	$375.00
9	Cajun Seasoning	Confections	0	0	$16.50	$22.00	$0.00
10	Olive Oil	Condiments	0	15	$16.01	$21.35	$240.19
11	Boysenberry Spread	Condiments	0	0	$18.75	$25.00	$0.00
12	Dried Pears	Fruits	0	0	$22.50	$30.00	$0.00
13	Curry Sauce	Sauces/Soups	0	0	$30.00	$40.00	$0.00
14	Walnuts	Produce	0	40	$17.44	$23.25	$697.50
15	Fruit Cocktail	Produce	0	0	$29.25	$39.00	$0.00
16	Chocolate Biscuits Mix	Confections	0	0	$6.90	$9.20	$0.00
17	Marmalade	Condiments	0	0	$60.75	$81.00	$0.00
18	Scones	Grains/Cereals	0	0	$7.50	$10.00	$0.00
19	Beer	Beverages	23	23	$10.50	$14.00	$241.50
20	Crab Meat	Seafood	0	0	$13.80	$18.40	$0.00
	DGET	DSUM	DCOUNT ⊕				

FIGURE 6-4: Use DCOUNT (or DCOUNTA) to tally a column's values based on your criteria.

TIP

If you just want to count records in a list, you can omit the `field` argument from the DCOUNT and DCOUNTA functions. When you don't specify a column name or number, the function counts the records in the table that match your criteria without regard to whether some field stores a value or is nonblank. For example, both of the following functions return the value 25:

```
DCOUNT(Inventory3[#All],, A3:G4)
DCOUNTA(Inventory3[#All],, A3:G4)
```

Note: To omit an argument, leave the space between the two commas empty.

TIP

Excel actually has a seemingly uncountable number of ways to count things. Besides DCOUNT, you can also use COUNT, COUNTA, COUNTIF, COUNTIFs, and COUNTBLANK. Check out Chapter 11, "Analyzing Data with Statistics," or the Excel online help for more information about these functions.

Averaging a Column's Values

The DAVERAGE function calculates an average for values in an Excel list. The unique and truly useful feature of DAVERAGE is that you can specify that you want only table records that meet specified criteria included in your average. DAVERAGE uses the following syntax:

```
DAVERAGE(database, field, criteria)
```

As an example of how the DAVERAGE function works, I return to the inventory table and ask a basic question: What's the average Unit Cost value for those products in the Beverages and Produce categories? To answer this query, you add the text Beverages under the Category header in the criteria range, and then add the text Produce below the Beverages cell, as shown in Figure 6-5. Remember that when you enter criteria using multiple rows, Excel selects those rows in the table that match at least one of the conditions. So, in the example, I'm asking Excel to look for only those products that have either Beverages or Produce in the Category column. Here's the DAVERAGE function that returns the average Unit Cost for those products (see cell B1 in Figure 6-5):

```
DAVERAGE(Inventory4[#All], "Unit Cost", A3:G5)
```

Notice that I expanded the *criteria* range to include both rows 4 and 5.

TIP

Excel offers an above-average number of functions for calculating averages, including not only the AVERAGE function (of course), but also the MEAN, MEDIAN, and MODE functions. I talk about these functions in Chapter 11.

FIGURE 6-5:
Use DAVERAGE
to average a
column's values
based on
your criteria.

Determining a Column's Maximum and Minimum Values

Often in data analysis work, looking for outliers is very useful. *Outliers* are values that are either much greater or much less than the average. One way to check for such anomalous values is to find the largest and smallest values in a column. You can certainly calculate such maxima and minima using every value in the column, but if you're interested only in those values that meet some criteria, then have I got two functions for you: DMAX and DMIN. These functions find the largest and smallest values, respectively, in a table column for those rows that match the criteria you specify. Both functions use the same standard-issue database function syntax, as shown here:

```
DMAX(database, field, criteria)
```

DMIN(*database, field, criteria*)As an example of how the DMAX and DMIN functions work, suppose you have an inventory table with a Value column that's the product of the number of units on hand and the unit cost. (For example, a product with 100 units on hand and a $5 unit cost has a total value of $500.) Here's a question for you: What are the maximum and minimum values for those items in the Produce category that are in stock?

To answer the preceding question, you add the text Produce under the Category header in the criteria range and then add the expression > 0 below the On Hand header, as shown in Figure 6-6. Remember that when you enter multiple conditions on a single row, Excel matches only those rows in the table that match all the conditions. So, in the example, I'm asking Excel to look for only those products that have Produce in the Category column and a value greater than 0 in the On Hand column. Here are the DMAX and DMIN functions that return the maximum and minimum, respectively, for those products (see cells B1 and B2 in Figure 6-6):

```
DMAX(Inventory5[#All], "Value", A4:G5)
DMIN(Inventory5[#All], "Value", A4:G5)
```

B1		▼	:	×	✓	fx	=DMAX(Inventory5[#All], "Value", A4:G5)		
	A	B		C	D	E	F	G
1	Maximum value:	$697.50						
2	Minimum value:	$5.00						
3								
4	Product Name	Category		On Hold	On Hand	Unit Cost	List Price	Value
5		Produce			>0			
6								
7	Product Name	Category		On Hold	On Hand	Unit Cost	List Price	Value
8	Chai	Beverages		25	25	$13.50	$18.00	$337.50
9	Syrup	Confections		0	50	$7.50	$10.00	$375.00
10	Cajun Seasoning	Confections		0	0	$16.50	$22.00	$0.00
11	Olive Oil	Condiments		0	15	$16.01	$21.35	$240.19
12	Boysenberry Spread	Condiments		0	0	$18.75	$25.00	$0.00
13	Dried Pears	Produce		0	0	$22.50	$30.00	$0.00
14	Curry Sauce	Sauces/Soups		0	0	$30.00	$40.00	$0.00
15	Walnuts	Produce		0	40	$17.44	$23.25	$697.50
16	Fruit Cocktail	Produce		0	0	$29.25	$39.00	$0.00
17	Chocolate Biscuits Mix	Confections		0	0	$6.90	$9.20	$0.00
18	Marmalade	Condiments		0	0	$60.75	$81.00	$0.00
19	Scones	Grains/Cereals		0	0	$7.50	$10.00	$0.00
20	Beer	Beverages		23	23	$10.50	$14.00	$241.50

◄ ► | DGET | DSUM | DCOUNT | DAVERAGE | **DMAX & DMIN** | ⊕ | : | ◄

FIGURE 6-6: Use DMAX and DMIN to return a column's largest and smallest values based on your criteria.

TIP

Excel provides several other functions for finding the minimum or maximum value, including MAX, MAXA, MIN, and MINA. Turn to Chapter 11 for more information about using these related functions.

Multiplying a Column's Values

Lots of table data contains the results of surveys or polls, meaning that the table values are percentages. One way you might want to interrogate such data is to ask, given two percentages, in what percentage are both true in the surveyed population? For example, if your survey says that 50% of people like item A and 50% of people like item B, what percentage of people like both items A and B? You get the answer by multiplying the percentages, so in this case, 25% of the surveyed population like both A and B.

You can perform this kind of table multiplication using the DPRODUCT function, which uses the usual syntax:

```
DPRODUCT(database, field, criteria)
```

For example, Figure 6-7 shows the results of a survey that asked people whether they liked certain items. What percentage of people like any two of the items? To calculate this, you set up a criteria range for the Item field and then add the items in separate rows below the Item header. In Figure 6-7, for example, you can see that I added Soggy cereal in the first row and Commuting in the second row. Here's the DPRODUCT function that calculates the answer (see cell B1 in Figure 6-7):

```
DPRODUCT(A6:B11, 2, A2:A4)
```

FIGURE 6-7: Use DPRODUCT to multiple a column's values based on your criteria.

Deriving a Column's Standard Deviation

One of the most important statistical measures is the *standard deviation*, which tells you how much the values in a collection vary with respect to the average. I talk about this in more detail in Chapter 11, but for now I can tell you that a low standard deviation means that the data values are grouped near the average, and a high standard deviation means that the values are spread out from the average.

For your table data analysis fun, the DSTDEV and DSTDEVP functions calculate the standard deviation: DSTDEV calculates the standard deviation when you're working with a sample of the population, whereas DSTDEVP calculates the standard deviation when you're working with the entire population. As with other database statistical functions, the unique and truly useful feature of DSTDEV and DSTDEVP is that you can specify that you want the calculation to include only those table records that meet your specified criteria.

REMEMBER

The DSTDEV and DSTDEVP functions use the same syntax:

```
=DSTDEV(database, field, criteria)
=DSTDEVP(database, field, criteria)
```

For example, in the inventory table, suppose you want to know the standard deviation of the Value column for products in the Condiments category and where the Value column is greater than 0. To set up this calculation, you enter the text Condiments under the criteria range's Category header and the expression > 10 under the Value header (see Figure 6-8), and then you add the DSTDEV function (as shown in cell B1 in Figure 6-8):

```
DSTDEV(Inventory6[#All], "Value", A3:G4)
```

B1	▼ : × ✓ fx	=DSTDEV(Inventory6[#All], "Value", A3:G4)					
	A	B	C	D	E	F	G
1	Standard deviation	$213.77					
2							
3	**Product Name**	**Category**	**On Hold**	**On Hand**	**Unit Cost**	**List Price**	**Value**
4		Condiments					>0
5							
6	**Product Name**	**Category**	**On Hold**	**On Hand**	**Unit Cost**	**List Price**	**Value**
7	Chai	Beverages	25	25	$13.50	$18.00	$337.50
8	Syrup	Confections	0	50	$7.50	$10.00	$375.00
9	Cajun Seasoning	Confections	0	0	$16.50	$22.00	$0.00
10	Olive Oil	Condiments	0	15	$16.01	$21.35	$240.19
11	Boysenberry Spread	Condiments	0	0	$18.75	$25.00	$0.00
12	Dried Pears	Produce	0	0	$22.50	$30.00	$0.00
13	Curry Sauce	Sauces/Soups	0	0	$30.00	$40.00	$0.00
14	Walnuts	Produce	0	40	$17.44	$23.25	$697.50
15	Fruit Cocktail	Produce	0	0	$29.25	$39.00	$0.00
16	Chocolate Biscuits Mix	Confections	0	0	$6.90	$9.20	$0.00
17	Marmalade	Condiments	0	0	$60.75	$81.00	$0.00
18	Scones	Grains/Cereals	0	0	$7.50	$10.00	$0.00
19	Beer	Beverages	23	23	$10.50	$14.00	$241.50

◄ ► ... DMAX & DMIN | DPRODUCT | **DSTDEV** ⊕

FIGURE 6-8:
Use DSTDEV (or DSTDEVP) to derive the standard deviation of a column's values based on your criteria.

TIP

If you want to calculate standard deviations without applying selection criteria, use one of Excel's nondatabase statistical functions such as STDEV, STDEVA, STDEVP, or STDEVPA. In Chapter 11, I describe and illustrate these other standard deviation functions.

Calculating a Column's Variance

The *variance* of a set is a measure of how dispersed the data is. The variance is actually the square of the standard deviation, so it's rarely used because it doesn't make intuitive sense. (For example, what does it mean to say that a result is in "dollars squared"?)

However, for the sake of completion, I include the fact that Excel does offer the DVAR and DVARP functions to calculate the variance. DVAR calculates the variance when your data is a sample of a larger population, whereas DVARP calculates the variance when your data is the entire population. As with other database statistical functions, using DVAR and DVARP enables you to specify that you want only those table records that meet selection criteria included in your calculations.

REMEMBER

As with standard deviation calculations, don't pick one of the two variance functions based on a whim, the weather outside, or how you're feeling. If you're calculating a variance using a sample or a subset of items from the entire data set or population, you use the DVAR function. To calculate a variance when you're dealing with all the items in the population, use the DVARP function.

The DVAR and DVARP functions use the same syntax:

```
=DVAR(database, field, criteria)
=DVARP(database, field, criteria)
```

For example, in the inventory table, suppose you want to know the variance of the Unit Cost column for products in the Confections category. To set up this calculation, you enter the text Confections under the criteria range's Category header (see Figure 6-9) and then add the DVAR function (as shown in cell B1 in Figure 6-8, shown previously):

```
DVAR(Inventory7[#All], "Unit Cost", A3:G4)
```

TIP

If you want to calculate variances without applying selection criteria, use one of the Excel nondatabase statistical functions such as VAR, VARA, VARP, or VARPA. I talk about these other variance functions in Chapter 11.

B1	▼ : × ✓ fx	=DVAR(Inventory7[#All], "Unit Cost", A3:G4)				

	A	B	C	D	E	F	G
1	Variance	26.84					
2							
3	**Product Name**	**Category**	**On Hold**	**On Hand**	**Unit Cost**	**List Price**	**Value**
4		Confections					
5							
6	**Product Name** ▾	**Category** ▾	**On Hold** ▾	**On Hand** ▾	**Unit Cost** ▾	**List Price** ▾	**Value** ▾
7	Chai	Beverages	25	25	$13.50	$18.00	$337.50
8	Syrup	Confections	0	50	$7.50	$10.00	$375.00
9	Cajun Seasoning	Confections	0	0	$16.50	$22.00	$0.00
10	Olive Oil	Condiments	0	15	$16.01	$21.35	$240.19
11	Boysenberry Spread	Condiments	0	0	$18.75	$25.00	$0.00
12	Dried Pears	Produce	0	0	$22.50	$30.00	$0.00
13	Curry Sauce	Sauces/Soups	0	0	$30.00	$40.00	$0.00
14	Walnuts	Produce	0	40	$17.44	$23.25	$697.50
15	Fruit Cocktail	Produce	0	0	$29.25	$39.00	$0.00
16	Chocolate Biscuits Mix	Confections	0	0	$6.90	$9.20	$0.00
17	Marmalade	Condiments	0	0	$60.75	$81.00	$0.00

| ◂ ▸ ... | DMAX & DMIN | DPRODUCT | DSTDEV | DVAR | ⊕ | ⋮ ◂ |

FIGURE 6-9:
Use DVAR (or DVARP) to derive the variance of a column's values based on your criteria.

2

Analyzing Data with PivotTables and PivotCharts

Use PivotTables to cross-tabulate data and gain new insights into your information.

Extend the power of Excel's PivotTables by creating your own customized formulas.

Display cross-tabulated data in a chart for new perspectives on opportunities and problems.

Customize PivotCharts to make sure that your graphical information communicates the right messages.

Chapter **7**

Creating and Using PivotTables

xcel tables and external databases can contain thousands of records. Let's face it: Figuring out how to glean useful insights from that much data will either keep you awake at night or cause nightmares if you do sleep. Want to get some quality shut-eye? No need for sleeping pills when Excel offers a powerful and versatile data-analysis tool called a *PivotTable,* which enables you to take those thousands of records and summarize them in a concise tabular format. You can then manipulate the layout of — or *pivot* — the PivotTable to see different views of your data.

This chapter shows you everything you need to know to get started with what is arguably Excel's most useful data-analysis tool. You learn how to create Pivot-Tables, refresh them, pivot them, group them, filter them, and much more.

Understanding PivotTables

In a general sense, PivotTables take a large amount of information and condense that data into a report that tells you something useful or interesting. For example, take a look at the table shown in Figure 7-1. This table contains well over 100 records, each of which is an order from a sales promotion. That's not a ton of data in the larger scheme of things, but trying to make sense of even this relatively small data set just by eyeballing the table's contents is futile. For example, how many earbuds were sold via social media advertising? Who knows? Ah, but now look at Figure 7-2, which shows a PivotTable built from the order data. This report tabulates the number of units sold for each product based on each promotion. From here, you can quickly see that 322 earbuds were sold via social media advertising. *That* is what PivotTables do.

	A	B	C	D	E	F
1	SUMMER SALES PROMOTION - ORDERS					
2	Date	Product	Quantity	Net $	Promotion	Advertisement
3	2019-06-01	Smartphone case	11	$119.70	1 Free with 10	Social media
4	2019-06-01	HDMI cable	6	$77.82	Extra Discount	Blog network
5	2019-06-01	USB car charger	15	$100.95	Extra Discount	Search
6	2019-06-01	HDMI cable	11	$149.71	1 Free with 10	Blog network
7	2019-06-02	USB car charger	22	$155.40	1 Free with 10	Blog network
8	2019-06-02	USB car charger	3	$20.19	Extra Discount	Search
9	2019-06-02	Earbuds	5	$33.65	Extra Discount	Social media
10	2019-06-02	Smartphone case	22	$239.36	1 Free with 10	Search
11	2019-06-02	HDMI cable	10	$129.70	Extra Discount	Blog network
12	2019-06-05	USB car charger	22	$155.40	1 Free with 10	Blog network
13	2019-06-05	Smartphone case	8	$82.96	Extra Discount	Social media
14	2019-06-05	Smartphone case	22	$239.40	1 Free with 10	Social media
15	2019-06-05	Earbuds	55	$388.50	1 Free with 10	Blog network
16	2019-06-05	USB car charger	25	$168.25	Extra Discount	Search
17	2019-06-05	HDMI cable	22	$299.42	1 Free with 10	Blog network
18	2019-06-06	USB car charger	33	$256.41	1 Free with 10	Blog network
19	2019-06-06	Smartphone case	11	$119.70	1 Free with 10	Blog network

FIGURE 7-1:
Some great data, but how do you make sense of it?

	A	B	C	D	E
1	Promotion	(All)			
2					
3	Sum of Quantity	Column Labels			
4	Row Labels	Blog network	Search	Social media	Grand Total
5	Earbuds	555	562	322	1439
6	HDMI cable	719	587	402	1708
7	Smartphone case	546	460	338	1344
8	USB car charger	1596	1012	752	3360
9	Grand Total	3416	2621	1814	7851
10					

FIGURE 7-2:
The PivotTable creates order out of data chaos.

PivotTables help you analyze large amounts of data by performing three operations: grouping the data into categories; summarizing the data using calculations; and filtering the data to show just the records you want to work with:

>> **Grouping:** A PivotTable is a powerful data-analysis tool in part because it automatically groups large amounts of data into smaller, more manageable chunks. For example, suppose you have a data source with a Region field in which each item contains one of four values: East, West, North, and South. The original data may contain thousands of records, but if you build your

PivotTable using the Region field, the resulting table has just four rows — one each for the four unique Region values in your data.

You can also create your own grouping after you build your PivotTable. For example, if your data has a Country field, you can build the PivotTable to group all the records that have the same Country value. When you have done that, you can further group the unique Country values into continents: North America, South America, Europe, and so on.

» **Summarizing:** In conjunction with grouping data according to the unique values in one or more fields, Excel also displays summary calculations for each group. The default calculation is Sum, which means that for each group, Excel totals all the values in some specified field. For example, if your data has a Region field and a Sales field, a PivotTable can group the unique Region values and display the total of the Sales values for each one. Excel has other summary calculations, including Count, Average, Maximum, Minimum, and Standard Deviation.

Even more powerful, a PivotTable can display summaries for one grouping broken down by another. For example, suppose your sales data also has a Product field. You can set up a PivotTable to show the total Sales for each Product, broken down by Region.

» **Filtering:** A PivotTable also enables you to view just a subset of the data. For example, by default, the PivotTable's groupings show all the unique values in the field. However, you can manipulate each grouping to hide those that you do not want to view. Each PivotTable also comes with a report filter that enables you to apply a filter to the entire PivotTable. For example, suppose your sales data also includes a Customer field. By placing this field in the PivotTable's report filter, you can filter the PivotTable report to show just the results for a single Customer.

Exploring PivotTable Features

You can get up to speed with PivotTables very quickly after you learn a few key concepts. You need to understand the features that make up a typical PivotTable, particularly the four areas — row, column, data, and filter — to which you add fields from your data. Figure 7-3 points out the following PivotTable features:

» **Row area:** Displays vertically the unique values from a field in your data.

» **Column area:** Displays horizontally the unique values from a field in your data.

>> **Value area:** Displays the results of the calculation that Excel applied to a numeric field in your data.

>> **Row field header:** Identifies the field contained in the row area. You also use the row field header to filter the field values that appear in the row area.

>> **Column field header:** Identifies the field contained in the column area. You also use the column field header to filter the field values that appear in the column area.

>> **Value field header:** Specifies both the calculation (such as Sum) and the field (such as Quantity) used in the value area.

>> **Filter area:** Displays a drop-down list that contains the unique values from a field. When you select a value from the list, Excel filters the PivotTable results to include only the records that match the selected value.

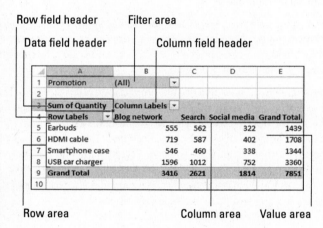

FIGURE 7-3:
The features of a typical PivotTable.

Building a PivotTable from an Excel Table

If the data you want to analyze exists as an Excel table, you can use the Summarize with PivotTable command to quickly build a PivotTable report based on your data. You need only specify the location of your source data and then choose the location of the resulting PivotTable.

Here are the steps to follow:

1. **Select a cell in the table that you want to use as the source data.**

2. **Choose Design ⇨ Summarize with PivotTable.**

   If your data resides in a regular Excel range instead of a table, you can still do the PivotTable thing. Select any cell in the range and then choose Insert⇨PivotTable.

TIP

   While I have your attention, I should also point out the Insert tab's Recommended PivotTables command. This command displays a dialog box that shows several predefined PivotTable layouts. These might not mean anything to you now if you're new to PivotTables, but keep the Recommended PivotTables command in mind down the road; it might save you a bit of time.

   The Create PivotTable dialog box appears with the Select a Table or Range radio button selected. The Table/Range box should show the name of your table (or the address of your range). If not, adjust the name or address as needed before moving on.

3. **Select the New Worksheet radio button.**

   Alternatively, if you want to add the PivotTable to an existing location, select the Existing Worksheet radio button and then use the Location range box to select the worksheet and cell where you want the PivotTable to appear.

4. **Click OK.**

   Excel creates a blank PivotTable and displays the PivotTable Fields pane, as shown in Figure 7-4. This pane contains two main areas:

   - A list of the column headers from your table, each of which has a check box to its left. These are your PivotTable fields.

   - Four boxes representing the four areas of the PivotTable: Filters, Columns, Rows, and Values. To complete the PivotTable, your job is to add one or more fields to some (or even all) of these areas.

5. **Drag a text field and drop it inside the Rows area.**

   For example, using the fields shown in Figure 7-4, you could drop the Product field into the Rows area.

   Excel adds the field's unique values to the PivotTable's row area.

6. **Drag a numeric field and drop it inside the Values area.**

   For example, using the fields shown in Figure 7-4, you could drop the Quantity field into the Values area.

   Excel sums the numeric values based on the row values.

Blank PivotTable   PivotTable fields

FIGURE 7-4:
You start with
a blank
PivotTable and
the PivotTable
Fields pane.

PivotTable areas

7. **If desired, drag fields and drop them in the Columns area and the Filters area.**

For example, using the fields shown in Figure 7-4, you could drop the Advertisement field into the Columns area and the Promotion field into the Filters area.

Each time you drop a field in an area, Excel updates the PivotTable to include the new data.

Excel offers a few shortcut techniques for building PivotTables:

TIP

- Select the check box for a text or date field to add it to the Rows area.

- Select the check box for a numeric field to add it to the Values area.

- Right-click a field and then select the area that you want to use.

Figure 7-5 shows a completed PivotTable, with fields in all four areas. Note, too, that when you select a cell inside the PivotTable, Excel displays the PivotTable Tools contextual tab, which includes two tabs — Analyze and Design — that offer lots of goodies for manipulating and formatting your PivotTable.

FIGURE 7-5:
The features of a
typical PivotTable.

To remove a field from a PivotTable area, you have two ways to proceed:

» Drag the field out of the PivotTable Fields pane.

» Click the field button in the PivotTable Fields pane to drop down the field menu, and then click Remove Field.

Creating a PivotTable from External Data

The data you're analyzing might not exist in an Excel range or table but rather outside Excel, in a relational database management system (RDBMS) such as Microsoft Access or SQL Server. With these programs, you can set up a table, query, or other object that defines the data you want to work with. Then, instead of building a PivotTable from data within an Excel worksheet, you create the PivotTable using the external data source. This enables you to build reports from extremely large data sets and from relational database systems.

Here are the steps to follow to build a PivotTable based on an external data source:

1. **Choose Data ⇨ Get Data ⇨ From Other Sources ⇨ From Microsoft Query.**

The Choose Data Source dialog box appears. I talk about this dialog box, as well as the general topics of external data and defining data sources, in Chapter 4, "Grabbing Data from External Sources." The steps that follow repeat those from the section about querying a data source in Chapter 4, so I leave out some of the details.

2. **Select the Use the Query Wizard to Create/Edit Queries check box.**

3. **On the Databases tab, select the database you want to query and then click OK.**

   If you choose one of the predefined database types, Excel displays the Select Database dialog box. In this dialog box, select the database that you want to query and then click OK.

   Excel displays the Query Wizard - Choose Columns dialog box.

4. **Add the columns you want to work with to the Columns in Your Query list and then select Next button.**

   Excel displays the Query Wizard - Filter Data dialog box.

5. **(Optional) Filter your data based on multiple filters by selecting the And or Or radio buttons; then select Next.**

   Excel displays the Query Wizard - Sort Order dialog box.

6. **(Optional) Choose a sort order for the query result data from the Query Wizard - Sort Order dialog box and then click Next.**

   Excel displays the Query Wizard - Finish dialog box.

7. **Select the Return Data to Microsoft Excel radio button and then click the Finish button.**

   Excel displays the Import Data dialog box, shown in Figure 7-6.

FIGURE 7-6:
Import the external data to a PivotTable Report.

8. **Select the PivotTable Report radio button, select the New Worksheet radio button, and then click OK.**

   Excel creates a blank PivotTable and the PivotTable Fields pane.

9. **Drag a text field and drop it inside the Rows area.**

   Excel adds the field's unique values to the PivotTable's row area.

10. **Drag a numeric field and drop it inside the Values area.**

   Excel sums the numeric values based on the row values.

11. **If desired, drag fields and drop them in the Columns area and the Filters area.**

   Each time you drop a field in an area, Excel updates the PivotTable to include the new data.

REMEMBER

When you create a PivotTable from external data, you don't need the external data to be imported to Excel. Rather, the external data resides only in the new Pivot-Table; you don't see the actual data in your workbook.

TECHNICAL STUFF

The most common drawback to using external data is that you often have no control over the data source. For example, if you attempt to refresh the PivotTable, as I describe in the next section, Excel might display an error message. If you suspect that the problem is a change to the database login data, click OK to display the Login dialog box and then find out the new login name and password from the database administrator.

Alternatively, the problem might be that the database file has been moved or renamed. Click OK in the error message and then click Database in the Login dialog box. Next, in the Select Database dialog box, find and select the database file.

Refreshing PivotTable Data

Whether your PivotTable is based on financial results, survey responses, or a database of collectibles such as rare books or cubic zirconia jewelry, the underlying data is probably not static. That is, the data changes over time as new results come in, new surveys are undertaken, and new items are added to the collection. You can ensure that the data analysis represented by the PivotTable remains up to date by refreshing the PivotTable.

Excel offers two methods for refreshing a PivotTable: manual and automatic. A manual refresh is one that you perform, usually when you know that the source data has changed, or if you simply want to be sure that the latest data is reflected in your PivotTable report. An automatic refresh is one that Excel handles for you.

Refreshing PivotTable data manually

To refresh your PivotTable data manually, you have two choices:

>> **Update a single PivotTable:** Select any cell inside the PivotTable and then choose Analyze ⇨ Refresh. You can also press Alt+F5.

>> **Update every PivotTable in the workbook:** Select a cell inside any PivotTable and then choose Analyze ⇨ Refresh ⇨ Refresh All. You can also update all PivotTables by pressing Ctrl+Alt+F5.

Excel dutifully updates the PivotTable data.

Refreshing PivotTable data automatically

Here are the steps to follow to convince Excel to refresh your PivotTable data automatically:

1. **Select any cell inside the PivotTable.**

2. **Choose Analyze ⇨ PivotTable ⇨ Options.**

   TIP

   You can also right-click any cell in the PivotTable and then choose PivotTable Options.

   The PivotTable Options dialog box appears.

3. **Click the Data tab.**

4. **Select the Refresh Data When Opening the File check box, as shown in Figure 7-7, and then click OK.**

   From now on, Excel will automatically refresh the PivotTable data each time you open the workbook.

TIP

If your PivotTable is based on external data, you can set up a schedule that automatically refreshes the PivotTable at a specified interval. Select any cell inside the PivotTable and then choose Analyze ⇨ Refresh ⇨ Connection Properties. In the Connection Properties dialog box, select the Refresh Every check box, use the spin buttons to specify the refresh interval, in minutes, and then click OK.

WARNING

Note, however, that when you set up an automatic refresh, it might be best not to have the source data updated too frequently. Depending on where the data resides and how much data you're working with, the refresh could take some time, which may slow down the rest of your work.

FIGURE 7-7:
Import the
external data
to a PivotTable
Report.

Adding Multiple Fields to a PivotTable Area

You can add two or more fields to any of the PivotTable areas. Having multiple fields is a powerful feature that enables you to perform further analysis of your data by viewing the data differently. For example, suppose you're analyzing the results of a sales campaign that ran different promotions in several types of advertisements. A basic PivotTable might show you the sales for each product (the row field) according to the advertisement used (the column field). You might also be interested in seeing, for each product, the breakdown in sales for each promotion. You can do that by adding the Promotion field to the row area.

REMEMBER

Excel doesn't restrict you to just two fields in any area. Depending on your data-analysis requirements, you're free to add three, four, or more fields to any Pivot-Table area.

Select a cell within the PivotTable and then use any of the following techniques to add another field to a PivotTable area:

>> **Add a field to the Rows area:** In the PivotTable Fields pane, select the check box of the text or date field that you want to add.

>> **Add a field to the Value area:** In the PivotTable Fields pane, select the check box of the numeric field that you want to add.

>> **Add a field to any area:** In the PivotTable Fields pane, drag the field and drop it inside the box of the area where you want the field to appear.

TIP

After you add a second field to the row or column area, you can change the field positions to change the PivotTable view. In the PivotTable Fields pane, drag the button of the field you want to move out of the Rows box or the Columns box and then drop the field above or below an existing field button.

When you add a second field to the value area, Excel moves the labels, such as Sum of Quantity and Sum of Net $, into the column area for easier reference. This is also reflected in the addition of a Values button in the Columns box section of the PivotTable Fields pane. This enables you to pivot the values within the report, as I describe in the next section.

Pivoting a Field to a Different Area

A PivotTable is a powerful data-analysis tool because it can take hundreds or even thousands of records and summarize them into a compact, comprehensible report. However, unlike most of the other data-analysis features in Excel, a PivotTable is not a static collection of worksheet cells. Instead, you can move a PivotTable's fields from one area of the PivotTable to another. Moving fields to various areas enables you to view your data from different perspectives, which can greatly enhance the analysis of the data. Moving a field within a PivotTable is called *pivoting* the data.

The most common way to pivot the data is to move fields between the row and column areas. However, you can also pivot data by moving a row or column field to the filter area. Either way, you perform the pivot by dragging the field from its current box in the PivotTable Fields pane and then dropping it inside the area where you want it moved.

You can move any row, column, or filter field to the PivotTable's value area. Moving a field to this location may seem strange because row, column, and page fields are almost always text values, and the default value area calculation is Sum. How can you sum text values? You can't, of course. Instead, the default Excel Pivot-Table summary calculation for text values is Count. So, for example, if you drag the Promotion field and drop it inside the value area, Excel creates a second value field named Count of Promotion.

Grouping PivotTable Values

To make a PivotTable with a large number of row or column items easier to work with, you can group the items. For example, you can group months into quarters, thus reducing the number of items from twelve to four. Similarly, a report that lists dozens of countries can group those countries by continent, thus reducing the number of items to four or five, depending on where the countries are located. Finally, if you use a numeric field in the row or column area, you may have hundreds of items, one for each numeric value. You can improve the report by creating just a few numeric ranges.

Grouping numeric values

Grouping numeric values is useful when you use a numeric field in a row or column field. Excel enables you to specify numeric ranges into which the field items are grouped. For example, suppose you have a PivotTable of invoice data that shows the extended price (the row field) and the salesperson (the column field). It would be useful to group the extended prices into ranges and then count the number of invoices each salesperson processed in each range.

Follow these steps to group numeric values in a PivotTable field:

1. Select any item in the numeric field you want to group.

2. Choose Analyze⇨Group⇨Group Field.

The Grouping dialog box appears, as shown in Figure 7-8.

FIGURE 7-8:
The Grouping
dialog box.

3. Use the Starting At text box to enter the starting numeric value.

Alternatively, select the Starting At check box to have Excel extract the minimum value of the numeric items and place that value in the text box.

4. **Use the Ending At text box to enter the ending numeric value.**

   Alternatively, select the Ending At check box to have Excel extract the maximum value of the numeric items and place that value in the text box.

5. **In the By text box, enter the size you want to use for each grouping.**

6. **Click OK.**

   Excel groups the numeric values.

Grouping date and time values

If your PivotTable includes a field with date or time data, you can use Excel's grouping feature to consolidate that data into more manageable or useful groups. Follow these steps:

1. **Select any item in the date or time field you want to group.**

2. **Choose Analyze ⇨ Group ⇨ Group Field.**

   The Grouping dialog box appears.

3. **In the Starting At text box, enter the starting date or time.**

   Alternatively, select the Starting At check box to have Excel extract the earliest date or time and place that value in the text box.

4. **Use the Ending At text box to enter the ending date or time.**

   Alternatively, select the Ending At check box to have Excel extract the latest date or time and place that value in the text box.

5. **From the By list, select the grouping you want, such as Months for dates or Hours for times.**

   If you select Days, you can also use the Number of Days spin buttons to set the days you want to use for the grouping interval.

   To use multiple groupings, select each type of grouping you want to use.

6. **Click OK.**

   Excel groups the date or time values.

Grouping text values

One common problem that arises when you work with PivotTables is that you often need to consolidate items, but you have no corresponding field in the data. For example, the data may have a Country field, but what if you need to consolidate the PivotTable results by continent? Your source data isn't likely to include a

Continent field. Similarly, your source data may include employee names, but you may need to consolidate the employees according to the people they report to. What happens if your source data does not include, say, a Supervisor field?

The solution in both cases is to use the Grouping feature to create custom groups. For the country data, you can create custom groups named North America, South America, Europe, and so on. For the employees, you can create a custom group for each supervisor.

Here are the steps to follow to create such a custom grouping for text values:

1. **Select the items that you want to include in the group.**

2. **Choose Analyze ⇨ Group ⇨ Group Selection.**

Excel creates a new group named Group*n* (where *n* means that this is the *n*th group you have created; the first group is Group1, the second is Group2, and so on) and restructures the PivotTable.

3. **Select the cell that contains the group label, type a new name for the group, and then press Enter.**

Excel renames the group.

4. **Repeat Steps 1 to 3 for the other items in the field until you have created all your groups.**

Filtering PivotTable Values

By default, each PivotTable report displays a summary for all the records in your source data. This is usually what you want to see. However, you may have situations in which you need to focus more closely on some aspect of the data. You can focus on a specific item from one of the source data fields by taking advantage of the PivotTable's report filter field.

Applying a report filter

Suppose you're dealing with a PivotTable that summarizes data from thousands of customer invoices over some period of time. A basic PivotTable might tell you the total amount sold for each product that you carry. That's interesting, but what if you want to see the total amount sold for each product in a specific country? If the Product field is in the PivotTable's row area, you can add the Country field to the column area. However, you may have dozens of countries, so adding the field to the column area isn't an efficient solution. Instead, you can add the Country field to the report filter and tell Excel to display the total sold for each product for the specific country that you're interested in.

Follow these steps to apply a PivotTable report filter:

1. **Select the filter field's drop-down arrow.**

Excel displays a list of the report filter field values.

2. **Select the report filter you want to view.**

In Figure 7-9, I use the report filter list to select Canada.

If you want to display data for two or more report filters, select the Select Multiple Items check box and then repeat Step 2 to select the other report filters.

To return later to showing all the items in the report field, select (All) from the filter field's drop-down list.

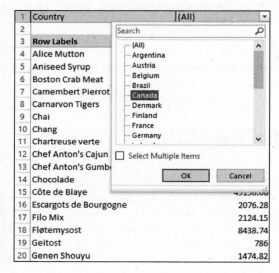

FIGURE 7-9: From the filter field's drop-down list, select a report filter.

3. **Select OK.**

Excel filters the PivotTable to show only the data for the report filter you selected.

Filtering row or column items

By default, your PivotTable shows all the items in whatever row and column fields you added to the report layout. Seeing all the items is usually what you want because the point of a PivotTable is to summarize all the data in the original source. However, sometimes you may not want to see every item. For example, in a PivotTable report that includes items from the ProductName field in the row area, you might want to see only those products with names that begin with the letter G or that contain the word *tofu*.

When you modify a PivotTable report to show only a subset of the row or column items, you are applying a *label filter* to the report, which is different from a *report filter*, which filters the entire PivotTable, as described in the previous section. Excel offers a number of label filters for text, including Equals, Does Not Equal, Begins With, Ends With, Contains, Greater Than, and Less Than.

If your PivotTable report includes a date field in the row or column area, you can apply a date filter to that field. Excel offers many different date filters, including Before, After, Between, Today, Yesterday, Last Week, Last Month, Last Quarter, This Year, and Year to Date.

Follow these steps to apply a label filter to row or column items:

1. **Click the drop-down arrow in the header of the field you want to filter.**

The field's Sorting & Filtering menu appears.

2. **Select Label Filters and then select the filter type you want to apply, such as Begins With.**

The Label Filter dialog box appears.

3. **Type the filter criteria and then click OK.**

Some filters, such as Between, require you to type two criteria values.

Excel filters the PivotTable report.

To remove a row or column label filter, click the drop-down arrow in the field's header and then select Clear Filter from *Field*, where *Field* is the name of the filtered field.

Filtering PivotTable values

Excel enables you to apply *value filters* that restrict the values you see in the value area. For example, you may want to see only those values that are larger than some amount or that fall between two specified amounts. Excel offers several value filters, including Equals, Does Not Equal, Greater Than, Greater Than or Equal To, Less Than, Less Than or Equal To, Between, and Not Between.

Similarly, you may be interested in only the highest or lowest values that appear in the PivotTable. For example, you might want to see just the top ten values. You can generate such a report by using Excel's Top 10 Filter, which filters the Pivot-Table to show just the top ten items based on the values in the value field.

For example, suppose you have a PivotTable report based on a database of invoices that shows the total sales for each product. The basic report shows all the products, but if you're interested in only the top performers for the year, you can activate the Top 10 Filter feature to see the ten products that sold the most. Despite its name, the Top 10 Filter can display more than just the top ten data values. You can specify any number between 1 and 2,147,483,647, and you can ask Excel to show the bottommost values as well.

Follow these steps to apply a value filter to your PivotTable:

1. **Click the drop-down arrow in the header of any row or column field.**

   The field's Sorting & Filtering menu appears.

2. **Select Value Filters and then select the filter type you want to apply, such as Top 10.**

   The dialog box for that value filter appears — for example, the Top 10 Filter dialog box.

3. **Type the filter criteria and then click OK.**

   Excel filters the PivotTable report.

To remove a value filter, click the drop-down arrow in the header of the filtered field and then choose Value Filters ⇨ Clear Filter.

Filtering a PivotTable with a slicer

As mentioned earlier in this chapter, you can filter a PivotTable either by using the report filter, which applies to the entire PivotTable, or by using either a label filter or a value filter, which apply only to the filter field. Whether it applies to the entire PivotTable or just the filter field, the filter is usable only with the PivotTable in which it's defined. However, requiring the same filter in multiple PivotTable reports is not unusual. For example, if you're a sales manager responsible for sales in a particular set of countries, you might often need to filter a PivotTable to show data from just those countries. Similarly, if you work with a subset of your company's product line, you might often have to filter PivotTable reports to show the results from just those products.

Applying these kinds of filters to one or two PivotTables is not difficult or time consuming, but if you have to apply the same filter over and over again, the process gets old in a hurry. To combat this repetition, Excel offers a PivotTable feature called the *slicer*. A slicer is very similar to a report filter, except that it's independent of any PivotTable. This means that you can use a single slicer to filter multiple PivotTables. Nice!

First, here are the steps to follow to create a slicer to filter a PivotTable:

1. **Select a cell inside your PivotTable.**

2. **Choose Analyze ⇨ Insert Slicer.**

    The Insert Slicers dialog box appears and displays a check box for every field in your PivotTable report.

3. **Select the check box beside each field for which you want to create a slicer; then click OK.**

    Excel displays one slicer for each field you selected. Each slicer is a box that contains a list of the items from its associated field. By default, all the items in the slicer are selected, so no filtering has yet been applied to the PivotTable. Your mission is to use the slicer to select just the field items you want to see in the PivotTable.

    Also, the Slicer Tools contextual tab appears when a slicer has the focus, and you can use the controls in its Options tab to customize each slicer.

4. **Select a field item that you want to include in your filter.**

    If you want to include multiple items in your filter, hold down Ctrl, select each item, and then release Ctrl. Alternatively, click the Multi-Select button (see Figure 7-10; you can also toggle Multi-Select by pressing Alt+S).

    Excel filters the PivotTable based on the field items you selected in each slicer. Figure 7-10 shows an example.

TIP

If a field contains lots of items, you may have to scroll a long way in the slicer to locate the item you want. In this case, configuring the slicer to display its items in multiple columns is often easier. Select the title of the slicer to select it, click the Options tab, and then click the Column spin buttons to set the number of columns.

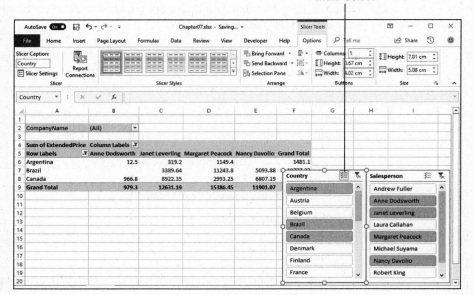

Multi-Select

FIGURE 7-10:
Excel filters the
PivotTable to
show just the
selected items in
each slicer.

If you find that you no longer need to use a slicer, you should remove it to avoid cluttering the PivotTable window. Either select the slicer and press Delete, or right-click the slicer and then select Remove *Slicer*, where *Slicer* is the name of the slicer (which is usually the field name). If you want only to temporarily hide the slicer, select any slicer, choose Options ➪ Selection Pane to display the Selection task pane, and then click the eye icon beside the slicer to hide it.

» **Working with PivotTable subtotals**

» **Using custom PivotTable calculations**

» **Creating a custom calculated PivotTable field and item**

Chapter **8**

Performing PivotTable Calculations

The near-ridiculous power and flexibility of a PivotTable is in contrast with the relative simplicity of what a PivotTable actually does, which is to take a mountain of data and turn it into a molehill of a report. With that report in place, the fun part begins when you pivot fields, group items, and filter the report (all of which I describe in painstaking detail in Chapter 7). Pivoting, grouping, and filtering represent the most visible aspects of a PivotTable's power, but lots of impressive things happening behind the PivotTable scenes as well. These "hidden" features include the massive number of calculations that Excel performs to summarize all that data so succinctly. That display of raw calculation horsepower is impressive enough, but you can actually harness that power for your own ends.

In this chapter, you open the PivotTable's hood to check out its calculation engine. You explore how the calculations work, swap out some parts to try different calculations, and even learn how to soup things up with your own custom calculations. Vroom vroom!

Messing around with PivotTable Summary Calculations

The calculation that Excel uses to populate the PivotTable data area is called the *summary calculation*. Most of the time, the default Sum calculation will get the job done, but Excel offers lots of options for taking the summary calculation to a higher analytical level. The next few sections fill you in on those options.

Changing the PivotTable summary calculation

The default summary calculation depends on the type of field you add to the data area:

>> If you add a numeric field to the data area, Excel uses Sum as the default summary calculation.

>> If you use a text field in the data area, Excel uses Count as the default summary calculation.

Sum and Count aren't the only calculation choices, however. If your data analysis requires a different calculation, you can configure the data field to use any one of Excel's 11 built-in summary calculations. Here's the complete list:

>> **Average:** Calculates the mean value in a numeric field.

>> **Count:** Displays the total number of cells in the source field.

>> **Count Numbers:** Displays the total number of numeric values in the source field.

>> **Max:** Displays the largest value in a numeric field.

>> **Min:** Displays the smallest value in a numeric field.

>> **Product:** Multiplies the values in a numeric field.

>> **StdDev:** Calculates the standard deviation of a population sample, which tells you how much the values in the source field vary with respect to the average.

>> **StdDevp:** Calculates the standard deviation when the values in the data field represent the entire population.

>> **Sum:** Adds the values in a numeric field.

>> **Var:** Calculates the variance of a population sample, which is the square of the standard deviation.

>> **Varp:** Calculates the variance when the values in the data field represent the entire population.

Here are the steps to follow to try a different summary calculation:

1. **Select any cell in the data field.**

2. **Choose Analyze⇨Field Settings.**

The Value Field Settings dialog box appears with the Summarize Values By tab displayed, as shown in Figure 8-1.

3. **In the Summarize Value Field By list, select the summary calculation you want to use.**

4. **Click OK.**

Excel recalculates the PivotTable results and renames the value field label to reflect the new summary calculation.

FIGURE 8-1:
Use the Value Field Settings dialog box to choose a summary calculation.

TIP

Another way to change the PivotTable summary calculation is to right-click any cell in the value field, choose the Summarize Values By command, and then select the calculation you want to use from the submenu that appears. If you don't see the calculation, choose the More Options command to open the Value Field Settings dialog box.

When you build your PivotTable, you may find that the results don't pass the smell test. For example, the numbers may appear to be far too small. In that case, check the summary calculation that Excel has applied to the field to see whether it's using Count instead of Sum. If the data field includes one or more text cells or one or more blank cells, Excel defaults to the Count summary function instead of Sum. If your field is supposed to be numeric, check the data to see whether any text values or blank cells are showing up.

When you add a second field to the row or column area, Excel displays a subtotal for each item in the outer field. (The *outer field* is the field "farthest" from the value area: the leftmost field if you have two fields in the row area; the topmost field if you have two fields in the column area. The other field is called the *inner field* because it's "closest" to the value area.) By default, the subtotals show the sum of the data results for each outer field item. However, the same 11 summary calculations — from Average to Varp — are also available for subtotals.

Trying out the difference summary calculation

The built-in summary calculations — Sum, Count, and so on — apply over an entire field. However, a major part of data analysis involves comparing one item with another. If you're analyzing sales to customers, for example, knowing how much you sold this year is useful, but even more useful is to compare this year's sales with last year's. Are the sales up or down? By how much? Are the sales up or down with all customers or only some? These are fundamental questions that help managers run departments, divisions, and companies.

Excel offers two difference calculations that can help with this kind of analysis:

>> **Difference From:** Compares one numeric item with another and returns the difference between them

>> **% Difference From:** Compares one numeric item with another and returns the percentage difference between them

Before you set up a difference calculation, you need to decide which field in your PivotTable to use as the comparison field, or *base field*, and which item within that field to use as the basis for all the comparisons, which is called the *base item*. For example, take a peek at Figure 8-2, which uses the Order Date field to show the sales in 2019 and the sales in 2018. In this example, Order Date is the base field and 2018 is the base item.

Sum of Extended Price	Order Date		
Customer	2018	2019	Grand Total
Alfreds Futterkiste	$2,250.50	$2,022.50	$4,273.00
Ana Trujillo Emparedados y helados	$603.20	$799.75	$1,402.95
Antonio Moreno Taquería	$1,063.20	$5,960.77	$7,023.97
Around the Horn	$6,983.75	$6,406.90	$13,390.65
Berglunds snabbköp	$11,078.57	$13,849.01	$24,927.58
Blauer See Delikatessen	$2,160.00	$1,079.80	$3,239.80
Blondel père et fils	$10,716.20	$7,817.88	$18,534.08
Bólido Comidas preparadas	$1,206.00	$3,026.85	$4,232.85
Bon app'	$10,754.89	$11,208.35	$21,963.24
Bottom-Dollar Markets	$13,171.35	$7,630.25	$20,801.60
B's Beverages	$2,910.40	$3,179.50	$6,089.90
Cactus Comidas para llevar	$1,576.80	$238.00	$1,814.80
Centro comercial Moctezuma	$100.80		$100.80
Chop-suey Chinese	$5,832.48	$6,516.40	$12,348.88

PT-Invoices 2018 vs 2019   Sales   PT-Sale ...   ⊕

FIGURE 8-2: A PivotTable that shows sales in two years: 2018 and 2019.

Here are the steps to follow to apply a difference summary calculation to a PivotTable:

1. **Select any cell in the value field.**

2. **Choose Analyze⇨Field Settings.**

   The Value Field Settings dialog box appears with the Summarize Values By tab displayed.

3. **Click the Show Values As tab.**

4. **In the Show Values As list, select Difference From.**

   If you want to see the difference in percentage terms, select % Difference From instead.

TIP

Another way to select the Difference Summary calculation is to right-click any cell in the value field, select Show Values As, and then select Difference From.

5. **In the Base Field list, select the field from which you want Excel to calculate the difference.**

6. **In the Base Item list, select a base item.**

   Figure 8-3 shows a completed Show Values As tab for the example PivotTable.

7. **Click OK.**

   Excel recalculates the PivotTable results to show the difference summary calculation. Figure 8-4 shows the PivotTable from Figure 8-2 with the Difference From calculation applied.

FIGURE 8-3:
Use the Value Field Settings dialog box to choose a summary calculation.

Sum of Extended Price	Order Date		
Customer	2018	2019	Grand Total
Alfreds Futterkiste		-$228.00	
Ana Trujillo Emparedados y helados		$196.55	
Antonio Moreno Taquería		$4,897.57	
Around the Horn		-$576.85	
Berglunds snabbköp		$2,770.44	
Blauer See Delikatessen		-$1,080.20	
Blondel père et fils		-$2,898.32	
Bólido Comidas preparadas		$1,820.85	
Bon app'		$453.46	
Bottom-Dollar Markets		-$5,541.10	
B's Beverages		$269.10	
Cactus Comidas para llevar		-$1,338.80	
Centro comercial Moctezuma		-$100.80	
Chop-suey Chinese		$683.92	

PT-Invoices 2018 vs 2019 | Sales | PT-Sale ...

FIGURE 8-4:
The PivotTable from Figure 8-2 is now using the Difference From calculation.

Applying a percentage summary calculation

When analyzing data, comparing two or more items as a percentage is often helpful because percentage calculations enable you to make apples-to-apples comparisons between values. For example, if your PivotTable shows quarterly sales by region (see Figure 8-5), you might want to know how the results in the second, third, and fourth quarters compare, as a percentage, to the results from the first quarter.

That kind of comparison sounds hard, but you can use Excel's percentage calculations to quickly view data items as a percentage of some other item or as a percentage of the total in the current row, column, or PivotTable. Excel offers seven percentage calculations that can help you perform this kind of analysis:

FIGURE 8-5:
A PivotTable that shows quarterly sales by region.

Sum of Sales	Quarter				
Region	1st	2nd	3rd	4th	Grand Total
East	$377,568	$343,706	$368,121	$374,260	$1,463,655
Midwest	$321,220	$307,992	$365,790	$370,213	$1,365,215
South	$346,345	$330,999	$376,658	$355,542	$1,409,544
West	$411,647	$390,493	$361,091	$314,653	$1,477,884
Grand Total	$1,456,780	$1,373,190	$1,471,660	$1,414,668	$5,716,298

PT-Sales By Region & Qtr   Invoices 2019   ...

>> **% Of:** Returns the percentage of each value with respect to a selected base item.

>> **% of Row Total:** Returns the percentage that each value in a row represents of the total value of the row.

>> **% of Column Total:** Returns the percentage that each value in a column represents of the total value of the column.

>> **% of Grand Total:** Returns the percentage that each value represents of the PivotTable grand total.

>> **% of Parent Row Total:** If you have multiple fields in the row area, this calculation returns the percentage that each value in an inner row represents with respect to the total of the parent item in the outer row.

>> **% of Parent Column Total:** If you have multiple fields in the column area, this calculation returns the percentage that each value in an inner column represents with respect to the total of the parent item in the outer column.

>> **% of Parent Total:** If you have multiple fields in the row or column area, this calculation returns the percentage of each value with respect to a selected base field in the outer row or column.

If you use the % Of or the % of Parent Total calculation, you must also choose a base field and a base item upon which Excel will calculate the percentages.

Here are the steps to follow to apply a percentage summary calculation:

1. **Select any cell in the value field.**

2. **Choose Analyze ⇨ Field Settings.**

   The Value Field Settings dialog box appears with the Summarize Values By tab displayed.

3. **Click the Show Values As tab.**

4. **In the Show Values As list, select the percentage calculation you want to use.**

   If you select % Of or % of Parent Total, continue with Step 5; otherwise, skip to Step 7.

5. **In the Base Field list, select the field from which you want Excel to calculate the percentages.**

6. **In the Base Item list, select a base item.**

7. **Click OK.**

   Excel recalculates the PivotTable results to show the percentage summary calculation. Figure 8-6 shows the PivotTable from Figure 8-2 with the % Of calculation applied.

Sum of Sales	Quarter				
Region	1st	2nd	3rd	4th	Grand Total
East	100.00%	91.03%	97.50%	99.12%	
Midwest	100.00%	95.88%	113.88%	115.25%	
South	100.00%	95.57%	108.75%	102.66%	
West	100.00%	94.86%	87.72%	76.44%	
Grand Total	100.00%	94.26%	101.02%	97.11%	

| ▶ | ... | PT-Sales By Region & Qtr | Invoices 2019 | ... | ⊕ | ⋮ | ◀ |

FIGURE 8-6:
The PivotTable from Figure 8-5, now using the % Of calculation.

Adding a running total summary calculation

A *running total* is the cumulative sum of the values that appear in a given set of data. Most running totals accumulate over a period of time. For example, suppose you have 12 months of sales figures. In a running total calculation, the first value is the first month of sales, the second value is the sum of the first and second months, the third value is the sum of the first three months, and so on.

You use a running total in data analysis when you need to see a snapshot of the overall data at various points. For example, suppose you have a sales budget for each month. As the fiscal year progresses, comparing the running total of the budget figures with the running total of the actual sales tells you how your department or company is doing with respect to the budget. If sales are consistently below budget, you might consider lowering prices, offering customers extra discounts, or increasing your product advertising.

Creating a running total seems like a job best left to a complex Excel formula. Sure, you could create such a formula, but I'm happy to report that you don't have to bother with any of that. That's because Excel offers a built-in Running Total In summary calculation that you can apply to your PivotTable results. No muss and not even any fuss.

REMEMBER

The Running Total In summary applies to not just the Sum calculation but also related calculations, such as Count and Average.

Before you configure your PivotTable to use a Running Total In summary calculation, you must choose the field on which to base the accumulation, called the *base field.* This field will most often be a date field, but you can also create running totals based on other fields, such as customer, division, product, and so on.

Here are the steps to follow to apply a Running Total In summary calculation to a PivotTable:

1. **Select any cell in the value field.**

2. **Choose Analyze ⇨ Field Settings.**

The Value Field Settings dialog box appears with the Summarize Values By tab displayed.

3. **Click the Show Values As tab.**

4. **In the Show Values As list, select Running Total In.**

If you want to see the running total in percentage terms, select % Running Total In instead.

Another way to select the Running Total In summary calculation is to right-click any cell in the value field, and then choose Show Values As ⇨ Running Total In.

TIP

5. **In the Base Field list, select the field from which you want Excel to accumulate the running totals.**

6. **Click OK.**

Excel recalculates the PivotTable results to show the running totals. Figure 8-8 shows the PivotTable from Figure 8-7 with the Running Total In calculation applied.

OrderDate	Sum of ExtendedPrice
Jan	$53,981.61
Feb	$42,386.08
Mar	$41,921.21
Apr	$53,032.95
May	$50,506.46
Jun	$39,637.61
Jul	$44,811.34
Aug	$53,497.15
Sep	$55,629.24
Oct	$65,354.48
Nov	$44,928.54
Dec	$71,398.41
Grand Total	**$617,085.08**

▸ ... PT-Monthly Sales | PT-Unit

FIGURE 8-7:
A PivotTable showing monthly order totals.

OrderDate	Sum of ExtendedPrice
Jan	$53,981.61
Feb	$96,367.69
Mar	$138,288.90
Apr	$191,321.85
May	$241,828.31
Jun	$281,465.92
Jul	$326,277.26
Aug	$379,774.41
Sep	$435,403.65
Oct	$500,758.13
Nov	$545,686.67
Dec	$617,085.08
Grand Total	

PT-Monthly Sales   PT-Unit

FIGURE 8-8: The PivotTable from Figure 8-7, with the Running Total In calculation applied.

Creating an index summary calculation

One of the most crucial aspects of data analysis is determining the relative importance of the results of your calculations. This determination is particularly vital in a PivotTable, whose results summarize a large amount of data but on the surface provide no clue as to the relative importance of the various value area results.

For example, suppose your PivotTable shows the units sold for various product categories broken down by region (see Figure 8-9). Suppose further that in Oregon, you sold 30 units of produce and 35 units of seafood. Does this mean that seafood sales are relatively more important in the Oregon market than produce sales? Not necessarily. To determine relative importance, you must take into account the larger picture, such as the total units sold of both produce and seafood across all states. Suppose the produce total is 145 units and the seafood total is 757 units. In that case, you can see that the 30 units of produce sold in Oregon represents a much higher portion of total produce sales than does Oregon's 35 units of seafood. A proper analysis would also take into account the total units sold in Oregon and the total units sold overall (the PivotTable's Grand Total).

Sum of Quantity CategoryName	Region Idaho	Oregon	Washington	Grand Total
Beverages	301	71	182	554
Condiments	240	32	99	371
Confections	359	79	72	510
Dairy Products	343	86	54	483
Grains/Cereals	247	42	25	314
Meat/Poultry	337	6	96	439
Produce	110	30	5	145
Seafood	637	35	85	757
Grand Total	2574	381	618	3573

PT-Units By Category & Region   PT-Custor ...

FIGURE 8-9: A PivotTable showing units sold by category and region.

Determining the relative importance of a PivotTable's results sounds headache-inducingly complex, but Excel offers the built-in Index calculation, which handles everything without the need for aspirin. The Index calculation determines the *weighted average* — the average taking into account the relative importance of each value — of each cell in the PivotTable results.

Put your math geek hat on because here's the formula Excel uses:

```
(Cell Value) * (Grand Total) / (Row Total) * (Column Total)
```

In the Index calculation results, the higher the value, the more important the cell is in the overall PivotTable report.

Follow these steps to apply the Index summary calculation to a PivotTable:

1. Select any cell in the value field.

2. Choose Analyze ⇨ Field Settings.

The Value Field Settings dialog box appears with the Summarize Values By tab displayed.

3. Click the Show Values As tab.

4. In the Show Values As list, select Index.

Alternatively, right-click any cell in the value field, and then choose Show Values As ⇨ Index.

TIP

5. Click OK.

Excel recalculates the PivotTable results to show the Index results.

Working with the Index calculation results is much easier if you format the data field to show just two decimal places. Select any cell in the value field, choose Analyze ⇨ Field Settings, click Number Format, select Number in the Category list, make sure that 2 appears in the Decimal places field, click OK, and then click OK again.

TIP

Figure 8-10 shows the PivotTable from Figure 8-9 with the Index calculation applied. Notice that under Oregon, the index value for the Produce category is 1.94, whereas the index value for Seafood is 0.43, which tells you that produce sales in Oregon are relatively more important than seafood sales.

Sum of Quantity	Region			
CategoryName	Idaho	Oregon	Washington	Grand Total
Beverages	0.75	1.20	1.90	1.00
Condiments	0.90	0.81	1.54	1.00
Confections	0.98	1.45	0.82	1.00
Dairy Products	0.99	1.67	0.65	1.00
Grains/Cereals	1.09	1.25	0.46	1.00
Meat/Poultry	1.07	0.13	1.26	1.00
Produce	1.05	1.94	0.20	1.00
Seafood	1.17	0.43	0.65	1.00
Grand Total	1.00	1.00	1.00	1.00

PT-Units By Category & Region   PT-Custor ...

FIGURE 8-10:
The PivotTable from Figure 8-9, with the Index calculation applied.

Working with PivotTable Subtotals

When you add a second field to the row or column area, as I describe in Chapter 7, Excel displays subtotals for the items in the outer field. Having these outer field subtotals available is a useful component of data analysis because it shows you not only how the data breaks down according to the items in the second (inner) field, but also the total of those items for each item in the first (outer) field. However, Excel lets you turn off subtotals that you don't want to see, and it lets you add multiple subtotals. The next two sections provide the details.

Turning off subtotals for a field

If you kick things up a notch and add a third field to the row or column area, Excel displays two sets of subtotals: one for the second (middle) field and one for the first (outer) field. And for every extra field you add to the row or column area, Excel mindlessly adds yet another set of subtotals.

Believe me, a PivotTable displaying two or more sets of subtotals in one area is no picnic to read. Do yourself a favor and reduce the complexity of the PivotTable layout by turning off the subtotals for one or more of the fields. Here's how:

1. **Select any cell in the field you want to work with.**

2. **Choose Analyze ⇨ Field Settings.**

    The Field Settings dialog box appears with the Subtotals & Filters tab displayed.

3. **In the Subtotals group, select the None radio button.**

    TIP

    Alternatively, right-click any cell in the field and then deselect the Subtotal "*Field*" command, where *Field* is the name of the field.

4. **Click OK.**

   Excel hides the field's subtotals.

Displaying multiple subtotals for a field

When you add a second field to the row or column area, as I discuss in Chapter 7, Excel displays a subtotal for each item in the outer field, and that subtotal uses the Sum calculation. If you prefer to see the Average for each item or the Count, you can change the field's summary calculation; see the section "Changing the Pivot-Table summary calculation," earlier in this chapter.

However, a common data analysis task is to view items from several different points of view. That is, you study the results by eyeballing not just a single summary calculation, but several: Sum, Average, Count, Max, Min, and so on.

That's awesome of you, but it's not all that easy to switch from one summary calculation to another. To avoid this problem, Excel enables you to view multiple subtotals for each field, with each subtotal using a different summary calculation. It's true. You can use as many of Excel's 11 built-in summary calculations as you need. That said, however, I should point out that using StdDev and StDevp at the same time doesn't make sense, because the former is for sample data and the latter is for population data. The same is true for the Var and Varp calculations.

Okay, here are the steps to follow to add multiple subtotals to a field:

1. **Select any cell in the field you want to mess with.**

2. **Choose Analyze ⇨ Field Settings.**

   The Field Settings dialog box appears with the Subtotals & Filters tab displayed.

3. **In the Subtotals group, select the Custom radio button.**

4. **In the list that appears below the Custom options, select each calculation that you want to appear as a subtotal.**

   Alternatively, right-click any cell in the field and then deselect the Subtotal "*Field*" command, where *Field* is the name of the field.

TIP

5. **Click OK.**

   Excel recalculates the PivotTable to show the subtotals you selected. Figure 8-11 shows an example PivotTable showing the Sum, Average, Max, and Min subtotals.

CompanyName	OrderID	Sum of ExtendedPrice
⊟ Around the Horn		
	10453	$407.70
	10558	$2,142.90
	10707	$1,641.00
	10741	$228.00
	10743	$319.20
	10768	$1,477.00
	10793	$191.10
Around the Horn Sum		$6,406.90
Around the Horn Average		$355.94
Around the Horn Max		$1,060.00
Around the Horn Min		$45.00

PT-Customer Orders | Orders | ⊕

FIGURE 8-11:
A PivotTable with multiple subtotals.

Introducing Custom Calculations

A *custom calculation* is a formula that you define yourself to produce PivotTable values that wouldn't otherwise appear in the report if you used only the source data and Excel's prefab summary calculations. Custom calculations let you to extend your data analysis to include results that are tailored to your company, department, or the daily whims of your boss.

For example, suppose your PivotTable shows employee sales by quarter and you want to award a 10 percent bonus to each employee with sales of more than $50,000 in any quarter. That's awfully generous of you! To help, you can create a custom calculation that checks for sales greater than $50,000 and then multiplies those by 0.1 to get the bonus number.

A custom calculation is an Excel formula that's applied to your source data to produce a summary result. In other words, in most cases the custom calculation is just like Excel's built-in PivotTable summary calculations, except that you define the specifics of the calculation yourself. Because you're creating a formula, you can use most of Excel's formula power, which gives you tremendous flexibility to create custom calculations that suit your data-analysis needs. And by placing these calculations within the PivotTable itself — as opposed to, for example, adding them to your source data — you can easily update the calculations as needed and refresh the report results.

Formulas for custom calculations

Custom calculations are formulas with certain restrictions imposed; see the section "Understanding custom calculation limitations," later in this chapter, for more details. A custom calculation formula always begins with an equals sign (=), followed by one or more operands and operators:

>> **Operands:** The values that the formula uses as the raw material for the calculation. In a custom PivotTable calculation, the operands can be numbers, worksheet functions, or fields from your data source.

>> **Operators:** The symbols that the formula uses to perform the calculation. In a custom PivotTable calculation, the available operators include addition (+), subtraction (–), multiplication (*), division (/), and comparison operators such as greater than (>) and less than or equal to (<=).

Checking out the custom calculation types

When building a custom calculation for a PivotTable, Excel offers two types:

>> **Calculated field:** A new data field in which the values are the result of a custom calculation formula. You can display the calculated field along with another data field or on its own. A calculated field is really a custom summary calculation, so in almost all cases, the calculated field references one or more fields in the source data. See the section "Inserting a Custom Calculated Field," later in this chapter.

>> **Calculated item:** A new item in a row or column field in which the values are the result of a custom calculation. In this case, the calculated item's formula references one or more items in the same field. See the section "Inserting a Custom Calculated Item," later in this chapter, for more on working with a custom calculated item.

Understanding custom calculation limitations

Custom calculations — whether they're calculated fields or calculated items — are powerful additions to your PivotTable analysis toolbox. However, although custom calculation formulas look like regular worksheet formulas, you can't assume that you can do everything with a custom PivotTable formula that you can do with a worksheet formula. In fact, Excel imposes a number of limitations on custom formulas.

The major limitation inherent in custom calculations is that, with the exception of constant values such as numbers, you can't reference anything outside the Pivot-Table's source data:

>> You can't use a cell reference, range address, or range name as an operand in a custom calculation formula.

>> You can't use any worksheet function that requires a cell reference, range, or defined name. However, you can still use many of Excel's worksheet functions by substituting either a PivotTable field or a PivotTable item in place of a cell reference or range name. For example, if you want a calculated item that returns the average of items named Jan, Feb, and Mar, you could use the following formula:

```
=AVERAGE(Jan, Feb, Mar)
```

>> You can't use the PivotTable's subtotals, row totals, column totals, or Grand Total as an operand in a custom calculation formula.

You also need to understand how references to other PivotTable fields work within your calculations and what limitations you face when using field references:

>> **Field references:** When you reference a PivotTable field in your formula, Excel interprets this reference as the *sum* of that field's values. For example, the formula =Sales + 1 does not add 1 to each Sales value and return the sum of these results; that is, Excel does not interpret the formula as =Sum of (Sales + 1). Instead, the formula adds 1 to the sum of the Sales values, and Excel interprets the formula as =(Sum of Sales) + 1.

>> **Field reference problems:** The fact that Excel defaults to a Sum calculation when you reference another field in your custom calculation can lead to problems. The trouble is that summing certain types of data doesn't make sense. For example, suppose you have inventory source data with UnitsInStock and UnitPrice fields. You want to calculate the total value of the inventory, so you create a custom field based on the following formula:

```
=UnitsInStock * UnitPrice
```

Unfortunately, this formula doesn't work because Excel treats the UnitPrice operand as Sum of UnitPrice. "Adding" the prices together doesn't make sense, so your formula produces an incorrect result.

Finally, Excel imposes the following limitations on the use of calculated items:

>> A formula for a calculated item can't reference items from any field except the one in which the calculated item resides.

>> You can't insert a calculated item into a PivotTable that has at least one grouped field. You must ungroup all the PivotTable fields before you can insert a calculated item.

» You can't group a field in a PivotTable that has at least one calculated item.

» You can't insert a calculated item into a filter field. Also, you can't move a row or column field that has a calculated item into the filter area.

» You can't insert a calculated item into a PivotTable in which a field has been used more than once.

» You can't insert a calculated item into a PivotTable that uses the Average, StdDev, StdDevp, Var, or Varp summary calculations.

Inserting a Custom Calculated Field

A custom calculated field might look much like an Excel worksheet formula, but you don't enter the formula for a calculated field into a worksheet cell. Instead, Excel offers the Calculated Field feature, which provides a dialog box for you to name the field and construct the formula. Excel then stores the formula along with the rest of the PivotTable data.

Here are the steps to follow to insert a custom calculated field into a PivotTable:

1. **Select any cell inside the PivotTable's value area.**

2. **Choose Analyze ⇨ Fields, Items, & Sets ⇨ Calculated Field.**

   The Insert Calculated Field dialog box appears.

3. **In the Name text box, enter a name for the calculated field.**

4. **In the Formula text box, start the formula.**

   Begin with an equals sign (=) and then add any constants or worksheet functions you need to get started.

5. **When you get to the point in your formula at which you need to add a field, select a field in the Fields list and then click Insert Field.**

   You can also double-click the field to add it to the formula.

6. **Keep building your formula, repeating Step 5 to add fields as needed.**

7. **When the formula is complete, click Add.**

   Figure 8-12 shows an example formula for a custom calculated field. In this case, the formula uses an IF() function to check whether the ExtendedPrice field is greater than 50,000. If it is, the formula returns the ExtendedPrice value multiplied by 0.1; otherwise, it returns 0.

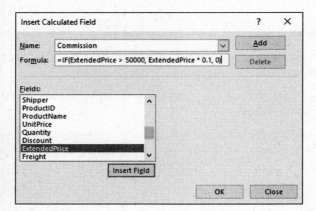

FIGURE 8-12:
A custom calculated field, ready for insertion into the PivotTable.

8. Click OK.

Excel adds the calculated field to the PivotTable's data area, as shown in Figure 8-13. Excel adds the calculated field to the PivotTable Fields pane.

Row Labels	Sum of ExtendedPrice	Sum of Commission
Andrew Fuller	$70,444.14	$ 7,044.41
Anne Dodsworth	$26,310.39	$ -
Janet Leverling	$108,026.13	$ 10,802.61
Laura Callahan	$56,032.60	$ 5,603.26
Margaret Peacock	$128,809.78	$ 12,880.98
Michael Suyama	$43,126.37	$ -
Nancy Davolio	$93,148.04	$ 9,314.80
Robert King	$60,471.19	$ 6,047.12
Steven Buchanan	$30,716.44	$ -
Grand Total	**$617,085.08**	**$ 61,708.51**

PT - Employee Total Sales   ⊕

FIGURE 8-13:
The custom calculated field in action.

WARNING

When you add a calculated field to the PivotTable, Excel also applies the custom calculation to the Grand Total value (refer to Figure 8-13). Unfortunately, this total is often inaccurate, and you should be careful not to assume that it's correct. The problem is that it's not a sum of the values in the calculated field, as you might think. Instead, Excel applies the calculated field's formula to the sum of whatever field or fields you referenced in the formula. In the example shown in Figure 8-13, Excel applies the formula to the Sum of Extended Price field's Grand Total value, which is not the correct way to calculate the total commission. If you want to see the correct total for the calculated field, set up a formula outside the PivotTable that sums the values.

Inserting a Custom Calculated Item

If your data analysis requires PivotTable results that are not available using just the data source fields and Excel's built-in summary calculations, no problem: You can insert a calculated item that uses a custom formula to derive the results you need. Sweet!

A calculated item uses a formula that's similar to an Excel worksheet formula, but you don't enter the formula for a calculated item into a worksheet cell. Instead, Excel offers the Calculated Item command, which displays a dialog box in which you name the item and construct the formula. Excel then stores the formula along with the rest of the PivotTable data.

The Calculated Item feature creates just a single item in a field. However, feel free to add as many calculated items as you need. For example, suppose you want to compare the sales of nonvegan items (such as meat, poultry, dairy, and seafood) with vegan items (grains, cereals, produce, and beverages). One approach would be to create one calculated item that returns the average sales of the nonvegan items and a second calculated item that returns the average sales of the vegan items.

Here are the steps to follow to insert a custom calculated item into a PivotTable:

1. **Select any cell inside the field to which you want to insert the item.**

2. **Choose Analyze⇨Fields, Items, & Sets⇨Calculated Item.**

   The Insert Calculated Item dialog box appears.

3. **In the Name text box, enter a name for the calculated field.**

4. **In the Formula text box, start the formula.**

   Begin with an equals sign (=) and then add any constants or worksheet functions you need to get started.

5. **When you get to the point in your formula at which you need to add a field, select the field in the Fields list and then click Insert Field.**

   You can also double-click the field to add it to the formula.

6. **When you get to the point in your formula at which you need to add an item, select the item in the Items list and then click Insert Item.**

   You can also double-click the item to add it to the formula.

7. **Keep building your formula, repeating Steps 5 and 6 to add fields and items as needed.**

8. **When the formula is complete, click Add.**

Figure 8-14 shows an example formula for a custom calculated item. In this case, I use the AVERAGE() function to calculate the average of several nonvegan food categories.

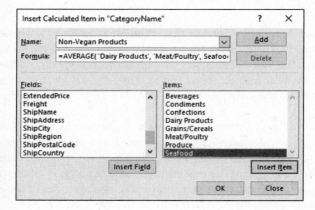

9. **Click OK.**

10. **Click OK.**

Excel adds the calculated item to the PivotTable field. Figure 8-15 shows two calculated items added to the PivotTable's row field. Notice, as well, that when you select a custom calculated item, Excel shows the item's custom formula in the Formula bar.

FIGURE 8-15:
Two custom calculated items added to the row area.

Editing a Custom Calculation

When you add a custom calculation to a PivotTable, Excel first checks the formula to make sure that it contains no syntax errors — such as a missing comma or parenthesis — or illegal operands — such as cell addresses, unknown field or item names, or functions not supported by custom calculations. If Excel finds an error, it displays a dialog box to scold you and refuses to add the custom calculation to the PivotTable.

However, just because a formula contains no syntax errors or illegal operands doesn't necessarily mean that its results are correct. In a calculated field, you might have used the wrong function for the result you're seeking. In a calculated item involving several field items, you might have accidentally missed an item.

Alternatively, your formula may be working perfectly, but it may no longer be the result you need if your data analysis needs have changed. For example, you might have a calculated field that determines whether employees get paid a bonus by looking for sales greater than $50,000. If that threshold changes to $75,000, your calculated field will no longer produce the results you want.

Whether your custom calculation contains an error or your data analysis needs have changed, Excel enables you to edit the formula to produce the result you want. Here's how to edit a custom calculation:

1. **To edit a calculated field, select any cell inside the PivotTable's data area.**

   To edit a calculated item, select any cell inside the field that contains the calculated item.

2. **Choose Analyze ⇨ Fields, Items, & Sets ⇨ Calculated Field.**

   The Insert Calculated Field dialog box appears.

   To edit a calculated item instead, choose Analyze ⇨ Fields, Items, & Sets ⇨ Calculated Item to open the Insert Calculated Item dialog box.

3. **In the Name list, select the calculation that you want to delete.**

4. **Edit the formula.**

5. **Click Modify.**

6. **Click OK.**

   Excel updates the custom calculation's results.

   You can also edit a calculated item by selecting the item's result. The formula appears in Excel's Formula bar, and you can edit it from there.

TIP

Deleting a Custom Calculation

Custom calculations don't always remain a permanent part of a PivotTable report. For example, it's common to add a calculated field or item temporarily to the PivotTable to test the data or get a number to use elsewhere. Similarly, you may find that you create several versions of a custom calculation and want to keep only the final version. Finally, although custom calculations are a powerful tool, they can't do everything, so you may find that a calculation does not provide the answer you seek or help you with your data analysis.

For all these situations, Excel enables you to delete those calculated fields or items that you no longer need by following these steps:

1. **Select any cell in the PivotTable.**

2. **To delete a calculated field, choose Analyze ⇨ Fields, Items, & Sets ⇨ Calculated Field.**

The Insert Calculated Field dialog box appears.

To delete a calculated item instead, choose Analyze ⇨ Fields, Items, & Sets ⇨ Calculated Item to open the Insert Calculated Item dialog box.

3. **In the Name list, select the calculation that you want to delete.**

4. **Click Delete.**

5. **Click OK.**

Excel removes the custom calculation.

Chapter **9**

Building PivotCharts

I f a PivotTable appeals to the left side of your brain — that is, the analytical side that likes numbers — the PivotChart will likely appeal to the right side of your brain — that is, the visual side that likes patterns. That's because a PivotChart is to a PivotTable what a regular chart is to a range. That is, the PivotChart is a graphical representation of the PivotTable. The PivotChart enables you to visualize the PivotTable results by displaying the value area results in chart form.

However, you can also say that a PivotChart is to a regular chart what a PivotTable is to a regular range. In other words, the PivotChart goes far beyond the capabilities of a simple chart because the PivotChart comes with most of the same features that make PivotTables so powerful: You can filter the results to see just the data you need, and you can pivot fields from one area of the PivotChart to another to get the layout you want. In this chapter, you discover what PivotCharts are all about, learn how to build PivotCharts, and explore ways to get the most out of your PivotCharts.

Introducing the PivotChart

As you might expect, PivotCharts have a number of elements in common with PivotTables, but some key differences also exist. The following list explains these differences and introduces you to some important PivotChart concepts:

>> **Chart Categories (X-Axis):** As does a PivotTable, a PivotChart automatically groups large amounts of data into smaller, more manageable groups. For

example, if you have data with a Category field containing values such as Beverages, Condiments, Confections, and so on and you build your PivotChart using the Category field, the resulting chart will display one chart category (X-axis value) for each unique Category field value. This is the equivalent of a row field in a PivotTable.

>> **Chart Data Series:** Also, as with a PivotTable, you can break down your data in terms of a second field. For example, your data might have an Order Date field. If you add that field to the PivotChart, Excel creates one data series for each unique value in that field. This is the equivalent of a column field in a PivotTable.

>> **Chart Values (Y-Axis):** You can't have a PivotTable without a value field, and the same is true of a PivotChart. When you add a numeric field for the summary calculation, Excel displays the results as chart values (Y-axis). This is the equivalent of a value field in a PivotTable.

>> **Dynamic PivotCharts:** Perhaps the biggest difference between a PivotChart and a regular chart is that each PivotChart is a dynamic object that you can reconfigure as needed, just as you can with a PivotTable. You can pivot fields from one area of the chart to another; you can add fields to different chart areas; and you can place multiple fields in any chart area.

>> **Filtering:** As with a PivotTable, you can use the unique values in another field to filter the results that appear in the PivotChart. For example, if your source data has a Country field, you can add it to the PivotChart and use it to filter the chart results to show just those from a specific country. This is the equivalent of a filter field in a PivotTable.

Understanding PivotChart pros and cons

PivotCharts have advantages and disadvantages, and understanding their strengths and weaknesses can help you decide when and if you should use them.

On the positive side, a PivotChart is a powerful data-analysis tool because it combines the strengths of Excel's charting capabilities — including most of the options available with regular charts — with the features of a PivotTable. Also, creating a basic PivotChart is just as straightforward as creating a PivotTable. In fact, if you already have a PivotTable, you can create the equivalent PivotChart by pressing a single key.

On the negative side, PivotCharts share the same caveats that come with regular charts, particularly the fact that if you don't choose the proper chart type or layout, your data will not be readily understood. Moreover, a PivotChart can quickly become extremely confusing when you have multiple Category fields or Data

Series fields. Finally, PivotCharts have inherent limitations that restrict the options and formatting that you can apply. I talk about these limitations a bit later in this chapter.

Taking a PivotChart tour

PivotCharts carry over some of the same terminology that I discussed in Chapter 7 for PivotTables, including the concepts of the *report filter*, *value area*, and *field button*. However, PivotCharts also use a number of unique terms that you need to understand to get the most out of PivotCharts (see Figure 9-1):

>> **Field buttons:** The PivotChart includes a button for each field, such as a Category field, Data Series field, or Report Filter. Each button displays a drop-down list with unique values from the field that you use to filter the PivotChart data.

>> **Category items:** The unique field values that define the chart's categories.

>> **Category axis:** The chart's X-axis (that is, the horizontal axis) that displays the category items.

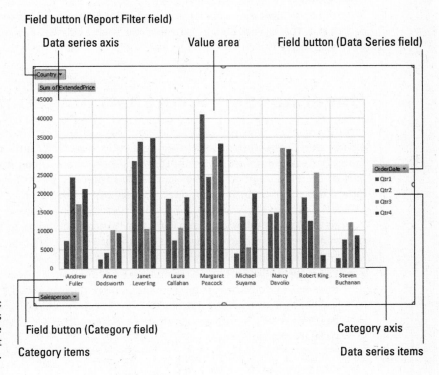

Field button (Report Filter field)

Data series axis   Value area   Field button (Data Series field)

FIGURE 9-1:
The major sights to see in the PivotChart landscape.

Field button (Category field)

Category items

Category axis

Data series items

>> **Data series items:** The unique field values that define the chart's data series. The item names appear in the chart legend.

>> **Data series axis:** The chart's Y-axis (that is, the vertical axis) that displays the values of the data series items.

>> **Value area:** Displays the charted results of the calculation that Excel applied to a numeric field in your data.

One of the main sources of PivotChart confusion is the fact that Excel uses different terminology with PivotCharts and PivotTables. In both, you have a value area that contains the numeric results, and you have a report filter that you can use to filter the data. However, understanding how Excel maps the PivotTable's row and column areas to the PivotChart is important:

>> **Row area versus category axis:** In a PivotTable, the row area contains the unique values that Excel has extracted from a field in the source data. The PivotChart equivalent is the category axis, which corresponds to the chart's X-axis. That is, each unique value from the source field has a corresponding category axis value.

>> **Column area versus series axis:** In a PivotTable, the column area contains the unique values that Excel has extracted from a field in the source data. The PivotChart equivalent is the series axis, which corresponds to the chart's Y-axis. That is, each unique value from the source field has a corresponding data series.

Understanding PivotChart limitations

PivotCharts are a powerful addition to your data-analysis toolkit, but they aren't always the ideal solution. Excel has rigid rules for which parts of a PivotTable report correspond to which parts of the PivotChart layout. Moving a field from one part of the PivotChart to another can easily result in a PivotChart layout that is either difficult to understand or doesn't make sense.

You also face a number of limitations that control the types of charts you can make and the formatting options you can apply:

>> **Chart types:** Excel offers a large number of chart types, and you can change the default PivotChart type to another that more closely suits your needs; see the section "Changing the PivotChart type," later in this chapter. However, the three chart types that you can't apply to a PivotChart are Bubble, XY (Scatter), and Stock.

>> **Adding and removing fields:** After you create the PivotChart, as long as you're working with the chart itself, you can't add or remove fields. If you want to reconfigure the PivotChart's fields, you have to add or remove the fields using the underlying PivotTable.

>> **Pivoting fields:** You can't pivot the fields from one part of the PivotChart to another. If you want to pivot a field, you have to use the underlying PivotTable.

Fortunately, these PivotChart limitations aren't onerous in most situations, so they should in no way dissuade you from taking advantage of the analytical and visualization power of the PivotChart.

Creating a PivotChart

Excel gives you three ways to create a PivotChart. That seems like a lot, but is that significant? Probably not, but you should at least be familiar with all three methods, which I outline in the sections that follow.

Creating a PivotChart from a PivotTable

I don't like using the word "easy" to describe anything computer related, because one person's easy is another person's I-have-no-idea-what's-going-on-here. However, if you already have a PivotTable, creating a PivotChart to visualize that PivotTable's data is as close to easy as things get in the data-analysis world. Why? Because convincing Excel to make that PivotChart requires just two measly steps:

1. **Select any cell in the PivotTable.**
2. **Press F11.**

Yep, that's all there is to it. Excel creates a new chart sheet and displays the PivotChart and the PivotChart Fields pane.

Embedding a PivotChart on a PivotTable's worksheet

When you create a PivotChart directly from an existing PivotTable by pressing F11, as described in the previous section, Excel places the chart on a new chart sheet. This is usually the best solution because it gives you the most room to view and manipulate the PivotChart. However, viewing the PivotChart together with its associated PivotTable is often useful. For example, when you change the Pivot-Table view, Excel automatically changes the PivotChart view in the same way. Rather than switching from one sheet to another to compare the results, having the PivotChart on the same worksheet lets you to compare the PivotChart and PivotTable immediately. Nice.

Creating a new PivotChart on the same worksheet as an existing PivotTable is called *embedding* the PivotChart. Here are the steps to follow to embed a PivotChart:

1. **Select any cell in the PivotTable.**

2. **Choose Analyze ⇨ PivotChart.**

   The Insert Chart dialog box appears.

REMEMBER

3. **In the list of chart types on the left side of the Insert Chart dialog box, select the chart type you want.**

   You can't use the XY (Scatter), Bubble, or Stock chart type with a PivotChart.

   Excel displays one or more chart subtypes for the chart type you selected.

4. **On the right side of the Insert Chart dialog box, select the chart subtype you want.**

5. **Click OK.**

   Excel embeds the PivotChart on the PivotTable's worksheet.

Excel embeds the PivotChart in the center of the visible worksheet area. In most cases, this location means that the new PivotChart overlaps your existing Pivot-Table, which makes comparing them more difficult. To fix this problem, you can move or resize the PivotChart:

>> To move the PivotChart, move the mouse pointer over an empty part of the chart area and then drag the chart object to the new position.

>> To resize the PivotChart, select the chart and then move the mouse pointer over any one of the selection handles that appear on the chart area's corners and sides. Drag a handle to the size you require.

REMEMBER

If you already have a PivotChart in a separate chart sheet, you can embed it in the PivotTable's worksheet. I describe how this works later in this chapter, in the section "Moving a PivotChart to another sheet."

Creating a PivotChart from an Excel table

If the data you want to summarize and visualize exists as an Excel table, you can build a PivotChart directly from that data. Note, too, that this method also works if your data exists as an Excel range instead of a table. Here are the steps to follow:

1. **Select a cell in the table that you want to use as the source data.**

If you're using a range, select any cell in the range instead.

2. **Choose Insert ➪ PivotChart.**

The Create PivotChart dialog box appears, with the Select a Table or Range radio button selected. The Table/Range box should show the name of your table (or the address of your range). If not, adjust the name or address as needed before moving on.

3. **Select the New Worksheet radio button.**

Alternatively, if you want to add the PivotTable to an existing location, select the Existing Worksheet radio button and then, in the Location range box, select the worksheet and cell where you want the PivotTable to appear.

4. **Click OK.**

Excel creates a blank PivotTable and a blank, embedded PivotChart, and it displays the PivotChart Fields pane, as shown in Figure 9-2. This pane contains two main areas:

- A list of the column headers from your table, each of which has a check box to its left. These are your PivotChart (and PivotTable) fields.

- Four boxes representing the four areas of the PivotChart: Filters, Legend (Series), Axis (Categories), and Values. To complete the PivotChart, add one or more fields to some or all of these areas.

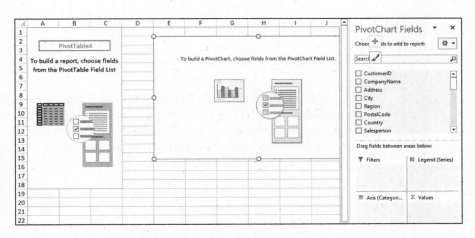

FIGURE 9-2: Excel kicks things off with a blank PivotTable and PivotChart, and the PivotChart Fields pane.

5. **Drag a text field and drop it inside the Axis (Categories) area.**

Excel adds a button for the field to the PivotChart's category (X) axis.

6. **Drag a numeric field and drop it inside the Values area.**

Excel sums the numeric values based on the row values.

7. **If desired, drag fields and drop them in the Legend (Series) area and the Filters area.**

Each time you drop a field into an area, Excel updates the PivotTable to include the new data. Figure 9-3 shows a completed PivotChart (and PivotTable), with fields in just the Axis (Categories), Values, and Filters boxes. Note, too, that when you select the PivotChart, Excel displays the PivotChart Tools contextual tab, which includes three tabs — Analyze, Design, and Format — that are bursting with options for manipulating and formatting your PivotChart.

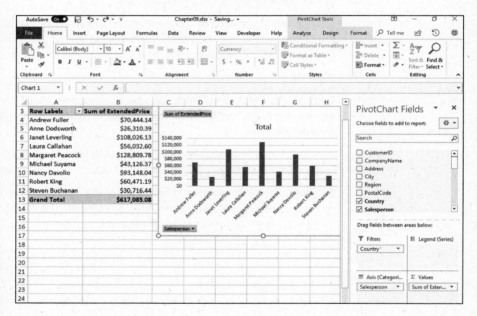

FIGURE 9-3:
An embedded PivotChart and its PivotTable.

If your PivotChart includes just a Category field, Excel displays the results using a standard bar chart. If the PivotChart includes both a Category field and a series field, Excel displays the results using a clustered column chart. I talk about how to view the PivotChart using a different type of chart in the section "Changing the PivotChart type," later in this chapter.

**TECHNICAL
STUFF**

The clustered column chart is a great way to visualize two-dimensional PivotTable results, but deciphering the chart isn't always easy — especially if you have a large number of data series, which usually means that most of the columns in each category are quite small. To get a better understanding of the chart, you might want to know what data is represented by specific columns.

You can find the specifics related to each column by moving the mouse pointer over the column in the plot area. Excel then displays a banner with data in the following format:

```
Series "Series Item" Point "Category Item" Value: Value
```

Here, `Series Item` is an item from the series field, `Category Item` is an item from the Category field, and `Value` is the value of the data point. For example, if the Shipper field has an item named United Package, the Salesperson field has an item named Steven Buchanan, and the value is 488, the banner shows the following:

```
Series "United Package" Point "Steven Buchanan" Value: 488
```

Working with PivotCharts

After you have a PivotChart up and charting, you might want to leave it as is. That's perfectly fine, but you're more likely to want to take advantage of the many ways Excel offers to manipulate and format a PivotChart. In the rest of this chapter, I run through a fistful of techniques for messing around with PivotCharts.

Moving a PivotChart to another sheet

In the section "Creating a PivotChart from a PivotTable," earlier in this chapter, I talk about creating a new PivotChart on a separate chart sheet. However, in some situations, this separate chart sheet might not be convenient. For example, if you want to compare the PivotChart and its associated PivotTable, that comparison is more difficult if the PivotChart and PivotTable reside in separate sheets. Similarly, you might prefer to place all your PivotCharts on a single sheet so that you can compare them or they're easy to find. Finally, if you plan on creating a number of PivotCharts, you might not want to clutter your workbook with separate chart sheets.

The solution in all these cases is to move your PivotChart or PivotCharts to the worksheet you prefer. To that worthy end, follow these steps to move a PivotChart to a new location:

1. **Select the PivotChart you want to move.**

2. **Choose Design⇨Move Chart.**

The Move Chart dialog box appears.

3. **Select the Object In radio button and open its drop-down list to select the sheet where you want the PivotChart moved (see Figure 9-4).**

4. **Click OK.**

Excel moves the PivotChart to the location you specified.

FIGURE 9-4:
Use the Move
Chart dialog box
to move a
PivotChart to
another
worksheet.

TIP

The steps in this section apply both to PivotCharts embedded in separate chart sheets and to PivotChart objects embedded in worksheets. For the latter, however, you can use a second technique. Select the PivotChart and then choose Home⇨Cut (or press Ctrl+X) to remove the PivotChart and store it in the Windows Clipboard. Switch to the sheet where you want the PivotChart moved. If you're moving the PivotChart to a worksheet, select the cell where you want the upper-left corner of the chart to appear. Choose Home⇨Paste (or press Ctrl+V). Excel pastes the PivotChart object to the sheet. Move and resize the PivotChart object to taste.

Filtering a PivotChart

By default, each PivotChart report displays a summary for all the records in your source data. This is usually what you want to see. However, you might have situations that require you to focus more closely on some aspect of the data. You can focus on a specific item from one of the source data fields by taking advantage of the PivotChart's report filter.

For example, suppose you're dealing with a PivotChart that summarizes data from thousands of customer invoices over some period of time. A basic PivotChart might tell you the total units sold for each product category. However, what if you want to see the units sold for each product in a specific country? If the Product field is in the PivotChart's Axis (Categories) area, you can add the Country field to the Legend (Series) area. However, dozens of countries might be involved, so that isn't an efficient way to go. Instead, you can add the Country field to the Report Filter area. You can then tell Excel to display the total sold for each product for the specific country in which you're interested.

As another example, suppose you ran a marketing campaign in the previous quarter and set up an incentive plan for your salespeople whereby they could earn bonuses for selling at least a specified number of units. Suppose, as well, that you have a PivotChart showing the sum of the units sold for each product. To see the numbers for a particular employee, you can add the Salesperson field to the Report Filter area and then select the employee you want to work with.

Here are the steps to follow to filter a PivotChart:

1. **Click the PivotChart's Report Filter button.**

Excel displays a list of the Report Filter field items.

2. **Select the item you want to view, as shown in Figure 9-5.**

If you want to display data for two or more items, select the Select Multiple Items check box and then repeat Step 2 to select the other items.

3. **Click OK.**

Excel filters the PivotChart to show only the data for the item (or items) you selected.

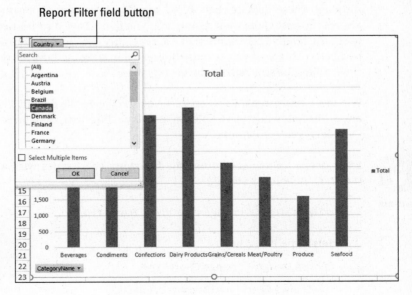

FIGURE 9-5:
Pull down the
Report Filter field
button and then
select an item.

If you want to return to seeing all the items, select the Report Filter field button, select (All), and then click OK.

You can also filter the items in the Axis (Categories) area. For example, in a PivotChart that includes items from the ProductName field in the row area, you might want to see only those products with names that begin with the letter G or contain the word *tofu*. You can do that by applying a filter to a Category field. Excel offers a number of text filters, including Equals, Doesn't Equal, Begins With, Ends With, Contains, Greater Than, and Less Than. If the field uses dates, you can apply a date filter such as Before, Yesterday, Last Month, and This Year.

In the PivotChart, click the button for the field you want to work with and then choose either the Label Filters or the Date Filters command. In the list that appears, select the filter type you want to apply, such as Begins With. Then type your filter criteria and click OK.

Changing the PivotChart type

If you don't include a series field in the PivotChart, Excel displays the report using regular columns, which is useful for comparing the values across the Category field's items. If you include a series field in the PivotChart, Excel displays the report using clustered columns, where each category shows several different-colored columns grouped beside one another, one for each item in the series field. These clustered columns are useful for comparing the series values for each item in the category.

Although these default chart types are fine for many applications, they're not always the best choice. For example, if you don't have a series field and you want to see the relative contribution of each category item to the total, a pie chart would be a better choice. If you're more interested in showing how the results trend over time, a line chart is usually the ideal type.

Whatever your needs, Excel enables you to change the default PivotChart type to any of the following types: Column, Bar, Line, Pie, Area, Doughnut, Radar, Surface, Cylinder, Cone, or Pyramid.

REMEMBER

Excel doesn't allow you to use the following chart types with a PivotChart: XY (Scatter), Bubble, or Stock.

Follow these steps to change your PivotChart's type:

1. **Select the PivotChart.**

2. **Choose Design ⇨ Change Chart Type.**

   The Change Chart Type dialog box appears.

3. **In the list of chart types on the left side of the Insert Chart dialog box, select the chart type you want to use.**

   Excel displays the available chart subtypes.

4. **On the right side of the Insert Chart dialog box, select the Chart subtype you want to use.**

5. **Click OK.**

   Excel redisplays the PivotChart with the new chart type. For example, Figure 9-6 shows the PivotChart from Figure 9-5 displayed using the Pie chart type.

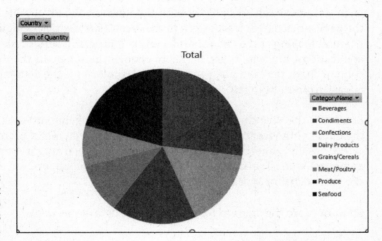

FIGURE 9-6: The PivotChart from Figure 9-5 now displayed as a pie chart.

Adding data labels to your PivotChart

Depending on the chart type you choose, augmenting the chart with the actual values from the report is often useful. For example, with a pie chart, you can add to each slice the value as well as the percentage the value represents of the grand total. In most cases, you can also add the series name and the category name.

To add these data labels to your PivotChart, follow these steps:

1. **Select the chart.**

2. **Choose Design ⇨ Add Chart Element ⇨ Data Labels.**

   Excel displays a menu of data label types.

3. **Select the data label position you want to use: Center, Inside End, Outside End, Best Fit (available only with certain chart types), or Data Callout.**

   You can also select More Data Label Options to open the Format Data Labels pane and then select the Value check box. Depending on the data, you might also be able to select the Series Name, Category Name, and Percentage check boxes.

Sorting the PivotChart

When you create a PivotChart and include a series field, Excel displays the data series based on the order of the field's items as they appear in the PivotTable. That is, as you move left to right through the items in the PivotTable's column field, the data series moves left to right in the PivotChart's series field (or top to bottom if you're looking at the PivotChart legend). This default series order is fine in most applications, but you might prefer to change the order. In the default clustered column chart, for example, you might prefer to reverse the data series so that they appear from right to left.

Similarly, the PivotChart categories appear in the same order as they appear in the underlying PivotTable's row field. In this case, you might prefer to display the categories in some custom order. For example, you might want to rearrange employee names so that those who have the same supervisor or who work in the same division appear together.

First, here are the steps to follow to sort the data series items:

1. **Select the PivotChart.**

2. **Select the field button for the PivotChart's Data Series field.**

   Excel displays a list of sort options for the field. The sort options you see vary depending on the field's data type:

   - **For a text field:** Sort A to Z (ascending) and Sort Z to A (descending).

   - **For a date field:** Sort Oldest to Newest (ascending) and Sort Newest to Oldest (descending).

   - **For a numeric field:** Sort Smallest to Largest (ascending) and Sort Largest to Smallest (descending)

3. **Select the sort order you want to use.**

   Excel redisplays the PivotChart using the new series order.

MANUALLY SORTING DATA SERIES OR CATEGORIES

Besides the standard ascending or descending sort orders shown in this section, Excel also enables you to sort the data series items or categories manually. Unfortunately, Excel doesn't offer a method for manually sorting series items or categories directly on the PivotChart. Instead, you must manually sort the data on the PivotTable itself. When you do this, Excel automatically applies the new sort order to the PivotChart.

To manually sort the data series items, select the PivotChart's underlying PivotTable and then select the label of the column field item you want to move. Move the mouse pointer to the right edge of the label cell (the pointer changes into a four-headed arrow) and then drag the label left or right to the new position.

To manually sort the categories, display the PivotChart's underlying PivotTable and select the label of the row field item you want to move. Move the mouse pointer to the bottom edge of the label cell (the pointer changes into a four-headed arrow) and then drag the label up or down to the new position.

When you return to the PivotChart, you see that the data series items or categories now appear in the new sort order.

Follow these steps to sort the category items:

1. **Select the PivotChart.**
2. **Select the field button for the PivotChart's Category field.**

   Excel displays a list of sort options for the field.

   The sort options you see vary depending on the field's data type, and the possible options are the same as those in Step 2 of the preceding steps.

3. **Select the sort order you want to use.**

   Excel redisplays the PivotChart using the new field order.

Adding PivotChart titles

By default, Excel doesn't add any titles to your PivotChart. This absence of titles isn't a big deal for most PivotCharts because the field names and item labels often provide enough context to understand the report. However, the data you use might have cryptic field names or coded item names, so the default PivotChart might be difficult to decipher. In that case, you can add titles to the PivotChart that make the report more comprehensible.

Excel offers three PivotChart titles:

» An overall chart title that sits either above the chart's plot area or is overlaid on the plot area.

» A category (X) axis title that sits below the category items.

» A data series (Y) axis title that sits to the left of the data series axis labels.

You can add one or more of these titles to your PivotChart. And although Excel doesn't allow you to move these titles to a different location, you can play around with the font, border, background, and text alignment.

WARNING

The downside to adding PivotChart titles is that most of them take up some space within the chart area, which means you have less space to display the PivotChart itself. (The exception is an overall chart title overlaid on the plot area.) This reduced space isn't usually a problem with a simple PivotChart, but if you have a complex chart — particularly if you have a large number of category items — you might prefer not to display titles at all, or you might prefer to display only one or two.

To get the PivotChart title ball rolling, here's how you add an overall chart title:

1. **Select the PivotChart.**

2. **Choose Design ⇨ Add Chart Element ⇨ Chart Title.**

3. **Select the type of chart title you want to add.**

    Besides None, you have two choices:

    • **Above Chart:** Places the title above the PivotChart's plot area, centered on the PivotChart.

    • **Centered Overlay:** Places the title centered within the PivotChart's plot area.

    Excel adds a default title to the PivotChart. The title that Excel adds depends on your data, but it's usually something generic such as "Chart Title" or "Total."

4. **Select the chart title.**

5. **Enter the title you want to use.**

6. **Click or tap outside the chart title to set it.**

Here are the steps to follow to add an axis title:

1. **Select the PivotChart.**

2. **Choose Design ⇨ Add Chart Element ⇨ Axis Titles.**

3. **Select the type of chart title you want to add.**

You have two choices:

- **Primary Horizontal:** Adds a category (X) axis title.
- **Primary Vertical:** Adds a data series (Y) axis title.

Excel adds a default axis title to the PivotChart. The title that Excel adds is usually something generic such as "Axis Title."

4. **Select the title.**

5. **Enter the title you want to use.**

6. **Click or tap outside the chart title to set it.**

To format a chart title, select the title and then choose Format ⇨ Format Selection. The pane that appears offers two tabs:

>> **Title Options:** This tab comes with three subtabs: Fill & Line (use the Fill and Border sections to format the title's background and borders); Effects (use the Shadow, Glow, Soft Edges, and 3-D Format sections to apply these effects to the title); and Size & Properties (use the Alignment options to align the title).

>> **Text Options:** This tab comes with three subtabs: Text Fill & Outline (use the Text Fill and Text Outline sections to format the title text background and outline); Text Effects (use the Shadow, Reflection, Glow, Soft Edges, 3-D Format, and 3-D Rotation sections to apply these effects to the title text); and Textbox (use the Text Box options to align the title text).

To edit a title, either double-click the title or right-click the title and then select Edit Text.

Excel gives you three methods for removing a title from a PivotChart:

>> Follow the steps in this section, and in the menu of title options, select None.

>> Right-click the title you want to remove and then choose the Delete command.

>> Select the title you want to remove and then press the Delete key.

Moving the PivotChart legend

The PivotChart legend displays the series field items along with a colored box that tells you which series belongs to which item. By default, Excel displays the legend to the right of the plot area. This position is usually the best because it doesn't interfere with other chart elements such as titles (which I describe in the previous section, "Add PivotChart Titles") or the axis labels.

However, displaying the legend on the right does mean that it takes up space that would otherwise be used by your PivotChart. If you have a number of category items in your PivotChart report, you might prefer to display the legend above or below the plot area to give the PivotChart more horizontal room.

Excel enables you to move the legend to one of five positions with respect to the plot area: right, left, bottom, top, and upper-right corner. Excel also gives you the option of having the legend overlapping the chart, which means that Excel doesn't resize the plot area to accommodate the legend. This position is useful if you have some white space on the chart (for example, at the top) where you can place the legend so that it doesn't hide any chart data.

Follow these steps to set the position of the PivotChart legend:

1. **Select the PivotChart.**

2. **Choose Design ⇨ Add Chart Element ⇨ Legend.**

   If you want, you can select a predefined legend position: Right, Top, Left, or Bottom.

3. **Select More Legend Options.**

   The Format Legend pane appears and displays the Legend Options tab.

4. **Click the Legend Options subtab and select the radio button for the legend position you want.**

   To display the legend overlapping the chart, deselect the Show the Legend Without Overlapping the Chart check box.

   Excel moves the legend to the new position.

In some cases, you might prefer to not display the legend at all. For example, if your PivotChart doesn't have a series field, Excel still displays a legend for the default "series" named Total. This legend isn't particularly useful, so you can gain some extra chart space by hiding the legend. To do this, follow the preceding Steps 1 and 2 to display the Legend menu and then select None. Alternatively, right-click the legend and then choose the Delete command.

Displaying a data table with the PivotChart

The point of a PivotChart is to combine the visualization effects of an Excel chart with the pivoting and filtering capabilities of a PivotTable. The visualization part helps your data analysis because it enables you to make at-a-glance comparisons among series and categories, and it enables you to view data points relative to other parts of the report.

However, although visualizing the data is often useful, it lacks a certain precision because you don't see the underlying data. Excel offers several ways to overcome this problem, including creating the PivotChart on the same worksheet as the PivotTable (see the section "Embedding a PivotChart on a PivotTable's worksheet"); moving a chart to the PivotTable worksheet (see the section "Moving a PivotChart to another sheet"); and displaying data labels (see the section "Adding data labels to your PivotChart"), all earlier in this chapter.

Yet another method is to display a data table along with the PivotChart. A *Pivot-Chart data table* is a table that displays the chart's categories as columns and its data series as rows, with the cells filled with the actual data values. Because these values appear directly below the chart, the data table gives you an easy way to combine a visual report with the specifics of the underlying data. To display a data table with the PivotChart, follow these steps:

1. **Select the PivotChart.**

2. **Choose Design⇨Add Chart Element⇨Data Table.**

   Select a predefined data table:

   - **With Legend Keys:** Displays the data table with the same colored squares that appear in the legend to identify each series.

   - **No Legend Keys:** Displays the data table without the colored squares.

   Excel displays the data table below the PivotChart. Figure 9-7 shows an example.

FIGURE 9-7: A data table shown below a PivotChart.

3

Discovering Advanced Data Analysis Tools

Use Excel's powerful worksheet functions and charting features to track trends over time and forecast future values.

Tap into the power of Excel's more than 70 statistical functions to calculate averages, determine ranking and percentiles, measure dispersions, and analyze distributions.

Gain extra insights into your data by using formulas, functions, and the Analysis ToolPak add-on tool for creating histograms, calculating moving averages, using exponential smoothing, and performing smart sampling.

Use the regression and correlation tools; the ANOVA data-analysis tool; and the z-test, t-test, and Fourier data-analysis tools to perform inferential statistics analysis.

IN THIS CHAPTER

» Charting the overall trend of a set of values

» Calculating values that show how data is trending

» Charting historical data into future periods

» Calculating future values given some historical data

» Charting exponential, logarithmic, power, and polynomial trends, what they are

Chapter **10**

Tracking Trends and Making Forecasts

When you're analyzing data, it certainly helps to run basic calculations such as the sum and average and to summarize the data either by using Excel's database functions or, even better, by constructing a PivotTable or PivotChart. It's all good. However, as useful as these tools are, they can't answer one seemingly fundamental question: Given some historical data — it could be profits or sales or expenses or defects or customer complaints — what's the overall direction of that data? Are profits going up? Are defects going down? Are sales cyclical (say, down in the winter, but up in the summer)? Answering these types of questions falls under the heading of *trend analysis*, and in this chapter you discover the powerful Excel tools that not only help you see the trends hiding in your data but also let you make forecasts of future values. It's all quite slick, as you soon see.

Plotting a Best-Fit Trend line

If you want to get a sense of the overall trend displayed by a set of data, the easiest way is to use a chart to plot a *best-fit trend line.* This is a straight line through the chart's data points where the differences between the chart points that reside above the line and those that reside below the line cancel each other out.

A best-fit trend line is an example of *regression analysis,* which is a statistical tool for analyzing the relationship between two phenomena, with one depending on the other. For example, housing sales depend on interest rates:

>> When interest rates go down, housing sales go up.

>> When interest rates go up, housing sales go down.

In regression analysis lingo, housing sales are known as the *dependent variable* and interest rates are called the *independent variable.*

When you're working with historical data — for example, sales over time — time is the independent variable, and the item you're measuring (such as sales) is the dependent variable.

REMEMBER

To add a best-fit trend line, you must plot your data series as an XY (Scatter) chart.

If you've already built an Excel chart for your data, here are the steps to follow to plot a best-fit trend line on that chart:

1. **Click the chart to select it.**

2. **If your chart has multiple data series, click the series you want to analyze.**

3. **Choose Design ⇨ Add Chart Element ⇨ Trendline ⇨ More Trendline Options.**

   The Format Trendline pane appears.

4. **Click the Trendline Options tab.**

5. **Select the Linear radio button.**

   Excel plots the best-fit trend line.

6. **(Optional) Select the Display Equation on Chart check box.**

   If you just want to see the trend line, feel free to pass over Steps 6 and 7, which introduce a bit of math to the trend analysis. It's useful math, however, so if you're interested, do Steps 6 and 7 and then read my explanation of what these numbers mean, which follows these steps.

7. **(Optional) Select the Display R-Squared Value on Chart check box.**

8. **Click Close.**

Excel displays the regression equation and the R^2 value (described below). Figure 10-1 shows a chart with the plotted trend line, the regression equation, and the R^2 value.

Regression equation R^2 value

$y = 1407.6x + 259800$
$R^2 = 0.7781$

Trendline

FIGURE 10-1: A chart with a trend line and some geeky numbers.

Okay, so what's up with those scary-looking numbers added to the chart above the trend line in Figure 10-1? The top line is called the *regression equation* and the bottom line is called the *R^2 value.*

The regression equation tells you the exact relationship between the dependent variable and the independent variable. With *linear regression*, in which the best-fit trend line is a straight line, the regression equation looks like this:

```
y = mx + b
```

y is the dependent variable; x is the independent variable; m is the slope of the trend line; and b is the starting value for the trend.

R² is the *coefficient of determination*, which is the square of the correlation, and it tells you how well the trend line fits the data. In general, the closer R^2 is to 1, the better the fit. Values of R^2 below 0.7 mean that the trend line isn't a very good fit for the data. I go on and on about correlation in Chapter 11.

Calculating Best-Fit Values

If your analysis requires exact trend values, you could plot the best-fit trend line and then use the regression equation to calculate the values. However, if the data values change, you need to recalculate the values. A better solution is to use the TREND function. TREND takes up to four arguments:

```
TREND(known_ys, known_xs, new_xs, const)
```

The only required argument is *known_ys*, which is a range reference or array of the dependent values. The *known_xs* argument is a range reference or array of the independent values (the default is the array {1,2,3,...],n}, where n is the number of *known_ys*). The *new_xs* argument is for forecasting, so it's not required here. (I talk about it a bit later in the "Calculating Forecasted Linear Values" section.) The *const* argument determines the y-intercept: FALSE places it at 0, and TRUE (the default) calculates the y-intercept based on the *known_ys*. (The *y-intercept* is the value of y at the point where the trend line crosses the y-axis.)

Here's the procedure to follow to calculate best-fit values using the TREND function:

1. **Select the cells in which you want the best-fit values to appear.**

2. **Type** =trend(.

3. **Type a reference or array that represents the dependent values.**

4. **Type a comma and then type a reference or array that represents the independent values.**

5. **If you prefer to use a trend starting point of 0, type two commas and then type** FALSE.

6. **Type**).

7. **Press and hold Ctrl+Shift and then click the Enter button or press Enter.**

Excel calculates the best-fit trend values and enters them as an array.

Figure 10-2 shows a worksheet that lists sales (column D) over three years by fiscal quarter. The TREND array is in column F, and you can see that the dependent variable (that is, the sales) is referenced by the range D2:D13, and the independent variable (that is, the period numbers) is referenced by the range C2:C13.

F2			× ✓ f_x	{=TREND(D2:D13, C2:C13)}	
	A	B	C	D	E	F
1	**Sales**		**Period**	**Actual**	**Trend (Equation)**	**TREND**
2		1st Quarter	1	259,846	261,208	261,208
3	**Fiscal**	2nd Quarter	2	262,587	262,615	262,615
4	**2017**	3rd Quarter	3	260,643	264,023	264,023
5		4th Quarter	4	267,129	265,430	265,431
6		1st Quarter	5	266,471	266,838	266,838
7	**Fiscal**	2nd Quarter	6	269,843	268,246	268,246
8	**2018**	3rd Quarter	7	272,803	269,653	269,654
9		4th Quarter	8	275,649	271,061	271,061
10		1st Quarter	9	270,117	272,468	272,469
11	**Fiscal**	2nd Quarter	10	275,315	273,876	273,876
12	**2019**	3rd Quarter	11	270,451	275,284	275,284
13		4th Quarter	12	276,543	276,691	276,692

FIGURE 10-2:
An array of best-fit trend values (column F).

REMEMBER

In the example shown in Figure 10-2, the independent values are the period numbers 1, 2, 3, and so on. However, these are the default values for the *known_xs* argument, so technically you could omit this argument in this example.

For the "fun" of it, column E shows the best-fit trend values calculated using the regression equation shown previously in Figure 10-1:

```
y = 1407.6x + 259800
```

For example, to calculate x for period 1 (cell C2), cell E2 contains the following formula:

```
y = 1407.6 * C2 + 259800
```

For the most part, the results in Columns E and F are identical, but not in every case. Why not? Because the TREND function uses higher precision than the regression equation. For example, while the regression equation uses 1407.6 for the slope of the trend line, the actual value (and the one used by TREND) is 1407.625874.

USING LINEST TO GET EXACT VALUES FOR THE REGRESSION EQUATION

How do I know the exact value of the trend line slope? I used Excel's LINEST function, which can calculate not only the slope (m) but also the y-intercept (b), which you can then plug into the general regression equation ($y = mx + b$) to calculate individual trend values. LINEST uses the following syntax:

```
LINEST(known_ys, known_xs, const, stats)
```

The first three arguments — *known_ys*, *known_xs*, and *const* — are identical to those used in the TREND function. A fourth argument, named stats, is an optional Boolean value that determines whether LINEST returns additional regression statistics besides the slope and intercept. The default is FALSE. When you use LINEST without the stats argument (or with *stats* set to FALSE), enter the function as a 1x2 array, where the value in the first column is the slope of the trend line and the value in the second column is the intercept. With stats set to TRUE, enter the function as a 5x2 array. Note that in this larger array, the R^2 value (the coefficient of determination) is given in the first column of the third row.

Plotting Forecasted Values

So far, I've mentioned two ways to determine the R^2 value (the coefficient of determination) that tells you whether the dependent and independent variables are well correlated:

» Plot the best-fit trend line and select the Display R-Squared Value on Chart check box.

» Use the LINEST function with the stats argument set to TRUE, and read the R^2 value in the first column of the third row.

If you find that either method indicates that the dependent and independent variables are well correlated (that is, the R^2 value is 0.7 or higher), give yourself a high-five and then take advantage of that correlation to forecast future values.

This sounds like magic, but it's nothing but statistics. The key here is the assumption that the major factors underlying the existing data will remain more or less constant over the number of periods in your forecast. If you're about to acquire another company or shed product lines, any forecast you produce based on your old data is likely to be useless.

With that caveat in mind, the most straightforward way to calculate forecasted values is to use a chart to extend the best-fit trend line into one or more future periods. Note, however, that to work with a best-fit trend line and use it to plot forecasted values, you must plot your data series as an XY (Scatter) chart.

Here are the steps to follow:

1. **Click the chart to select it.**

2. **If your chart has multiple data series, click the series you want to analyze.**

3. **Choose Design ⇨ Add Chart Element ⇨ Trendline ⇨ More Trendline Options.**

   The Format Trendline pane appears.

4. **Click the Trendline Options tab.**

5. **Select the Linear radio button.**

   Excel plots the best-fit trend line.

6. **In the Forecast section, use the Forward text box to type the number of units you want to project the trend line into in the future.**

   Excel extends the best-fit trend line, as shown in Figure 10-3.

FIGURE 10-3: A best-fit trend line, extended four periods into the future.

The extended trend line

7. (Optional) Select the Display Equation on Chart check box.

8. (Optional) Select the Display R-Squared Value on Chart check box.

9. Click Close.

Excel displays the regression equation and the R^2 value beside the extended trend line.

TECHNICAL STUFF

Another way to come up with forecasted dependent variable values is to calculate them directly using the regression equation that Excel generates when you select the Display Equation on Chart check box in the Format Trendline pane. The general regression equation for a linear model is as follows:

$$y = mx + b$$

y is the dependent variable; x is the independent variable; m is the slope of the trend line; and b is the starting value for the trend. Both m and b are constants, so to calculate the dependent variable value for the next period in your forecast, substitute that period's independent variable value for x.

Extending a Linear Trend

With a *linear trend*, the dependent variable is related to the independent variable by some constant amount. For example, you might find that housing sales (the dependent variable) increase by 100,000 units whenever interest rates (the independent variable) decrease by 1 percent. Similarly, you might find that company revenue (the dependent variable) increases by $250,000 for every $50,000 you spend on advertising (the independent variable).

If forecasting is part of your data analysis, you can take advantage of a linear relationship to forecast future periods. Excel kindly offers a couple of tools you can use to extend a linear trend into one or more future periods: the fill handle and the Series command.

Extending a linear trend using the fill handle

Excel's fill handle — the little green square that appears in the lower-right corner of the selected cell or range — wears many hats, but perhaps the most surprising use for this handy tool is to extend a linear trend one or more periods into the future. Here's how it works:

1. **Select the existing data.**

   The fill handle appears in the lower-right corner of the selected range.

2. **Click and drag the fill handle to extend the selection over the number of future periods you want to forecast.**

   Excel extends the existing data with the forecasted values.

Extending a linear trend using the Series command

The second method that Excel offers for extending a linear trend is the Series command. Here's how it works:

1. **Select the existing data and the cells where you want the forecasted data to appear.**

2. **Choose Home ⇨ Fill ⇨ Series.**

   Excel displays the Series dialog box, shown in Figure 10-4. Notice that Excel automatically fills in the Step Value text box with the slope of the trend line for the existing data.

3. **Select the AutoFill radio button.**

4. **Click OK.**

   Excel extends the existing linear trend with the forecasted values.

FIGURE 10-4:
The Series dialog box: your best-fit trend best friend.

TIP

If your data analysis requires that you see the actual values that make up a linear trend, the Series command can help:

1. **Copy the historical data into an adjacent row or column.**

2. **Select the range that includes both the copied historical data and the blank cells that will contain the projections.**

3. **Choose Home ⇨ Fill ⇨ Series.**

   Excel displays the Series dialog box.

4. **Select the Linear radio button.**

5. **Select the Trend check box.**

6. **Click OK.**

   Excel replaces the copied historical data with the best-fit trend numbers and projects the trend onto the blank cells.

Calculating Forecasted Linear Values

If your analysis requires exact forecast values, you could extend the best-fit trend line and then use the regression equation to calculate the values, or you could use the fill handle or Series command to extend the linear trend. These are straight-forward methods, but if the historical values change, you need to repeat these procedures to recalculate the forecasted values. A more efficient solution is to use the TREND function. Here's a recap of the TREND syntax:

```
TREND(known_ys, known_xs, new_xs, const)
```

In this situation, you need to use TREND not only with the *known_ys* argument (a reference to the dependent values) and optionally the *known_xs* argument (a reference to the independent values), but also the *new_xs* argument. The *new_xs* argument is a range reference or array that represents the new independent values for which you want forecasted dependent values.

Here's the procedure to follow to calculate forecasted linear trend values using the TREND function:

1. **Select the cells in which you want the forecasted values to appear.**

2. **Type** =trend(.

3. **Type a reference or array that represents the dependent values.**

4. **Type a comma and then type a reference or array that represents the independent values.**

5. **Type a comma and then a reference or array that represents the new independent values.**

6. **If you prefer to use a trend starting point of 0, type a comma and then type** FALSE.

7. **Type).**

8. **Press and hold Ctrl+Shift and then click the Enter button or press Enter.**

   Excel calculates the forecasted trend values and enters them as an array.

Figure 10-5 shows a worksheet that lists historical sales (D2:D13) over three years by fiscal quarter. The TREND forecast array is in D14:D17.

D14		▼	:	×	✓	fx	{=TREND(D2:D13, C2:C13, C14:C17)}		

	A	B	C	D	E	F
1	**Sales**		**Period**	**Actual**		
2		1st Quarter	1	259,846		
3	**Fiscal**	2nd Quarter	2	262,587		
4	**2017**	3rd Quarter	3	260,643		
5		4th Quarter	4	267,129		
6		1st Quarter	5	266,471		
7	**Fiscal**	2nd Quarter	6	269,843		
8	**2018**	3rd Quarter	7	272,803		
9		4th Quarter	8	275,649		
10		1st Quarter	9	270,117		
11	**Fiscal**	2nd Quarter	10	275,315		
12	**2019**	3rd Quarter	11	270,451		
13		4th Quarter	12	276,543		
14		1st Quarter	13	278,099		
15	**Fiscal**	2nd Quarter	14	279,507		
16	**2020**	3rd Quarter	15	280,915		
17	**(Projected)**	4th Quarter	16	282,322		
18						

— Forecasted values

FIGURE 10-5: An array of forecasted trend values (see the range D14:D17).

TECHNICAL STUFF

When you use the LINEST function to calculate the linear trend's slope (m) and y-intercept (b), you can use these results to forecast new values. That is, given a new independent value x, the forecasted dependent value is given by the regression equation:

```
y = mx + b
```

You can also calculate a forecasted linear trend value by using the FORECAST. LINEAR function, which takes three arguments:

```
TREND(x, known_ys, known_xs)
```

x is the new independent value for which you want to forecast a new dependent value; known_ys and known_xs are the same as with the TREND function, except that with FORECAST.LINEAR, the known_xs argument is required.

Plotting an Exponential Trend Line

Up to now, I cover doing regression analysis only on linear data, which changes at a constant rate. However, you can also apply regression analysis to nonlinear data, where the trend line isn't straight.

A common example of nonlinear data is an *exponential* trend, which rises or falls at an increasing rate. It's called exponential because the trend line resembles the graph of a number being raised to successively higher values of an exponent. For example, the series 2^1, 2^2, 2^3 starts off slowly (2, 4, 8, and so on), but by the time you get to 2^{20}, the series value is up to 1,048,576, and 2^{100} is a number that's 31 digits long!

To visualize such a trend, you can plot an *exponential trend line.* This is a curved line through the data points where the differences between the points on one side of the line and those on the other side of the line cancel each other out.

Here are the steps to follow to plot an exponential trend line:

1. **Click the chart to select it.**

2. **If your chart has multiple data series, click the series you want to analyze.**

3. **Choose Design ⇨ Add Chart Element ⇨ Trendline ⇨ More Trendline Options.**

    The Format Trendline pane appears.

4. **Click the Trendline Options tab.**

5. **Select the Exponential radio button.**

    Excel plots the exponential trend line.

6. **(Optional) Select the Display Equation on Chart check box.**

    If you just want to see the trend line, feel free to pass over steps 6 and 7.

7. **(Optional) Select the Display R-Squared Value on Chart check box.**

8. **Click Close.**

    Excel displays the regression equation and the R^2 value (described below). Figure 10-6 shows a chart with the plotted exponential trend line, the regression equation, and the R^2 value.

With nonlinear regression, when the best-fit trend line is an exponential curve, the regression equation takes the following general form:

$$y = be^{mx}$$

y is the dependent variable; x is the independent variable; b and m are constants; and e is a constant (approximately 2.71828) that represents the base of the natural logarithm.

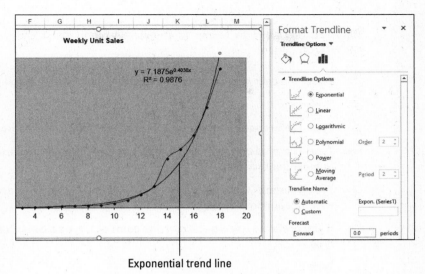

FIGURE 10-6:
A chart with an
exponential
trend line.

Exponential trend line

Calculating Exponential Trend Values

Eyeballing an exponential trend line, as I discuss in the previous section, is a fun way to pass the time. The trend line is a great visual tool, but it doesn't help if you require exact exponential trend values. Yep, you could plot the trend line and then use the exponential version of the regression equation to calculate the exact values:

```
y = be^mx
```

However, if the data values change, you need to replot the trend line and recalculate the trend values. Too much work!

A better solution is to use the GROWTH function, which takes up to four arguments:

```
GROWTH(known_ys, known_xs, new_xs, const)
```

The *known_ys* argument is required and is a reference to the dependent values. The *known_xs* argument is a reference to the independent values (the default is the array {1,2,3,...},n}, where n is the number of *known_ys*). The *new_xs* argument is a reference to the new independent values for which you want forecasted dependent values. The *const* argument determines the value of b in the exponential regression equation: FALSE places it at 1, whereas TRUE (the default) calculates b based on the *known_ys*.

Here are the steps to follow to calculate exponential trend values using the GROWTH function:

1. **Select the cells in which you want the exponential values to appear.**

2. **Type** =growth(.

3. **Type a reference or array that represents the dependent values.**

4. **Type a comma and then type a reference or array that represents the independent values.**

5. **Type a comma and then type a reference or array that represents the new independent values.**

6. **If you prefer to use a trend starting point of 1, type a comma and then type** FALSE.

7. **Type**).

8. **Press and hold Ctrl+Shift and then click the Enter button or press Enter.**

   Excel calculates the exponential trend values and enters them as an array.

Figure 10-7 shows a worksheet that lists units sold (column B) over 18 weeks. The GROWTH array for the historical trend is in column C, and you can see that the dependent variable (that is, the units sold) is referenced by the range B3 : B20, and the independent variable (that is, the week numbers) is referenced by the range A3 : A20.

C3			f_x	{=GROWTH(B3:B20, A3:A20)}	

	A	B	C	D	E	F
1	Historical Data				Future Data	
2	Week	Units	Trend		Week	Forecast
3	1	11	11		19	
4	2	15	16		20	
5	3	27	24		21	
6	4	44	36		22	
7	5	59	54			
8	6	112	81			
9	7	125	121			
10	8	136	182			
11	9	157	272			
12	10	298	408			
13	11	503	610			
14	12	875	914			
15	13	1,452	1,369			
16	14	3,293	2,049			
17	15	3,902	3,069			
18	16	4,837	4,596			
19	17	6,693	6,882			
20	18	9,283	10,306			

FIGURE 10-7: An array of exponential trend values (column C) and forecast values (column F).

USING LOGEST TO GET EXACT VALUES FOR THE EXPONENTIAL REGRESSION EQUATION

You can use the LOGEST function to calculate the exponential trend equation's m and b constants, which you can then plug into the equation, $y = be^{mx}$, to calculate individual trend values. LOGEST uses the syntax shown here:

```
LINEST(known_ys, known_xs, const, stats)
```

The first three arguments — *known_ys*, *known_xs*, and *const* — are the same as those used in the GROWTH function. A fourth argument, named stats, is an optional Boolean value that determines whether LOGEST returns additional regression statistics. The default is FALSE. When you use LOGEST without the stats argument (or with stats set to FALSE), enter the function as a 1x2 array, where the value in the second column is b; to derive m, you must use the LN function to take the natural logarithm of the value in the first column of the array. With stats set to TRUE, enter the function as a 5x2 array. Note that in this larger array, the R^2 value (the coefficient of determination) is given in the first column of the third row.

REMEMBER

In the example shown in Figure 10-7, the independent values are the week numbers 1, 2, 3, and so on. However, these are the default values for the *known_xs* argument, so technically you could omit this argument in this example.

Plotting a Logarithmic Trend Line

A *logarithmic trend* is one in which the data rises or falls very quickly at the beginning but then slows down and levels off over time. An example of a logarithmic trend is the sales pattern of a highly anticipated new product, which typically sells in large quantities for a short time and then levels off.

To visualize such a trend, you can plot a *logarithmic trend line.* This is a curved line through the data points where the differences between the points on one side of the line and those on the other side of the line cancel each other out.

Here are the steps to follow to plot a logarithmic trend line:

1. **Click the chart to select it.**
2. **If your chart has multiple data series, click the series you want to analyze.**

3. **Choose Design ⇨ Add Chart Element ⇨ Trendline ⇨ More Trendline Options.**

The Format Trendline pane appears.

4. **Click the Trendline Options tab.**

5. **Select the Logarithmic radio button.**

Excel plots the logarithmic trend line.

6. **(Optional) Select the Display Equation on Chart check box.**

If you just want to see the trend line, feel free to pass over Steps 6 and 7.

7. **(Optional) Select the Display R-Squared Value on Chart check box.**

8. **Click Close.**

Excel displays the regression equation and the R^2 value (described below). Figure 10-8 shows a chart with the plotted exponential trend line, the regression equation, and the R^2 value.

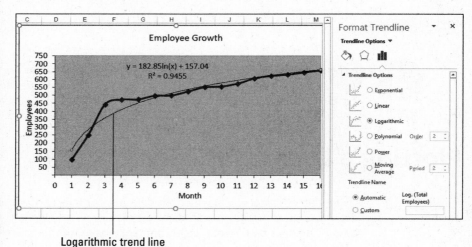

FIGURE 10-8:
A chart with a logarithmic trend line.

Logarithmic trend line

When the best-fit trend line is a logarithmic curve, the regression equation takes the following general form:

$$y = m * \ln(x) + b$$

y is the dependent variable; x is the independent variable; b and m are constants; and ln is the natural logarithm, for which you can use the Excel function LN.

TECHNICAL STUFF

Excel doesn't have a function that calculates the values of b and m directly. However, you can use the LINEST function if you "straighten out" the logarithmic curve by using a logarithmic scale for the independent values:

```
{=LINEST(known_ys, LN(known_xs), const, stats)}
```

Plotting a Power Trend Line

In many cases of regression analysis, the best fit is provided by a *power trend,* in which the data increases or decreases steadily. Such a trend is clearly not exponential or logarithmic, both of which imply extreme behavior, either at the end of the trend (in the case of exponential) or at the beginning of the trend (in the case of logarithmic). Examples of power trends include revenues, profits, and margins in successful companies, all of which show steady increases in the rate of growth year after year.

A power trend sounds linear, but plotting the *power trend line* shows a curved best-fit line through the data points. In your analysis of such data, it's usually best to try a linear trend line first. If that doesn't give a good fit, switch to a power trend line.

Follow these steps to plot a power trend line:

1. **Click the chart to select it.**

2. **If your chart has multiple data series, click the series you want to analyze.**

3. **Choose Design ⇨ Add Chart Element ⇨ Trendline ⇨ More Trendline Options.**

   The Format Trendline pane appears.

4. **Click the Trendline Options tab.**

5. **Select the Power radio button.**

   Excel plots the power trend line.

6. **(Optional) Select the Display Equation on Chart check box.**

   If you just want to see the trend line, skip Steps 6 and 7.

7. **(Optional) Select the Display R-Squared Value on Chart check box.**

8. **Click Close.**

   Excel displays the regression equation and the R^2 value (described below). Figure 10-9 shows a chart with the plotted power trend line, the regression equation, and the R^2 value.

FIGURE 10-9:
A chart with a
power trend line.

Power trend line

When the best-fit trend line is a power curve, the regression equation takes the following general form:

$$y = m * x^b$$

y is the dependent variable; x is the independent variable; and b and m are constants.

TECHNICAL STUFF

There's no worksheet function available to directly calculate the values of b and m. However, you can use the LINEST function if you "straighten out" the power curve by applying a logarithmic scale to the dependent and independent values:

```
{=LINEST(LN(known_ys), LN(known_xs), const, stats)}
```

Plotting a Polynomial Trend Line

In many real-world scenarios, the relationship between the dependent and independent variables doesn't move in a single direction. That would be too easy. For example, rather than constantly rising — uniformly, as in a linear trend, sharply, as in an exponential or logarithmic trend, or steadily, as in a power trend — data such as unit sales, profits, and costs might move up and down.

To visualize such a trend, you can plot a *polynomial trend line,* which is a best-fit line of multiple curves derived using an equation that uses multiple powers of x. The number of powers of x is the *order* of the polynomial equation. Generally, the higher the order, the tighter the curve fits your existing data, but the more unpredictable your forecasted values are.

If you have a chart already, follow these steps to add a polynomial trend line:

1. **Click the chart to select it.**

2. **If your chart has multiple data series, click the series you want to analyze.**

3. **Choose Design ⇨ Add Chart Element ⇨ Trendline ⇨ More Trendline Options.**

   The Format Trendline pane appears.

4. **Click the Trendline Options tab.**

5. **Select the Polynomial radio button.**

6. **Click the Order spin button arrows to set the order of the polynomial equation you want.**

   Excel plots the polynomial trend line.

7. **(Optional) Select the Display Equation on Chart check box.**

   If you just want to see the trend line, bypass Steps 7 and 8.

8. **(Optional) Select the Display R-Squared Value on Chart check box.**

9. **Click Close.**

   Excel displays the regression equation and the R^2 value. Figure 10-10 shows a chart with the plotted polynomial trend line, the regression equation, and the R^2 value.

When the best-fit trend line is a polynomial curve, the regression equation takes the following form:

$$y = m_n x^n + \ldots + m_2 x^2 + m_1 x + b$$

y is the dependent variable; x is the independent variable; and b and m_n through m_1 are constants.

Polynomial trend line

$$y = 0.0148x^5 - 0.442x^4 + 4.808x^3 - 22.869x^2 + 45.045x - 10.713$$
$$R^2 = 0.6236$$

FIGURE 10-10:
A chart with a polynomial trend line.

TECHNICAL STUFF

To calculate the values b and m_n through m_1, you can use LINEST if you raise the *known_xs* values to the powers from 1 to n for an nth-order polynomial:

```
{=LINEST(known_ys, known_xs ^ {1,2,...,n}, const, stats)}
```

Alternatively, you can use the TREND function:

```
{=TREND(known_ys, known_xs ^ {1,2,...,n}, new_xs, const)}
```

» **Calculating the mean, median, mode, and other averages**

» **Figuring out a value's rank in relation to the rest of the data**

» **Grouping your data into a frequency distribution**

» **Messing around with statistical powerhouses such as standard deviation and correlation**

Chapter **11**

Analyzing Data with Statistics

Excel is a statistics powerhouse that boasts more than 100 statistical worksheet functions. That's great if you're a statistician, but do you really need all that stats muscle if you're just doing basic data analysis? You'll no doubt be relieved to hear that the answer is a resounding "No!" Most of Excel's statistical features redefine the word *esoteric*. Believe me when I tell you that you can safely do without Excel features such as cumulative beta probability density and Fourier analysis. I merrily skip over those features and many more in this chapter as I focus on Excel's most important and most useful statistical methods, including calculating the average, rank, largest and smallest values, variance, standard deviation, and correlation. Will it be fun? No, don't be silly. Will it be useful? You bet.

Counting Things

The simplest statistical method you can apply to your data is to count the items in that data set. Of course, Excel being Excel, just because counting things is simple, counting things in Excel is complex because the program offers — count 'em — *four* functions related to counting items a worksheet: COUNT, COUNTA, COUNT-BLANK, and COUNTIF. As if that's not enough, Excel also provides two extra functions — PERMUT and COMBIN — that handle permutations and combinations, respectively.

Counting numbers

The COUNT function tallies the number of cells within a specified range that hold numeric values. That is, COUNT ignores cells that contain text (including numbers values that are formatted as text), that contain the logical values TRUE or FALSE, and that are empty. (It's worth noting that COUNT does include cells that contain dates or times, because Excel treats those data types as numbers.) Here's the syntax:

```
=COUNT(value1[, value2, ...])
```

Here, *value1*, *value2*, and so on are cell or range references. For example, to use the COUNT function to return how many numeric values are in the range B3:B12 in the worksheet shown in Figure 11-1, use the following formula:

```
=COUNT(B3:B12)
```

As shown in cell E3, COUNT returns 6 (five numbers plus one date).

FIGURE 11-1: COUNT returns the tally of the numeric values in a range.

Counting nonempty cells

The COUNTA function counts the number of cells within a specified range that are nonempty. It doesn't matter what data types the cells use — they could be numbers, dates, times, logical values, or text. As long as a cell contains something, it gets included in the COUNT A total. Here's the COUNTA syntax:

```
=COUNTA(value1[, value2, ...])
```

Here, *value1*, *value2*, and so on are cell or range references. For example, to use COUNTA to calculate how many nonempty values are in the range B3:B12 in the worksheet shown earlier in Figure 11-1, use the following formula:

```
=COUNTA(B3:B12)
```

As you can see in cell E4 in Figure 11-1, COUNTA returns the value 9.

Counting empty cells

The COUNTBLANK function is the functional opposite of COUNTA in that it counts the number of cells within a specified range that are empty. Here's the COUNTBLANK syntax:

```
=COUNTBLANK(value1[, value2, ...])
```

Here, *value1*, *value2*, and so on are cell or range references. For example, to use COUNTBLANK to return how many empty values are in the range B3:B12 in the worksheet shown earlier in Figure 11-1, use the following formula:

```
=COUNTBLANK(B3:B12)
```

As you can see in cell E5 in Figure 11-1, COUNTBLANK returns the value 1.

Counting cells that match criteria

The COUNT, COUNTA, and COUNTBLANK functions count numbers, nonempty cells, and empty cells, respectively, so they have, in a sense, built-in criteria for what they count and what they ignore. If you have your own criteria for what should get counted and what shouldn't, you can turn to the COUNTIF function to apply that condition. Here's the syntax:

```
=COUNTIF(range, criteria)
```

Here, *range* is the worksheet range over which you want to count cells, and *criteria* is a logical expression, enclosed in quotation marks, that specifies which cells in the range should be counted.

For example, looking back at the range B3:B12 in Figure 11-1, suppose you want to know how many cells contain a value greater than 800. Here's a formula that'll get the job done:

```
=COUNTIF(B3:B12,">800")
```

As you can see in cell E6 in Figure 11-1, this formula returns the value 3. (There are two numbers greater than 800, plus the date value is equal to 43700, so it also meets the criteria.)

TIP

You can use any of the standard logical operators when building your criteria expression: Use the < operator for a less-than comparison; the <= operator for a less-than-or-equal-to comparison; the > operator for a greater-than comparison; the >= operator for a greater-than-or-equal-to comparison; the = operator for an equal-to comparison; and the <> operator for a not-equal-to comparison.

Counting cells that match multiple criteria

The COUNTIF function applies a single condition to a single range, but sometimes you might need to apply multiple criteria

>> To a single range

>> To multiple ranges

To handle both scenarios, may I introduce you to the COUNTIFS function, which uses the following syntax:

```
=COUNTIFS(range1, criteria1[, range2, criteria2, ...])
```

Here, *criteria1* gets applied to *range1*, *criteria2* gets applied to *range2*, and so on. COUNTIFS includes in the tally only those cells that match all the criteria.

For example, looking back at the range B3:B12 in Figure 11-1, suppose you want to know how many cells contain a value greater than 800 but less than 1000. Here's a formula that will do just that:

```
=COUNTIFS(B3:B12, ">800", B3:B12, "<1000")
```

As you can see in cell E7 in Figure 11-1, this formula returns the value 2.

Counting permutations

An often useful way to count things is to calculate the *permutations*, which, given a data set, is the number of ways that a subset of that data can be grouped, in any order, without repeats. For example, suppose your data set consists of the letters A, B, C, D. Here are all the ways you can group any two of these letters, without repeats:

AB, AC, AD, BA, BC, BD, CA, CB, CD, DA, DB, DC

The two crucial characteristics of a permutation are as follows:

>> Order is important, so AB and BA are considered to be different groupings.

>> Repeats aren't allowed, so the groupings AA, BB, CC, and DD aren't included in the permutations.

Excel's PERMUT function counts the number of permutations possible when selecting a subset from a data set (or a sample from a population). Here's the PERMUT syntax:

```
=PERMUT(number, number_chosen)
```

Here, *number* is the number of items in the set, and *number_chosen* is the number of items in each subset. Given a population of four items and two items in each subset, for example, you calculate the number of permutations by using the formula

```
=PERMUT(4, 2)
```

The function returns the value 12, indicating that 12 different ways exist in which two items can be selected from a set of four.

A variation on the permutation theme is when you allow repetitions in the subset (such as AA, BB, CC, and DD from the ABCD set). In that case, you need to use Excel's PERMUTATIONA function, which uses the same syntax as PERMUT:

```
=PERMUTATIONA(number, number_chosen)
```

For example, to calculate the number of permutations in which two items are selected from a population of four items, with repeats allowed, you use the following formula:

```
=PERMUTATIONA(4, 2)
```

The result is 16.

Counting combinations

It's often useful to count things by calculating the *combinations*, which, given a data set, is the number of ways that a subset of that data can be grouped, without repeats, when the order isn't important (that is, each subset is unique). For example, suppose your data set consists of the letters A, B, C, D. Here are all the unique ways you can group any two of these letters, without repeats:

AB, AC, AD, BC, BD, CD

A combination has two key characteristics:

>> The subsets must be unique, which is another way of saying that order isn't important. For example, the subsets AB and BA are considered to be the same subset.

>> Repeats aren't allowed, so the groupings AA, BB, CC, and DD aren't included in the combinations.

Excel's COMBIN function counts the number of combinations possible when selecting unique subsets from a data set (or a sample from a population). Here's the COMBIN syntax:

```
=COMBIN(number, number_chosen)
```

Here, *number* is the number of items in the set, and *number_chosen* is the number of items in each subset. Given a population of four items and two items in each subset, for example, you calculate the number of combinations by using the formula

```
=COMBIN(4, 2)
```

The function returns the value 6, indicating that six different ways exist in which two items can be selected uniquely from a set of four.

If you want repeats included (such as AA, BB, CC, and DD from the ABCD set), use Excel's COMBINA function, which uses the same syntax as COMBIN:

```
=COMBINA(number, number_chosen)
```

For example, to calculate the number of unique combinations in which two items are selected from a population of four items, with repeats allowed, you use the following formula:

```
=COMBINA(4, 2)
```

The result is 10.

Averaging Things

An *average* is the sum of two or more numeric values divided by the count of the numeric values. If you want, you can calculate the average by creating a custom formula, but that's practical for only a small number of items. For larger collections, using the Excel worksheet functions for calculating averages is way faster and more efficient.

REMEMBER

Statisticians refer to an average as the *mean. Central tendency* is defined as a typical value in a distribution or a value that represents the majority of cases. The most commonly used measures of central tendency are mean, median, and mode.

Calculating an average

The go-to worksheet function for calculating the average (or mean) of a set of values is the AVERAGE function, which uses the following syntax:

```
AVERAGE(number1[, number2, ...])
```

You can enter up to 255 arguments, and each can be a number, a cell, a range, a range name, or an array (that is, a list of values enclosed in curly braces, such as {20, 25, 25, 30}). If a cell contains zero, Excel includes it in the calculation, but if a cell is blank, Excel doesn't include it.

For example, to determine the average of the values in the range D3:D19, you use the following formula:

```
=AVERAGE(D3:D19)
```

Calculating a conditional average

In your data analysis, you might need to average the values in a range, but only those values that satisfy some condition. You can do this by using the AVERAGEIF function, an amalgam of AVERAGE and IF, which averages only those cells in a range that meet the condition you specify. AVERAGEIF takes up to three arguments:

```
=AVERAGEIF(range, criteria[, average_range])
```

The *range* argument is the range of cells you want to use to test the condition; the *criteria* argument is a logical expression, surrounded by double quotation marks, that determines which cells in *range* to average; and the optional *average_range* argument is the range from which you want the average values to be taken. If you omit *average_range*, Excel uses *range* for the average.

Excel sums only those cells in *average_range* that correspond to the cells in *range* and meet the *criteria*.

For example, consider the parts database shown in Figure 11-2. If you want to get the average of the values in the Gross Margin column, you use the AVERAGE function:

```
=AVERAGE(H3:H10)
```

F13		✕	✓	*fx*	=AVERAGEIF(E3:E10, "<10", H3:H10)			
	A	B	C	D	E	F	G	H
1	Parts Database							
2	Division	Description	Number	Quantity	Cost	Total Cost	Retail	Gross Margin
3	4	Gangley Pliers	D-178	57	$10.47	$ 596.79	$17.95	71.4%
4	3	HCAB Washer	A-201	856	$ 0.12	$ 102.72	$ 0.25	108.3%
5	3	Finley Sprocket	C-098	357	$ 1.57	$ 560.49	$ 2.95	87.9%
6	2	6" Sonotube	B-111	86	$15.24	$1,310.64	$19.95	30.9%
7	4	Langstrom 7" Wrench	D-017	75	$18.69	$1,401.75	$27.95	49.5%
8	3	Thompson Socket	C-321	298	$ 3.11	$ 926.78	$ 5.95	91.3%
9	1	S-Joint	A-182	155	$ 6.85	$1,061.75	$ 9.95	45.3%
10	2	LAMF Valve	B-047	482	$ 4.01	$1,932.82	$ 6.95	73.3%
11								
12				Total cost of Division 3 parts:		$ 1,589.99		
13				Average gross margin for parts under $10:		81.2%		
14			Average gross margin for parts over $15 and less than 100 units:			40.2%		

FIGURE 11-2:
A parts database.

But if, instead, you want the average of the Gross Margin values, but only for those parts with a Cost value under $10, you're into AVERAGEIF territory:

```
=AVERAGEIF(E3:E10, "<10", H3:H10)
```

This function says to Excel, in effect, "look in the range E3:E10, and each time you come across a value that's less than 10, grab the corresponding value from the range H3:H10 and include that value in the average. Best regards, AVERAGEIF."

Calculating an average based on multiple conditions

If you want to calculate an average based on multiple criteria applied to one or more ranges, check out the AVERAGEIFS function:

```
=AVERAGEIFs(average_range, range1, criteria1[, range2,
    criteria2...])
```

The *average_range* argument is the range from which you want the average values to be taken. *criteria1* gets applied to *range1*, *criteria2* gets applied to *range2*, and so on. AVERAGEIFS includes in the calculation only those cells that match all the criteria.

Referring back to the parts database shown in Figure 11-2, suppose you want the average of the Gross Margin values, but only for those parts with a Quantity value (D3:D10) less than 100 and a Cost value (E3:E10) greater than $15. AVERAGEIFS is on it:

```
=AVERAGEIFS(H3:H10, D3:D10, "<100", E3:E10, ">15")
```

This formula appears in cell F14 of Figure 11-2, and you can see that the result is 40.2%.

Calculating the median

When analyzing data, you may need to find the *median,* which is the midpoint in a series of numbers: the point at which half the values are greater and half the values are less when you arrange the values in numerical order. What about when you have an even number of values? Great question! In that case, the median is the average of the two values that lie in the middle.

To calculate the median, you use Excel's MEDIAN function:

```
MEDIAN(number1[, number2, ...])
```

You can enter up to 255 arguments, and each can be a number, cell, range, range name, or array. Excel includes zeroes in the calculation, but not blanks.

In the Product Defects worksheet shown in Figure 11-3, the median value of the Defects column (D3:D19) is given by the following formula in cell I2:

```
=MEDIAN(D3:D19)
```

Calculating the mode

The *mode* is the most common value in a list of values. To calculate the mode for a set of numbers, fire up Excel's MODE function:

```
MODE(number1[, number2, ...])
```

I2	▼	:	×	✓	fx	=MEDIAN(D3:D19)		

	A	B	C	D	E	F	G	H	I
1		Product Defects							
2		Workgroup	Group Leader	Defects	Units	% Defective		Median Defects:	9
3		A	Hammond	8	969	0.8%		Mode Defects:	11
4		B	Hammond	4	815	0.5%			
5		C	Hammond	14	1,625	0.9%			
6		D	Hammond	3	1,453	0.2%			
7		E	Hammond	9	767	1.2%			
8		F	Hammond	11	1,023	1.1%			
9		G	Hammond	15	1,256	1.2%			
10		H	Hammond	8	781	1.0%			
11									
12		L	Bolter	7	1,109	0.6%			
13		M	Bolter	11	1,021	1.1%			
14		N	Bolter	6	812	0.7%			
15		O	Bolter	11	977	1.1%			
16		P	Bolter	5	1,182	0.4%			
17		Q	Bolter	7	961	0.7%			
18		R	Bolter	12	689	1.7%			
19		T	Bolter	19	1,308	1.5%			
20									

FIGURE 11-3: MEDIAN returns the median value of a set of numeric values.

You can specify up to 255 arguments; each argument can be a number, cell, range, range name, or array. Excel includes zeroes in the calculation, but it doesn't include blanks.

In the Product Defects worksheet, shown earlier in Figure 11-3, the mode value of the Defects column (D3:D19) is given by the following formula in cell I3:

```
=MODE(D3:D19)
```

REMEMBER Excel interprets the logical value TRUE as 1 and the logical value FALSE as 0, so you can use logical values as arguments when calculating the median or mode. However, if an array or a range of cells contains a logical value, MEDIAN and MODE don't include them in the calculation.

Finding the Rank

Finding how one item ranks relative to the other items in a list is often useful. For example, you might want to find out how a student's test score ranks in relation to the other students. You can do this by sorting the list, but in some situations, sorting isn't advisable. For example, if the original data was constantly changing, it would require constant resorting. Instead, you can use Excel's RANK.EQ function to determine an item's rank relative to other items in a list:

```
RANK.EQ(number, ref[, order])
```

RANK.EQ takes three arguments: *number* is the item you want to rank; *ref* is the range that holds the list of items; and *order* is the optional sort order you want Excel to use. The default is descending, but you can use any nonzero value for ascending.

For example, Figure 11-4 shows a worksheet that contains student grades in the range B3:B48. To find out the rank of the grade in cell B3, you use the following formula:

```
=RANK.EQ(B3, $B$3:$B$48)
```

	A	B	C	D	E	F
1	Student Grades					
2	Student ID	Grade	Rank			
3	64947	82	6			
4	69630	66	28			
5	18324	52	44			
6	89826	94	1			
7	63600	40	46			
8	25089	62	39			
9	89923	88	2			
10	13000	75	10			
11	16895	66	28			
12	24918	62	39			
13	45107	71	19			
14	64090	53	43			
15	94395	74	14			
16	58749	65	34			
17	26916	66	28			
18	59033	67	27			
19	15450	68	25			

C3 — fx =RANK.EQ(B3, $B$3:$B$48)

RANK | LARGE or SMALL | FREQUENCY | VAR.P

FIGURE 11-4: RANK returns the ranking of a value in a set.

As you can see in cell C3, the returned value is 6.

TIP

Note the use of absolute references for the *ref* argument in Figure 11-4. I used absolute references because after entering the formula in cell C3, I filled the formula down from C4 to C48. By using an absolute range reference, I ensured that the *ref* argument is the same for all the filled cells.

You can also use the RANK.AVG function to calculate the rank. With RANK.AVG, if two or more numbers have the same rank, Excel averages the rank. For example, in the list 100, 95, 90, 85, 85, 80, 70, the RANK.AVG function ranks the number 85 as 4.5, which is the average of 4 and 5. By contrast, RANK.EQ would give both instances of 85 the rank 4. With both RANK.EQ and RANK.AVG, if two or more numbers have the same rank, subsequent numbers are affected. In the preceding list, the number 80 ranks sixth. The RANK.AVG function takes the same three arguments as RANK.EQ:

```
RANK.AVG(number, ref[, order])
```

While you're here, I might as well mention Excel's PERCENTRANK.INC function, which you can wield to determine the rank of a value as a percentage of all the values in your data set. PERCENTRANK.INC takes three arguments:

```
PERCENTRANK.INC(array, x[, significance])
```

Here, array is the array or range you want to use; x is the value you want to rank; and significance is the optional number of significant digits you want your results to return (the default is three). PERCENTRANK.INC gives equal values the same rank.

Excel also includes PERCENTRANK.EXC to comply with industry standards for calculating the rank of a value as a percentage of all the values in a data set:

```
PERCENTRANK.EXC(array, x[, significance])
```

As you can see, PERCENTRANK.EXC takes the same arguments as PERCENTRANK. INC, but it excludes the ranks of 0 and 100.

Determining the Nth Largest or Smallest Value

When given a list of values and an item from that list, you can use RANK.EQ (or RANK.AVG) to determine that item's rank (ascending or descending) within that list. A slightly different approach to this problem is to determine, given a list of values, what item in that list has a specified rank, such as first, third, or tenth.

You can solve this problem by sorting the list, but if the values change constantly, a better approach is to use Excel's LARGE or SMALL function, as I describe in the next two sections.

Calculating the nth highest value

Excel's LARGE worksheet function returns the *n*th highest value in a list. Here's the syntax:

```
LARGE(array, n)
```

LARGE takes two arguments: `array` is the array or range you want to work with, and *n* is the rank order of the value you seek.

For example, given a list of student grades shown in the range B3:B48 in Figure 11-5, what's the minimum mark required to crack the top 10 grades? That's a piece of cake for the LARGE function, where the following formula (see cell D4 in Figure 11-5) returns the value 75:

```
=LARGE(B3:B48, 10)
```

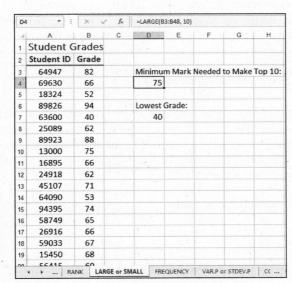

Calculating the *n*th smallest value

Excel's SMALL worksheet function returns the *n*th smallest value in an array or range. Here's the syntax:

```
SMALL(array, n)
```

SMALL takes two arguments: *array* is the array or range you want to work with, and *n* is the rank order of the value you want.

For example, given the student grades shown in the range B3:B48 in Figure 11-5, what's the lowest grade? The following formula (see cell D7 in Figure 11-5) returns the value 40:

```
=SMALL(B3:B48, 1)
```

Creating a Grouped Frequency Distribution

Organizing a large amount of data into a grouped frequency distribution can help you see patterns within the data. With student test scores, for example, the first group might be scores less than or equal to 50, the second group might be 51 to 60, and so on, up to scores between 91 and 100. You can use the Excel FREQUENCY function to return the number of occurrences in each group:

```
FREQUENCY(data_array, bins_array)
```

FREQUENCY takes two arguments: *data_array* is the list of values you want to group; *bins_array* is the list of groupings (known as *bins*) you want to use. You enter FREQUENCY as an array formula into the same number of cells as you have groups. For example, if you have six groups, you enter the formula into six cells. Here are the steps to follow:

1. **Select the cells where you want the grouped frequency distribution to appear.**

2. **Type =frequency(.**

3. **Enter or select the items you want to group.**

4. **Type a comma and then enter or select the list of groupings.**

   When you create your frequency distribution, keep the number of groups reasonable: between five and ten is good. If you have too few or too many groups, you can lose your ability to convey information easily. Too few intervals can hide trends, and too many intervals can mask details. You should also keep your intervals simple. Intervals of 5, 10, or 20 are good because they are easy to understand. Start your interval with a value that's divisible by the interval size, which will make your frequency distribution easy to read. Finally, all intervals should have the same number of values. Again, this makes your frequency distribution easy to understand.

5. Type).

6. **Hold down Ctrl+Shift and then click the Enter button or press Ctrl+Shift+Enter.**

Excel enters the array formula and returns the number of items in each grouping. Figure 11-6 shows a FREQUENCY array formula entered into the range E3:E8.

FIGURE 11-6: FREQUENCY tells you how many items in a range appear in each bin.

Calculating the Variance

Part of your analysis might involve determining how, on average, some values deviate from the mean. One method is to take the difference each number varies from the mean, square those differences, sum those squares, and then divide by the number of values. The result is called the *variance*, and in Excel you calculate it using VAR.S or VAR.P:

```
VAR.S(number1[, number2, ...])
VAR.P(number1[, number2, ...])
```

Use VAR.S if your data represents a sample of a larger population; use VAR.P if your data represents the entire population. In both cases, you can enter up to 255 arguments.

For example, in the Product Defects worksheet, shown in Figure 11-7, I calculate the variance of the Defects column (D3:D19) with the following formula (see cell H3):

```
=VAR.P(D3:D19)
```

H3	▼	:	×	✓	fx	=VAR.P(D3:D19)		

▲ A	B	C	D	E	F	G	H	I
1	Product Defects							
2	Workgroup	Group Leader	Defects	Units	% Defective		Defects Variance:	
3	A	Hammond	8	969	0.8%		17.2	
4	B	Hammond	4	815	0.5%		Defects Standard Deviation:	
5	C	Hammond	14	1,625	0.9%		4.2	
6	D	Hammond	3	1,453	0.2%			
7	E	Hammond	9	767	1.2%			
8	F	Hammond	11	1,023	1.1%			
9	G	Hammond	15	1,256	1.2%			
10	H	Hammond	8	781	1.0%			
11								
12	L	Bolter	7	1,109	0.6%			
13	M	Bolter	11	1,021	1.1%			
14	N	Bolter	6	812	0.7%			
15	O	Bolter	11	977	1.1%			
16	P	Bolter	5	1,182	0.4%			
17	Q	Bolter	7	961	0.7%			
18	R	Bolter	12	689	1.7%			
19	T	Bolter	19	1,308	1.5%			
20								

FIGURE 11-7: VAR.P returns the variance of data that represents an entire population.

Calculating the Standard Deviation

I introduce the variance in the previous section, but because the variance is a squared value, it's difficult to interpret relative to the mean. Therefore, statisticians often calculate the *standard deviation*, which is the square root of the variance.

If two data sets have a similar mean, the set with a higher standard deviation has more variable data. If your data is distributed normally, about 68 percent of the data is found within one standard deviation of the mean; about 95 percent is within two standard deviations; and about 99 percent is within three standard deviations.

To calculate the standard deviation, you can use the STDEV.S or STDEV.P function.

```
STDEV.S(number1[, number2, ...])
STDEV.P(number1[, number2, ...])
```

Use STDEV.S if your data is a sample of a population; use STDEV.P if your data is the entire population. In both cases, you can enter up to 255 arguments.

For example, in the Product Defects worksheet shown earlier in Figure 11-7, I calculated the standard deviation of the Defects column (D3:D19) with the following formula (see cell H3):

```
=STDEV.P(D3:D19)
```

WARNING

The relation of the values to each other in the data set affects the standard deviation. For example, a single outlier can distort the standard deviation, and a data set consisting of identical values gives you a standard deviation of zero.

Finding the Correlation

Correlation is a measure of the relationship between two sets of data. For example, if you have monthly figures for advertising expenses and sales, you might wonder whether higher advertising expenses lead to more sales, that is, whether the two values are related.

WARNING

Keep in mind that a correlation does not prove that one thing causes another. The most you can say is that one number varies with the other.

To find a correlation in Excel, you use the CORREL function:

```
CORREL(array1, array2)
```

CORREL takes two arguments: *array1* and *array2*, which are two lists of numbers. CORREL returns the *correlation coefficient*, which is a number between −1 and 1. The sign suggests whether the relationship is positive (+) or negative (−). See the following table to help interpret the result.

Correlation Coefficient	Interpretation
1	The data sets are perfectly and positively correlated. For example, a 10-percent increase in advertising produces a 10-percent increase in sales.
Between 0 and 1	The data sets are positively correlated. The higher the number is, the higher the correlation is between the data.

Correlation Coefficient	Interpretation
0	No correlation exists between the data.
Between 0 and –1	The data sets are negatively correlated. The lower the number is, the more negatively correlated the data is.
–1	The data sets have a perfect negative correlation. For example, a 10-percent increase in advertising leads to a 10-percent decrease in sales.

Figure 11-8 shows a worksheet that has advertising costs in the range C3:C14 and sales in the range D3:D14. Cell F3 calculates the correlation between these two ranges as follows:

```
=CORREL(C3:C14, D3:D14)
```

FIGURE 11-8: CORREL calculates the correlation between two sets of values.

IN THIS CHAPTER

» **Getting Excel's Analysis ToolPak on the job**

» **Generating oodles of descriptive statistics**

» **Calculating moving averages, ranks, and percentiles**

» **Generating random numbers, for some reason**

» **Creating frequency distributions and histograms**

Chapter **12**

Analyzing Data with Descriptive Statistics

When you're analyzing your Excel data using statistics, you can generate results that either describe something about the data or let you infer something about the data.

Describing the data, statistically speaking, means measuring various aspects of the data, including the sum, count, average, maximum, minimum, standard deviation, and so on. All these measures fall under the heading of *descriptive statistics*.

Making inferences about the data means taking a subset of the total population (which could be people, products, or panda bears) and measuring various aspects of the data that enable you to reach conclusions — *inferences* — about the population as a whole. The tools and techniques that enable you to analyze your data in this way fall under the heading of *inferential statistics*.

In this chapter, you dive into the useful world of descriptive statistics, particularly those you can generate with just a few clicks and key presses using Excel's powerful Analysis ToolPak add-in. For the inferential statistics fun, you'll have to wait until Chapter 13.

Loading the Analysis ToolPak

You can get access to a number of powerful statistical analysis tools by loading Excel's Analysis ToolPak add-in. The Analysis ToolPak consists of 19 statistical tools that calculate not only a basic set of descriptive statistics (such as the sum, average, and standard deviation) but also more sophisticated results, such as the moving average and the rank and percentile. You can also use the analysis tools to generate random numbers and frequency distributions, and to perform inferential statistical analysis, such as correlation and regression.

Many of these tools have equivalent worksheet functions. For example, you can calculate correlation using the CORREL function, rank and percentile using the RANK.* and PERCENTILE.* functions, and so on. However, each Analysis ToolPak tool displays a dialog box that makes it easier for you to configure the tool and select the options you need for your analysis.

If all that sounds too good to be true, know that using the Analysis ToolPak has a downside: All the tool results are static values, not formulas, so if your data changes, you need to run the tool all over again.

Here are the steps to plow through to load the Analysis ToolPak:

1. **Choose File ⇨ Options.**

   The Excel Options dialog box appears.

2. **Click Add-Ins.**

3. **In the Manage drop-down list, click Excel Add-ins and then click Go.**

   The Add-Ins dialog box appears.

4. **Select the Analysis ToolPak check box, as shown in Figure 12-1, and then click OK.**

   Excel loads the Analysis ToolPak add-in.

FIGURE 12-1:
Loading
the Analysis
ToolPak add-in.

The Analysis ToolPak creates a new group named Analysis on the Ribbon's Data tab. To use one of the Analysis ToolPak's statistical tools, choose Data➪Data Analysis. In the Data Analysis dialog box that appears (see Figure 12-2), click the tool you want to use and then click OK. Excel displays a dialog box for the tool. Use the dialog box to specify the tool settings you want to use (the controls vary from tool to tool), and then click OK.

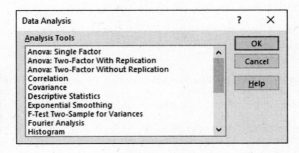

FIGURE 12-2:
The Analysis
ToolPak's tools
appear in the
Data Analysis
dialog box.

If you no longer need the Analysis ToolPak, you can disable the add-in to reduce clutter on the Ribbon's Data tab and to save space on your computer's hard drive. Follow Steps 1 through 3 to display the Add-Ins dialog box, deselect the Analysis ToolPak check box, and then click OK.

Generating Descriptive Statistics

You can speed up your data analysis by using the Descriptive Statistics tool to quickly generate up to 16 different statistical measurements. When you use this tool on a range of data, Excel assumes that you're working with a sample of a larger population and produces a table containing statistical calculations for that sample data, including the measures outlined in Table 12-1.

TABLE 12-1 **Measures Generated By the Descriptive Statistics Tool**

Measure	What It Returns
Mean	The average of the sample data.
Standard Error	The standard error of the sample data, which is a measure of how much the sample data's mean deviates from the population's mean.
Median	The middle value in the sample data (that is, the value that separates the largest half of the values from the smallest half of the values).
Mode	The most common value in the sample data.
Standard Deviation	The standard deviation measure of the sample data. This is a measure of the relative spread of the data: A larger standard deviation means that the data is more spread out; a smaller standard deviation means that the data is bunched together.
Sample Variance	The variance for the sample data. The variance is the square of the standard deviation.
Kurtosis	A measure that indicates whether the curve formed by the sample data (if you charted it) is peaked (positive kurtosis) or flat (negative kurtosis).
Skewness	A measure that indicates whether the curve formed by the charted sample data is bunched below the mean (positive skewness) or above the mean (negative skewness).
Range	The difference between the largest and smallest values in the sample data.
Minimum	The smallest value in the sample data.
Maximum	The largest value in the sample data.
Sum	The total of all the values in the sample data.
Count	The number of values in the sample data.
Largest(X)	The Xth largest value in the sample data.
Smallest(X)	The Xth smallest value in the sample data.
Confidence Level(X%)	The confidence interval for the mean, which is the sample mean plus or minus the returned value. There is X% probability that the mean value for the population data falls within the confidence interval.

The sharp-eyed reader will have noticed two things about the Confidence Level statistic. First, that it's slightly misnamed because it actually returns the confidence interval, not the confidence level. Second, because it enables you to infer something about the population from the sample, it's really an inferential statistic, not a descriptive statistic.

No matter; here are the steps to follow to generate all these statistics for your data:

1. Choose Data ⇨ Data Analysis.

The Data Analysis dialog box appears.

2. In the Analysis Tools list, select Descriptive Statistics and then click OK.

The Descriptive Statistics dialog box appears.

3. Use the Input Range box to specify the range of cells you want to analyze.

Most data will be in columns, but if your data is in rows, be sure to select the Rows radio button. Also, if your data range has labels, select the Labels in First Row check box (or the Labels in First Column check box, if your data is in rows).

4. To specify a location for the output data, select the Output Range radio button and then type or click the upper-left corner of the output range.

Alternatively, you can select New Worksheet Ply to plop the stats in a new worksheet, or select New Workbook to create an entirely new file for the results.

5. Select the Summary Statistics check box.

This tells Excel to generate the mean, standard error, median, mode, standard deviation, sample variance, kurtosis, skewness, range, minimum, maximum, sum, and count.

6. To calculate the confidence interval, select the Confidence Level for Mean check box and then type the confidence level in the text box.

Remember that the confidence level is the probability that the population mean falls with the calculated confidence interval of the sample mean. The default confidence level of 95% is fine for most uses.

7. To calculate the Kth largest value in the sample data, select the Kth Largest check box and then type a value for K in the text box.

8. To calculate the Kth smallest value in the sample data, select the Kth Smallest check box and then type a value for K in the text box.

Figure 12-3 shows a completed version of the Descriptive Statistics dialog box.

Descriptive Statistics ? ✕

Input
Input Range: $D$2:$D$22 ⬆

Grouped By: ◉ Columns
     ○ Rows

☑ Labels in first row

Output options
◉ Output Range: $H$2 ⬆
○ New Worksheet Ply:
○ New Workbook

☑ Summary statistics
☑ Confidence Level for Mean: 95   %
☑ Kth Largest: 5
☑ Kth Smallest: 5

OK
Cancel
Help

FIGURE 12-3:
The Descriptive
Statistics dialog
box, ready to run.

9. **Click OK.**

Excel calculates the descriptive statistics and then displays them in the location
you specified in Step 4. Figure 12-4 shows an example. In this case, the sample
data is the Defects column of the table (D3 : D22).

TIP

If you see General instead of the numbers generated by the Descriptive Statistics
tool, you need to format the results to see the values. Select the output range,
click the Home tab, and then use the Number Format list to select Number.

I4   ✕ ✓ fx   8.9

	Workgroup	Group Leader	Defects	Units	% Defective				
1	Product Defects Database								
2	Workgroup	Group Leader	Defects	Units	% Defective			Defects	
3	A	Hammond	8	969	0.8%				
4	B	Brimson	4	816	0.5%		Mean		8.90
5	C	Reilly	14	1,625	0.9%		Standard Error		0.99
6	D	Richardson	3	1,453	0.2%		Median		8.50
7	E	Durbin	9	767	1.2%		Mode		8.00
8	F	O'Donoghue	10	1,024	1.0%		Standard Deviation		4.41
9	G	Voyatzis	15	1,256	1.2%		Sample Variance		19.46
10	H	Granick	8	782	1.0%		Kurtosis		0.51
11	I	Aster	13	999	1.3%		Skewness		0.25
12	J	Shore	9	1,172	0.8%		Range		19.00
13	K	Fox	0	936	0.0%		Minimum		0.00
14	L	Bolter	7	1,109	0.6%		Maximum		19.00
15	M	Renaud	8	1,022	0.8%		Sum		178.00
16	N	Ibbitson	6	812	0.7%		Count		20.00
17	O	Harper	11	978	1.1%		Largest(5)		12.00
18	P	Ferry	5	1,183	0.4%		Smallest(5)		6.00
19	Q	Richens	7	961	0.7%		Confidence Level(95.0%)		2.06
20	R	Munson	12	690	1.7%				
21	S	Little	10	1,105	0.9%				
22	T	Jones	19	1,309	1.5%				
23									

FIGURE 12-4:
The statistics
generated by the
Descriptive
Statistics tool.

Calculating a Moving Average

A *moving average* smoothes a data series by averaging the series values over a specified number of preceding periods. For example, a seven-day moving average takes the average of the first seven days; then, for each subsequent day to the end of the series, calculates a new average based on the previous seven days. In this example, seven is called the *interval* of the moving average.

Using a moving average can reveal trends that are masked when you use a simple average because a simple average gives equal weight to each value. A moving average weighs recent values equally and ignores older values, thereby enabling you to spot trends. You can use a moving average to forecast sales, stock prices, or other trends.

Follow these steps to crank out some moving averages for your data:

1. **Choose Data ⇨ Data Analysis.**

   Excel displays the Data Analysis dialog box.

2. **Use the Analysis Tools list to select Moving Average and then click OK.**

   The Moving Average dialog box shows up.

3. **Use the Input Range box to specify the range of cells you want to analyze.**

   TIP

   Your range reference should use absolute cell addresses, where you precede both the column letter and the row number with $, as in $C$2:$C$121.

   If your data range has labels, select the Labels in First Row check box.

4. **Use the Interval text box to enter the interval you want to use for the moving average.**

5. **Use the Output Range box to enter or click the upper-left corner of the range where you want the results to appear.**

   Alternatively, you can select New Worksheet Ply to plop the stats in a new worksheet, or select New Workbook to create an entirely new file for the results.

6. **(Optional) Select the Chart Output check box to display a chart that plots the moving average results.**

7. **(Optional) Select the Standard Errors check box if you want to calculate standard errors for the data**

   Excel places standard error values next to the moving average values.

   Figure 12-5 shows a completed version of the Moving Average dialog box.

FIGURE 12-5:
The Moving Average dialog box, good to go.

8. **Click OK.**

Excel calculates the moving averages and then displays them in the location you specified in Step 5, as shown in Figure 12-6. In this case, the sample data is the Actual column of the worksheet (C2:C:121). In this example, cell D13 shows the moving average for cells C2 through C13.

	A	B	C	D
1	**Monthly Sales - Data**		**Actual**	**12-Month Moving Avg**
2		January, 2010	90.0	#N/A
3		February, 2010	95.0	#N/A
4		March, 2010	110.0	#N/A
5		April, 2010	105.0	#N/A
6		May, 2010	100.0	#N/A
7	2010	June, 2010	100.0	#N/A
8		July, 2010	105.0	#N/A
9		August, 2010	105.0	#N/A
10		September, 2010	110.0	#N/A
11		October, 2010	120.0	#N/A
12		November, 2010	130.0	#N/A
13		December, 2010	140.0	109.17
14		January, 2011	90.0	109.17
15		February, 2011	95.0	109.17
16		March, 2011	115.0	109.58
17		April, 2011	110.0	110.00
18		May, 2011	105.0	110.42
19	2011	June, 2011	105.0	110.83
20		July, 2011	110.0	111.25
21		August, 2011	115.0	112.08
22		September, 2011	115.0	112.50
23		October, 2011	125.0	112.92

FIGURE 12-6:
Some moving averages generated by the Moving Average tool.

When you use the Moving Average tool, the first few values in the column contain the value #N/A (see, for example, the range D2:D12 in Figure 12-6). The number of cells that contain #N/A is one less than the number specified for the Interval value because for those initial cells, Excel doesn't yet have enough values to calculate the moving average.

TIP

To use a formula to create a custom moving average of interval *n* using the AVERAGE function, enter the initial formula =AVERAGE(*range*), where *range* is a reference to the first *n* values in the series. Be sure to use relative references in the range coordinates. That way, when you fill the formula down to the subsequent cells to the end of the series, Excel updates the formula to automatically create a moving average. Thanks!

Determining Rank and Percentile

One common form of data analysis is calculating where an item ranks relative to the other items in a group. For example, in a data set that shows the number of product defects by workgroup, you might want to find out how one group's defects total ranks in relation to the other groups. You might also want to calculate the *percentile*, which is the percentage of items in the sample that are at the same level or a lower level than a given value.

As I talk about in Chapter 11, "Analyzing Data with Statistics," you can calculate the rank using Excel's RANK.EQ and RANK.AVG functions, and you can calculate the percentile using the PERCENTILE.EXC and PERCENTILE.INC functions. These are perfectly good worksheet functions, but if you do not mind using static results, you can calculate these values faster and with less effort by using the Analysis ToolPak's Rank and Percentile tool.

Here's how it works:

1. **Choose Data ➪ Data Analysis.**

Excel opens the Data Analysis dialog box.

2. **Use the Analysis Tools list to select Rank and Percentile and then click OK.**

Excel opens the Rank and Percentile dialog box.

3. **Use the Input Range box to specify the range of cells you want to analyze.**

If your data is in rows, be sure to select the Rows radio button. Also, if your data range has labels, select the Labels in First Row check box (or the Labels in First Column check box, if your data is in rows).

4. **Use the Output Range box to enter or click the upper-left corner of the range where you want the results to appear.**

Alternatively, you can select New Worksheet Ply to toss the stats into a new worksheet, or select New Workbook to create a new file to hold the results.

Figure 12-7 shows a completed version of the Rank and Percentile dialog box.

FIGURE 12-7:
A completed
version of the
Rank and
Percentile
dialog box.

5. **Click OK.**

Excel calculates the rank and percentile values and displays them in the
location you specified in Step 4, as shown in Figure 12-8. In this case, the
sample data is the Defects column of the worksheet (D3:D:22).

Workgroup	Group Leader	Defects	Units	% Defective		Point	Defects	Rank	Percent
A	Hammond	8	969	0.8%		20	19	1	100.00%
B	Brimson	4	816	0.5%		7	15	2	94.70%
C	Reilly	14	1,625	0.9%		3	14	3	89.40%
D	Richardson	3	1,453	0.2%		9	13	4	84.20%
E	Durbin	9	767	1.2%		18	12	5	78.90%
F	O'Donoghue	10	1,024	1.0%		15	11	6	73.60%
G	Voyatzis	15	1,256	1.2%		6	10	7	63.10%
H	Granick	8	782	1.0%		19	10	7	63.10%
I	Aster	13	999	1.3%		5	9	9	52.60%
J	Shore	9	1,172	0.8%		10	9	9	52.60%
K	Fox	0	936	0.0%		1	8	11	36.80%
L	Bolter	7	1,109	0.6%		8	8	11	36.80%
M	Renaud	8	1,022	0.8%		13	8	11	36.80%
N	Ibbitson	6	812	0.7%		12	7	14	26.30%
O	Harper	11	978	1.1%		17	7	14	26.30%
P	Ferry	5	1,183	0.4%		14	6	16	21.00%
Q	Richens	7	961	0.7%		16	5	17	15.70%
R	Munson	12	690	1.7%		2	4	18	10.50%
S	Little	10	1,105	0.9%		4	3	19	5.20%
T	Jones	19	1,309	1.5%		11	0	20	0.00%

Product Defects Database

FIGURE 12-8:
The product
defects with their
respective ranks
and percentiles.

Excel creates a four-column table containing the rank and percentile data.
Table 12-2 explains what each column tells you.

TABLE 12-2 **The Rank and Percentile Tool's Output Columns**

Column	Description
Point	The location of the data value within the specified input range. For example, if the value was originally the third numeric value in the input data, the point value is 3.
Column Name	The input values, sorted based upon their ranking. *Column Name* refers to the name of the original input data column.
Rank	The rank for each input value, with 1 being the highest-ranking value in the list.
Percent	The percentile result for each input value.

Generating Random Numbers

When you're building a data analysis model in Excel, that model won't be worth a hill of beans if it doesn't contain any data so that you can take the model for a test drive. If you don't have data lying around, you can enter some placeholder test values by hand, but that sounds like way too much work. Fortunately, you can skip that tedious and time-consuming chore in favor of a faster and more efficient approach: the Analysis ToolPak's Random Number Generation tool, which is happy to generate a set of random values for your model.

True, Excel offers worksheet functions for generating random numbers, but these functions, although useful, have limited capabilities. For example, the RAND function generates random numbers between 0 and 1, and the RANDBETWEEN function generates random numbers between two specified values. If either function provides what you need for your data, go for it.

However, in many cases the numbers coughed up by RAND and RANDBETWEEN aren't useful because they aren't realistic. For example, if your data model uses student test scores, random numbers between, say, 40 and 100 are unrealistic because student scores are almost always distributed as a bell curve, with most of the result bunched in the middle, and just a few results on the high and low ends.

To help you get more realistic random numbers, the Random Number Generation tool enables you to generate random values using various *distributions* that specify the pattern of the values. Here's a quick look:

>> **Uniform:** Generates numbers with equal probability from the range of values you provide (which makes the Uniform distribution similar to the RANDBETWEEN worksheet function).

>> **Normal:** Produces numbers in a bell curve distribution based on a mean and standard deviation.

>> **Bernoulli:** Generates a random series of 1s and 0s based on the probability of success on a single trial.

>> **Binomial:** Generates random numbers characterized by the probability of success over a number of trials.

>> **Poisson:** Generates random numbers based on the probability of a designated number of events occurring in a time frame.

>> **Patterned:** Generates random numbers according to a pattern given by a lower and upper bound, step value, and repetition rate.

>> **Discrete:** Generates random numbers from a series of values and probabilities for these values.

Don't worry if you don't understand all these distributions or if you aren't sure how to even pronounce some of them. Feel free to experiment with each one to see the results you get.

Here are the steps to follow to use the Random Number Generation tool:

1. **Choose Data ⇨ Data Analysis.**

   Excel displays the Data Analysis dialog box.

2. **Use the Analysis Tools list to select Random Number Generation and then click OK.**

   The Random Number Generation dialog box appears.

3. **Specify how many random numbers you want to generate.**

   Use the Number of Variables text box to enter how many random number sets you want. This is the number of columns that will appear in the generated output.

   Use the Number of Random Numbers text box to enter how many random numbers you want in each set. This is the number of rows that will appear in the generated output.

4. **Use the Distribution list to select the type of distribution you want to use.**

5. **Use the controls in the Parameters group to specify the distribution parameters.**

   The options you see depend on the distribution you selected in Step 4. For example, the Random Number Generation dialog box shown in Figure 12-9 shows the Normal distribution selected, so the parameters are a mean value and a standard deviation.

FIGURE 12-9:
The parameters change depending on the Distribution value.

6. **(Optional) Use the Random Seed text box to enter a starting point for the random number generation.**

   You have the option of entering a value that Excel will use to start its generation of random numbers. The benefit of using a Random Seed value, as Excel calls it, is that you can later produce the same set of random numbers by planting the same "seed."

7. **Use the Output Range box to enter or click the upper-left corner of the range where you want the random numbers to appear.**

   Alternatively, you can select New Worksheet Ply to add the random numbers to a new worksheet, or select New Workbook to create a new file for the output.

8. **Click OK.**

   Excel generates the random numbers and then displays them in the location you specified in Step 7, as shown in Figure 12-10.

	A	B	C
1	Student Test Scores		
2	**Student**	**Score**	
3	A	72	
4	B	79	
5	C	77	
6	D	79	
7	E	76	
8	F	57	
9	G	89	
10	H	65	
11	I	70	
12	J	55	
13	K	61	
14	L	61	
15	M	61	
16	N	90	
17	O	75	
18	P	61	
19	Q	66	
20	R	43	
21	S	83	
22	T	74	
23	U	71	

FIGURE 12-10:
Random test
scores generated
by the Random
Number
Generation tool.

Creating a Frequency Distribution

When analyzing a large amount of data, you might require a *frequency distribution*, which organizes the data into numeric ranges called *bins* and then tells you the number of observations that fall within each bin. For example, when analyzing student grades, you might want to know the number of students who received grades between 90 and 100, between 80 and 89, between 70 and 79, and so on.

Although you could generate a frequency distribution using Excel's FREQUENCY function (as I describe in Chapter 11), Excel offers an easier and faster method: the Analysis ToolPak's Histogram tool. This tool requires two worksheet ranges: the *input range* of observations and the *bin range,* which is a range of numbers in which each number defines a boundary of the bin. In Figure 12-11, for example, the grades in column C (C3:C48) are the input range, and the numbers in column E (E3:E8) are the bin range. In this case, there are six bins: 0–50, 51–60, 61–70, 71–80, 81–90, and 91–100.

REMEMBER

Why is it called the Histogram tool and not, say, the Frequency Distribution tool? No idea. However, I can tell you that a *histogram* is a chart of a frequency distribution and, as I show in the steps that follow, the Histogram tool does offer an option for including a chart in the output.

FIGURE 12-11:
A worksheet with
student grades
and a bin
range for the
distribution.

	A	B	C	D	E
1		Student Grades			
2		Student ID	Grade		Bin
3		64947	82		50
4		69630	66		60
5		18324	52		70
6		89826	94		80
7		63600	40		90
8		25089	62		100
9		89923	88		
10		13000	75		
11		16895	67		
12		24918	62		
13		45107	71		
14		64090	53		

Here are the steps to follow to create a frequency distribution using the Histogram tool:

1. **Choose Data ⇨ Data Analysis.**

   Excel displays the Data Analysis dialog box.

2. **Use the Analysis Tools list to select Histogram and then click OK.**

   The Histogram dialog box appears.

3. **Use the Input Range box to specify the range of cells you want to analyze.**

4. **Use the Bin Range box to specify the range of cells that contain your bins.**

   If your input and bin ranges have labels, select the Labels check box.

5. **Use the Output Range box to enter or click the upper-left corner of the range where you want the results to appear.**

   Alternatively, you can select New Worksheet Ply to add the frequency distribution to a new worksheet, or select New Workbook to create a new file for the output.

6. **(Optional) Customize the histogram.**

   Select the Pareto (Sorted Histogram) check box to have Excel sort the bins in descending order.

   Select the Cumulative Percentage check box to have Excel add a Cumulative % column to the output. This column adds the bin percentages as it moves down the bins.

   Select the Chart Output check box to have Excel include a histogram chart with the frequency distribution. If you selected the Cumulative Percentage check box, Excel also includes in the histogram a line showing the cumulative percentages.

   Figure 12-12 shows a ready-to-roll version of the Histogram dialog box.

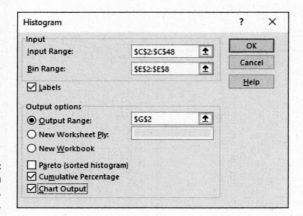

FIGURE 12-12:
The Histogram
dialog box,
all dressed up.

7. **Click OK.**

Excel calculates the frequency distribution and then displays the bin frequencies in the location you specified in Step 5, as shown in Figure 12-13. In this case, the bin values are repeated in column G, the frequencies appear in column H, and (because I selected the Cumulative Percentage check box in Figure 12-12) the cumulative percentages in column I. Figure 12-13 also shows an example histogram (because I selected the Chart Output check box in Figure 12-12).

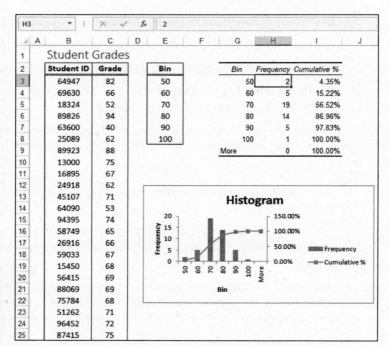

FIGURE 12-13:
A frequency
distribution and
histogram for
some student
grades.

IN THIS CHAPTER

» **Sampling data**

» **Discovering Excel's t-test and z-test tools**

» **Doing a regression analysis and determining the correlation**

» **Implementing the ANOVA data analysis tools**

» **Comparing variances with the f-test tool**

Chapter **13**

Analyzing Data with Inferential Statistics

I n this chapter, I talk about the more sophisticated tools provided by the Excel Analysis ToolPak add-in, such as sampling, t-test, z-test, scatter plot, regression, correlation, ANOVA, and f-test. With these other tools, you can perform inferential statistics, which you use to first look at a set of sample observations drawn from a population and then draw conclusions — that is, make inferences — about the population's characteristics. (To read about the simpler descriptive statistical tools that Excel supplies through the Analysis ToolPak add-in, skip back to Chapter 12. You should also jump back to Chapter 12 to learn how to install the Analysis ToolPak add-in, if you haven't done so already.)

It's worth pointing out right off the top that to use these tools, you need to already have a decent background in statistics. I'm talking a good basic statistics course in college or graduate school, and perhaps even a follow-up course. Armed with this reasonable knowledge of statistics and a bit of patience, you can use all these tools to good advantage.

Sampling Data

With the Sampling tool that's part of the Analysis ToolPak, you can select items from a data set either randomly or regularly, with "regular" meaning that you select every *n*th item. Why would you want to do such a thing? The most common reason is that your full data set (the population) is huge, so analyzing it would take up too much time and computing resources. So, instead, you extract a sample and then use this chapter's inferential statistical techniques on the sample to draw conclusions about the population.

For example, suppose that as part of an internal audit, you want to randomly select 20 orders from a table of invoices. Why, that's a perfect task for the Sampling tool! As an example, I use the table of invoices shown in Figure 13-1.

	ShippedDate	Shipper	ProductID	ProductName	UnitPrice	Quantity	Discount	ExtendedPrice	Freight	Shipp
2	1/16/2019	Federal Shipping	29	Thüringer Rostbratwurst	$99.00	21	0%	$2,079.00	$83.93	Easte
3	1/16/2019	Federal Shipping	35	Steeleye Stout	$14.40	35	0%	$504.00	$83.93	Easte
4	1/16/2019	Federal Shipping	49	Maxilaku	$16.00	30	0%	$480.00	$83.93	Easte
5	1/10/2019	Speedy Express	30	Nord-Ost Matjeshering	$20.70	18	0%	$372.60	$12.51	Rattle
6	1/10/2019	Speedy Express	56	Gnocchi di nonna Alice	$30.40	70	0%	$2,128.00	$12.51	Rattle
7	1/10/2019	Speedy Express	65	Louisiana Fiery Hot Pepper Sauce	$16.80	20	0%	$336.00	$12.51	Rattle
8	1/10/2019	Speedy Express	71	Fløtemysost	$17.20	60	0%	$1,032.00	$12.51	Rattle
9	1/10/2019	United Package	23	Tunnbröd	$7.20	60	0%	$432.00	$67.88	Ernst
10	1/10/2019	United Package	63	Vegie-spread	$35.10	65	0%	$2,281.50	$67.88	Ernst
11	1/9/2019	Federal Shipping	16	Pavlova	$13.90	21	15%	$248.11	$73.79	Ernst
12	1/9/2019	Federal Shipping	48	Chocolade	$10.20	70	15%	$606.90	$73.79	Ernst
13	1/8/2019	Speedy Express	26	Gumbär Gummibärchen	$24.90	30	5%	$709.65	$155.97	Maga
14	1/8/2019	Speedy Express	42	Singaporean Hokkien Fried Mee	$11.20	40	5%	$425.60	$155.97	Maga
15	1/8/2019	Speedy Express	49	Maxilaku	$16.00	30	5%	$456.00	$155.97	Maga
16	1/22/2019	Speedy Express	3	Aniseed Syrup	$8.00	50	0%	$400.00	$34.82	LINO-
17	1/13/2019	Speedy Express	1	Chai	$14.40	10	0%	$144.00	$108.04	Quee
18	1/13/2019	Speedy Express	21	Sir Rodney's Scones	$8.00	30	10%	$216.00	$108.04	Quee
19	1/13/2019	Speedy Express	28	Rössle Sauerkraut	$36.40	42	10%	$1,375.92	$108.04	Quee
20	1/13/2019	Speedy Express	36	Inlagd Sill	$15.20	5	10%	$68.40	$108.04	Quee
21	1/13/2019	Speedy Express	40	Boston Crab Meat	$14.70	2	10%	$26.46	$108.04	Quee
22	1/30/2019	United Package	11	Queso Cabrales	$16.80	30	0%	$504.00	$91.48	Ottili
23	1/30/2019	United Package	69	Gudbrandsdalost	$28.80	15	0%	$432.00	$91.48	Ottili
24	1/30/2019	United Package	71	Fløtemysost	$17.20	15	0%	$258.00	$91.48	Ottili
25	1/14/2019	Speedy Express	37	Gravad lax	$20.80	10	0%	$208.00	$11.26	Folies
26	1/14/2019	Speedy Express	54	Tourtière	$5.90	6	0%	$35.40	$11.26	Folies
27	1/14/2019	Speedy Express	62	Tarte au sucre	$39.40	35	0%	$1,379.00	$11.26	Folies
28	1/14/2019	Speedy Express	14	Tofu	$18.60	12	0%	$223.20	$29.83	Océa

FIGURE 13-1:
A table of invoice data from which you might select a sample.

To sample items from a worksheet like the one shown in Figure 13-1, take the following steps:

1. Choose Data ⇨ Data Analysis.

   The Data Analysis dialog box appears.

2. In the Analysis Tools list, select Sampling and then click OK.

   The Sampling dialog box appears.

3. **Use the Input Range box to specify the range of cells from which you want to extract your sample.**

   The range you select must contain only numeric values. If your data range has a label, select the Labels check box.

4. **Choose a sampling method.**

   Excel provides two sampling methods for extracting items in your data set:

   - **Periodic:** Extracts every nth item from the data set, such as every fifth item or every tenth item. To use this method, select the Periodic radio button and then enter the period you want to use in the Period text box.

   - **Random:** Extracts items randomly from the data set. To use this method, select the Random radio button and then enter the number of items that you want to extract in the Number of Samples text box.

5. **To specify a location for the output data, select the Output Range radio button and then type or click the upper-left corner of the output range.**

   Alternatively, you can select New Worksheet Ply to plop the sample in a new worksheet, or select New Workbook to create an entirely new file for the results.

   Figure 13-2 shows a completed version of the Sampling dialog box. In this case, I ask for a random sample of 20 items from Q2:Q1060, which is the Quantity column in the Invoices table.

FIGURE 13-2: The Sampling dialog box, ready to sample.

6. **Click OK.**

   Excel extracts the sample and displays it in the location you specified in Step 5. Figure 13-3 shows an example. In this case, the sample data is the Defects column of the table (D3:D22).

	A	B
1	20	
2	60	
3	30	
4	60	
5	8	
6	7	
7	40	
8	30	
9	21	
10	8	
11	40	
12	35	
13	3	
14	10	
15	10	
16	10	
17	15	
18	4	
19	35	
20	8	
21		

FIGURE 13-3:
The sample
extracted by the
Sampling tool.

Using the t-Test Tools

The Excel Analysis ToolPak add-in provides three tools for working with t-values and t-tests, which can be useful when you want to make inferences about very small data sets:

>> t-Test: Paired Two Sample for Means

>> t-Test: Two-Sample Assuming Equal Variances

>> t-Test: Two-Sample Assuming Unequal Variances

Briefly, here's how these three tools work. For the sake of illustration, assume that you're working with the values shown in Figure 13-4. The worksheet range A1:A21 contains the first set of values. The worksheet range B1:B21 contains the second set of values.

To perform a t-test calculation, follow these steps:

1. **Choose Data ⇨ Data Analysis.**

   The Data Analysis dialog box appears.

	A	B
1	Sample 1	Sample 2
2	0.390639	0.597253
3	0.960314	0.247645
4	0.002978	0.76919
5	0.073425	0.83317
6	0.311795	0.450877
7	0.451693	0.08733
8	0.989853	0.247164
9	0.946743	0.036413
10	0.88257	0.591507
11	0.846565	0.475535
12	0.817594	0.06112
13	0.933039	0.703724
14	0.013688	0.003346
15	0.08753	0.887344
16	0.017276	0.11998
17	0.642356	0.393307
18	0.782696	0.070239
19	0.391383	0.837355
20	0.142597	0.707126
21	0.241643	0.757264
22		

FIGURE 13-4: Some sample data you can use to perform t-test calculations.

2. **Use the Analysis Tools list to select the t-test tool you want to use and then click OK.**

   - **t-Test: Paired Two-Sample for Means:** Choose this tool when you want to perform a paired two-sample t-test.

   - **t-Test: Two-Sample Assuming Equal Variances:** Choose this tool when you want to perform a two-sample test and you have reason to assume that the variances of both samples equal each other.

   - **t-Test: Two-Sample Assuming Unequal Variances:** Choose this tool when you want to perform a two-sample test but you assume that the two-sample variances are unequal.

   Excel displays the corresponding t-test dialog box. Figure 13-5 shows the t-Test: Two-Sample Assuming Equal Variances dialog box. The other t-test dialog boxes look very similar.

3. **In the Variable 1 Range and Variable 2 Range input text boxes, identify the sample values by telling Excel in what worksheet ranges you've stored the two samples.**

   You can enter a range address into these text boxes. Or you can click in the text box and then select a range by clicking and dragging. If the first cell in the variable range holds a label and you include the label in your range selection, select the Labels check box.

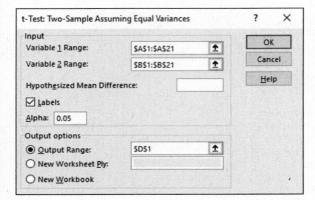

FIGURE 13-5:
The t-Test:
Two-Sample
Assuming Equal
Variances
dialog box.

4. **Use the Hypothesized Mean Difference text box to indicate whether you hypothesize that the means are equal.**

If you think that the means of the samples are equal, either enter **0** (zero) into this text box or leave the text box empty. If you hypothesize that the means are not equal, enter the mean difference.

5. **In the Alpha text box, state the confidence level for your t-test calculation.**

The confidence level is between 0 and 1. By default, the confidence level is equal to 0.05, which is equivalent to a 5-percent confidence level.

6. **In the Output Options section, indicate where the t-test tool results should be stored.**

Here, select one of the radio buttons and enter information in the text boxes to specify where Excel should place the results of the t-test analysis. For example, to place the t-test results into a range in the existing worksheet, select the Output Range radio button and then identify the range address in the Output Range text box. If you want to place the t-test results someplace else, select one of the other option radio buttons.

7. **Click OK.**

Excel calculates the t-test results. Figure 13-6 shows the t-test results for a Two-Sample Assuming Equal Variances test. The t-test results show the mean for each of the data sets, the variance, the number of observations, the pooled variance value, the hypothesized mean difference, the degrees of freedom (abbreviated as *df*), the t-value (or t-stat), and the probability values for one-tail and two-tail tests.

	A	B	C	D	E	F
1	Sample 1	Sample 2		t-Test: Two-Sample Assuming Equal Variances		
2	0.390639	0.597253				
3	0.960314	0.247645			Sample 1	Sample 2
4	0.002978	0.76919		Mean	0.496319	0.443844
5	0.073425	0.83317		Variance	0.138465	0.097277
6	0.311795	0.450877		Observations	20	20
7	0.451693	0.08733		Pooled Variance	0.117871	
8	0.989853	0.247164		Hypothesized Mean Difference	0	
9	0.946743	0.036413		df	38	
10	0.88257	0.591507		t Stat	0.48333	
11	0.846565	0.475535		P(T<=t) one-tail	0.315817	
12	0.817594	0.06112		t Critical one-tail	1.685954	
13	0.933039	0.703724		P(T<=t) two-tail	0.631635	
14	0.013688	0.003346		t Critical two-tail	2.024394	
15	0.08753	0.887344				
16	0.017276	0.11998				
17	0.642356	0.393307				
18	0.782696	0.070239				
19	0.391383	0.837355				
20	0.142597	0.707126				
21	0.241643	0.757264				

FIGURE 13-6:
The results of a t-test.

Performing a z-Test

If you know the variance or standard deviation of the underlying population, you can calculate z-test values by using the Analysis ToolPak's z-Test: Two Sample for Means tool. You might typically work with z-test values to calculate confidence levels and confidence intervals for normally distributed data. To perform a z-test, take these steps:

1. **Choose Data ⇨ Data Analysis.**

   The Data Analysis dialog box appears.

2. **Use the Analysis Tools list to select the z-Test: Two Sample for Means tool and then click OK.**

   Excel displays the z-Test: Two Sample for Means dialog box.

3. **In the Variable 1 Range and Variable 2 Range text boxes, identify the sample values by telling Excel in what worksheet ranges you've stored the two samples.**

   You can enter a range address into the text boxes here or you can click in the text box and then select a range by clicking and dragging. If the first cell in the variable range holds a label and you include the label in your range selection, select the Labels check box.

4. **Use the Hypothesized Mean Difference text box to indicate whether you hypothesize that the means are equal.**

If you think that the means of the samples are equal, enter **0** (zero) into this text box or leave the text box empty. If you hypothesize that the means are not equal, enter the difference.

5. **Use the Variable 1 Variance (Known) and Variable 2 Variance (Known) text boxes to provide the population variance for the first and second samples.**

6. **In the Alpha text box, state the confidence level for your z-test calculation.**

The confidence level is between 0 and 1. By default, the confidence level equals 0.05 (equivalent to a 5-percent confidence level).

7. **In the Output Options section, indicate where the z-test tool results should be stored.**

To place the z-test results into a range in the existing worksheet, select the Output Range radio button and then identify the range address in the Output Range text box. If you want to place the z-test results someplace else, use one of the other options.

Figure 13-7 shows a completed version of the dialog box (using the same sample data as shown earlier in Figure 13-4).

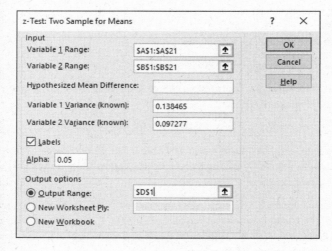

FIGURE 13-7: The z-Test: Two Sample for Means dialog box.

8. **Click OK.**

   Excel calculates the z-test results. Figure 13-8 shows the z-test results for a Two Sample for Means test. The z-test results show the mean for each of the data sets, the variance, the number of observations, the hypothesized mean difference, the z-value, and the probability values for one-tail and two-tail tests.

	A	B	C	D	E	F
1	Sample 1	Sample 2		z-Test: Two Sample for Means		
2	0.390639	0.597253				
3	0.960314	0.247645			Sample 1	Sample 2
4	0.002978	0.76919		Mean	0.496319	0.443844
5	0.073425	0.83317		Known Variance	0.138465	0.097277
6	0.311795	0.450877		Observations	20	20
7	0.451693	0.08733		Hypothesized Mean Difference	0	
8	0.989853	0.247164		z	0.48333	
9	0.946743	0.036413		P(Z<=z) one-tail	0.314431	
10	0.88257	0.591507		z Critical one-tail	1.644854	
11	0.846565	0.475535		P(Z<=z) two-tail	0.628861	
12	0.817594	0.06112		z Critical two-tail	1.959964	
13	0.933039	0.703724				
14	0.013688	0.003346				
15	0.08753	0.887344				
16	0.017276	0.11998				
17	0.642356	0.393307				
18	0.782696	0.070239				
19	0.391383	0.837355				
20	0.142597	0.707126				
21	0.241643	0.757264				

FIGURE 13-8: The z-test calculation results.

Determining the Regression

In Chapter 10, "Tracking Trends and Making Forecasts," I talk about adding trend lines to scatter charts to help you visualize the overall trend of your data. You can move beyond the visual regression analysis that the scatter plot technique provides by using the Analysis ToolPak's Regression tool. For example, say that you used the scatter plotting technique, as I describe earlier, to begin looking at a simple data set. And, after that initial examination, suppose that you want to look more closely at the data by using full-blown, take-no-prisoners regression. To perform regression analysis by using the Regression tool, do the following:

1. **Choose Data ⇨ Data Analysis.**

   The Data Analysis dialog box appears.

2. **Use the Analysis Tools list to select the Regression tool and then click OK.**

   Excel displays the Regression dialog box.

3. **Identify your Y and X values.**

   Use the Input Y Range text box to identify the worksheet range holding your dependent variables. Then use the Input X Range text box to identify the worksheet range reference holding your independent variables.

   If your input ranges include a label select the Labels check box.

4. **(Optional) Set the constant to zero.**

   If the regression line should start at zero — in other words, if the dependent value should equal zero when the independent value equals zero — select the Constant is Zero check box.

5. **(Optional) Calculate a confidence level in your regression analysis.**

   To do this, select the Confidence Level check box and then (in the Confidence Level text box) enter the confidence level you want to use.

6. **Select a location for the regression analysis results.**

   Use the Output Options radio buttons and text boxes to specify where Excel should place the results of the regression analysis. To place the regression results into a range in the existing worksheet, for example, select the Output Range radio button and then identify the range address in the Output Range text box. To place the regression results someplace else, select one of the other option radio buttons.

7. **Identify what data you want returned.**

   Select from the Residuals check boxes to specify what residuals results you want returned as part of the regression analysis.

   Similarly, select the Normal Probability Plots check box to add residuals and normal probability information to the regression analysis results.

   Figure 13-9 shows a completed version of the dialog box.

8. **Click OK.**

   Figure 13-10 shows a portion of the regression analysis results including three stacked visual plots of data from the regression analysis. There is a range that supplies some basic regression statistics, including the R-square value, the standard error, and the number of observations. Below that information, the Regression tool supplies *analysis of variance* (or ANOVA) data, including information about the degrees of freedom, sum-of-squares value, mean square value, the f-value, and the significance of F. Beneath the ANOVA information, the Regression tool supplies information about the regression line calculated from the data, including the coefficient, standard error, t-stat, and probability values for the intercept — as well as the same information for the independent variable, which is the number of ads in the example I discuss here. Excel also plots some of the regression data using simple scatter charts. In Figure 13-10, for example, Excel plots residuals, predicted dependent values, and probabilities.

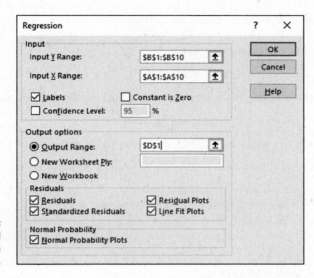

FIGURE 13-9:
The completed
Regression
dialog box.

FIGURE 13-9:
The completed
Regression
dialog box.

FIGURE 13-10:
The regression
analysis results.

Calculating the Correlation

The Correlation analysis tool (which is also available through the Analysis Tool-Pak) quantifies the relationship between two sets of data. You might use this tool to explore such things as the effect of advertising on sales, for example. To use the Correlation analysis tool, follow these steps:

1. **Choose Data⇨Data Analysis.**

The Data Analysis dialog box appears.

2. **Use the Analysis Tools list to select the Correlation tool and then click OK.**

Excel displays the Correlation dialog box.

3. **Identify the range of X and Y values that you want to analyze.**

Use the Input Range box to identify the worksheet range holding your data.

Excel assumes that your data is in columns, so it automatically selects the Columns radio button in the Grouped By section. If your data is in rows, select the Rows radio button instead. If the input range includes labels in the first row (or first column), select the Labels in First Row (or Labels in First Column) check box.

4. **Select an output location.**

Use the Output Options radio buttons and text boxes to specify where Excel should place the results of the correlation analysis. To place the correlation results into a range in the existing worksheet, select the Output Range radio button and then identify the range address in the Output Range text box. If you want to place the correlation results someplace else, select one of the other radio buttons.

Figure 13-11 shows a completed version of the dialog box.

FIGURE 13-11: The completed Correlation dialog box.

5. **Click OK.**

Excel calculates the correlation coefficient for the data that you identified and places it in the specified location. Figure 13-12 shows the correlation results for list price versus units sold. The key value is shown in cell E3. The value –0.96666 suggests that a strong negative correlation exists between list price and units sold. That is, as the list price goes up, the unit sales go down.

	A	B	C	D	E	F
1	List Price	Units Sold			List Price	Units Sold
2	$6.99	9,985		List Price	1	
3	$7.99	8,110		Units Sold	-0.96666	1
4	$8.99	6,039				
5	$9.99	5,721				
6	$10.99	4,555				
7	$11.99	4,075				
8	$12.99	3,290				
9	$13.99	2,592				
10	$14.99	2,289				

FIGURE 13-12: The worksheet showing the correlation results for the list price and units sold data.

Calculating the Covariance

The Covariance tool, also available through the Analysis ToolPak add-in, quantifies the relationship between two sets of values. The Covariance tool calculates the average of the product of deviations of values from the data set means.

To use this tool, follow these steps:

1. **Choose Data ⇨ Data Analysis.**

The Data Analysis dialog box appears.

2. **Use the Analysis Tools list to select the Covariance tool and then click OK.**

Excel displays the Covariance dialog box.

3. **Identify the range of X and Y values that you want to analyze.**

Use the Input Range box to identify the worksheet range holding your data.

Excel assumes that your data is in columns, so it automatically selects the Columns radio button in the Grouped By section. If your data is in rows, select the Rows radio button instead. If the input range includes labels in the first row (or first column), select the Labels in First Row (or Labels in First Column) check box.

4. Select an output location.

Use the Output Options radio buttons and text boxes to specify where Excel should place the results of the covariance analysis. To place the results into a range in the existing worksheet, select the Output Range radio button and then identify the range address in the Output Range text box. If you want to place the results someplace else, select one of the other Output Options radio buttons.

Figure 13-13 shows a completed version of the dialog box.

5. Click OK after you select the output options.

Excel calculates the covariance information for the data that you identified and places it in the specified location. Figure 13-14 shows the covariance results for the list price and units sold data.

	A	B	C	D	E	F	G
1	**List Price**	**Units Sold**				List Price	Units Sold
2	$6.99	9,985			List Price	6.666667	
3	$7.99	8,110			Units Sold	-6053.56	5882524
4	$8.99	6,039					
5	$9.99	5,721					
6	$10.99	4,555					
7	$11.99	4,075					
8	$12.99	3,290					
9	$13.99	2,592					
10	$14.99	2,289					

Using the Anova Tools

The Analysis ToolPak add-in also provides three Anova (analysis of variance) tools: Anova: Single Factor, Anova: Two-Factor With Replication, and Anova: Two-Factor Without Replication. With the Anova tools, you can compare sets of data by looking at the variance of values in each set.

Here are the steps to follow to use an Anova tool:

1. **Choose Data ⇨ Data Analysis.**

   The Data Analysis dialog box appears.

2. **Use the Analysis Tools list to select the Anova tool you want to work with and then click OK.**

   Excel displays the corresponding Anova dialog box.

3. **Describe the data to be analyzed.**

   Use the Input Range box to identify the worksheet range holding your data.

   Excel assumes that your data is in columns, so it automatically selects the Columns radio button in the Grouped By section. If your data is in rows, select the Rows radio button instead. If the input range includes labels in the first row (or first column), select the Labels in First Row (or Labels in First Column) check box.

4. **Describe the location for the Anova results.**

   Use the Output Options buttons and boxes to specify where Excel should place the results of the Anova analysis. If you want to place the Anova results into a range in the existing worksheet, for example, select the Output Range radio button and then identify the range address in the Output Range text box. To place the Anova results someplace else, select one of the other Output Options radio buttons.

   Figure 13-15 shows a completed version of the Anova: Single Factor dialog box.

FIGURE 13-15: The completed Anova: Single Factor dialog box.

5. **Click OK.**

   Excel returns the Anova calculation results, as shown in Figure 13-16.

	A	B	C	D	E	F	G	H	I	J
1	**List Price**	**Units Sold**		Anova: Single Factor						
2	$6.99	9,985								
3	$7.99	8,110		SUMMARY						
4	$8.99	6,039		*Groups*	*Count*	*Sum*	*Average*	*Variance*		
5	$9.99	5,721		List Price	9	98.91	10.99	7.5		
6	$10.99	4,555		Units Sold	9	46656	5184	6617840		
7	$11.99	4,075								
8	$12.99	3,290								
9	$13.99	2,592		ANOVA						
10	$14.99	2,289		*Source of Variation*	*SS*	*df*	*MS*	*F*	*P-value*	*F crit*
11				Between Groups	1.2E+08	1	1.2E+08	36.39254	1.74E-05	4.493998
12				Within Groups	52942778	16	3308924			
13										
14				Total	1.73E+08	17				
15										

Performing an f-test

The Excel Analysis ToolPak add-in also provides a tool for calculating two-sample f-test calculations. An f-test analysis enables you to compare variances from two populations.

Here are the steps to follow to use the f-test tool:

1. **Choose Data ⇨ Data Analysis.**

   The Data Analysis dialog box appears.

2. **Use the Analysis Tools list to select the F-Test Two-Sample for Variances tool and then click OK.**

   Excel displays the F-Test Two-Sample for Variances dialog box.

3. **In the Variable 1 Range and Variable 2 Range input text boxes, identify the sample values by telling Excel in what worksheet ranges you've stored the two samples.**

   You can enter a range address into these text boxes. Or you can click in the text box and then select a range by clicking and dragging. If the first cell in the variable range holds a label and you include the label in your range selection, select the Labels check box.

4. **In the Alpha text box, state the confidence level for your t-test calculation.**

   The confidence level is between 0 and 1. By default, the confidence level is equal to 0.05, which is equivalent to a 5-percent confidence level.

5. Describe the location for the f-test results.

Use the Output Options buttons and boxes to specify where Excel should place the results of the f-test analysis. If you want to place the results into a range in the existing worksheet, for example, select the Output Range radio button and then identify the range address in the Output Range text box. To place the results someplace else, select one of the other Output Options radio buttons.

Figure 13-17 shows a completed version of the F-Test Two-Sample for Variances dialog box.

FIGURE 13-17: The completed F-Test Two-Sample for Variances dialog box.

6. Click OK.

Excel returns the f-test calculation results, as shown in Figure 13-18.

FIGURE 13-18: The worksheet showing the F-Test Two-Sample for Variances results for the list price and units sold data.

	A	B	C	D	E	F
1	List Price	Units Sold		F-Test Two-Sample for Variances		
2	$6.99	9,985				
3	$7.99	8,110			List Price	Units Sold
4	$8.99	6,039		Mean	10.99	5184
5	$9.99	5,721		Variance	7.5	6617840
6	$10.99	4,555		Observations	9	9
7	$11.99	4,075		df	8	8
8	$12.99	3,290		F	1.13E-06	
9	$13.99	2,592		P(F<=f) one-tail	0	
10	$14.99	2,289		F Critical one-tail	0.290858	
11						

An f-test analysis tests to see whether two population variances equal each other. Essentially, the analysis compares the ratio of two variances. The assumption is that if variances are equal, the ratio of the variances should equal 1.

4

The Part of Tens

IN THIS PART . . .

Buff up your basic statistics skills so that you're more easily and comfortably doing data analysis with Excel.

Learn how to analyze financial data over, under, sideways, and down.

Get secrets for building better, more powerful PivotTables.

» **Why averages aren't as simple as they might seem**

» **Some observations about observations**

» **Making sense (to a point) of inferential statistics**

» **Mercifully brief looks at probability distributions and confidence intervals**

Chapter **14**

Ten Things You Ought to Know about Statistics

A big part of the "analysis" portion of "data analysis" involves things like counting, averaging, adding, and standard deviation-ing the data. In a word, much of data analysis involves *statistics*. Here's the thing about statistics, though: After you get beyond the basics, it's a subject that gets complicated in a hurry. Fortunately, you can leap gazelle-like over many of these early statistics hurdles by learning a few basics, and that's what this chapter is all about.

And when I say "basics," I mean *basics*. In the paragraphs that follow, you won't see any mention of statistical esoterica such as chi-squared distributions and Fourier analysis. There are no Greek letters in this chapter.

If you've never been exposed to statistics in school or a decade or two have passed since you were, you should find some useful background here to help you use some of the statistical tools that Excel provides.

Descriptive Statistics Are Straightforward

The first thing that you ought to know about statistics is that some statistical analysis and some statistical measures are pretty darn straightforward. Descriptive statistics, which include things such as the pivot table cross-tabulations (presented in Chapters 7 through 9), as well as some of the statistical functions, make sense even to somebody who's not all that quantitative.

For example, if you sum a set of values, you get a sum. Pretty easy, right? And finding the biggest value or the smallest value in a set of numbers is pretty straightforward, too.

I mention this point about descriptive statistics because people often freak out when they hear the word *statistics.* That's too bad, because many of the most useful statistical tools available to you are simple, easy-to-understand descriptive statistics.

Averages Aren't So Simple Sometimes

Here's a weird thing that you might remember if you ever took a statistics class. When someone uses the term *average,* what she usually refers to is the most common average measurement, which is a *mean.* But you ought to know that several other commonly accepted average measurements exist, including mode, median, and some special mean measurements such as the geometric mean and harmonic mean.

I want to quickly cover some of these . . . not because you need to know all this stuff, but because understanding that the term *average* is imprecise makes some of the discussions in this book and much of Excel's statistical functionality more comprehensible.

To make this discussion more concrete, assume that you're looking at a small set of values: 1, 2, 3, 4, 5. The mean in this small set of values is 3, which you calculate by adding all the numbers in the set (1+2+3+4+5) and then dividing this sum (15) by the total number of values in the set (5).

Two other common average measurements are mode and median. I start with the discussion of the median measurement because it's readily understood using the data set that I introduce in the preceding paragraph. The *median* is the middle value in the sense that there are the same number of values larger than the median as there are values smaller than the median. In the data set 1, 2, 3, 4, 5, the median is 3. Why? Because this data set has two larger values (4 and 5) and two smaller values (1 and 2).

TIP

When you have an even number of values in your data set, you calculate the median by averaging the two middle values. For example, the data set 1, 2, 3, and 4 has no middle value. Add the two middle values — 2 and 3 — and then divide by 2. This calculation produces a median value of 2.5. With the median value of 2.5, half the values in the data set are above the median value, and half the values in the data set are below the median value.

The mode measurement is a third common average. The *mode* is the most common value in the data set. For example, consider the data set 1, 2, 2, 2, 3, 5, 5. The values 1 and 3 occur only once, the value 5 occurs twice, but the value 2 occurs three times. That makes 2 the most common value, so the mode of this data set is 2.

REMEMBER

As I mention earlier, other common statistical measures of the average exist. The mean measurement that I refer to earlier in this discussion is actually an arithmetic mean because the values in the data set get added together arithmetically as part of the calculation. You can, however, combine the values in other ways. Financial analysts and scientists sometimes use a geometric mean, for example. There's also something called a harmonic mean.

You don't need to know about (much less understand) these other average measurements, but you should remember that, because there you have so many different ways to calculate an average, using the term *average* all by itself is imprecise. Make sure that people know what type of average you're using. What if someone else uses the term *average* without specifying the type? That person is probably referring to the *mean*, but you can't be certain, and a lack of certainty is dangerous when you're talking statistics.

Standard Deviations Describe Dispersion

Statistical reports usually include some vague or scary reference to either the standard deviation or its close relative, the variance. Although the formula for standard deviation is terrifying to look at — at least if you're not comfortable with the Greek alphabet — intuitively, the formula and the logic are pretty straightforward to understand.

A *standard deviation* describes how values in a data set are dispersed around the mean. In general, if a data set has a low standard deviation, it means the values are clustered close to the mean; if the data has a high standard deviation, it means the values are spread out away from the mean.

For example, a bit later in this chapter I talk about the normal distribution, which is an arrangement of the items in a data set that, if charted, would produce the classic bell curve: low at the beginning for the smallest values, curving up to a peak at the mean value, curving down from the mean, and then low again for the largest values. That's all annoyingly vague, but you can use standard deviation to make things much more precise. That's because the standard deviation tells you something about how the items are clustered in the normal distribution:

>> 68 percent of the values in the data set lie within plus or minus one standard deviation of the mean. For example, if the mean is 50 and the standard deviation is 10, then 68 percent of the values lie between 40 and 60.

>> 95 percent of the values in the data set lie within plus or minus two standard deviations of the mean. For a mean of 50 and a standard deviation of 10, 95 percent of the values lie between 30 and 70.

>> 99.7 percent of the values in the data set lie within plus or minus three standard deviations of the mean. For a mean of 50 and a standard deviation of 10, 99.7 percent of the values lie between 20 and 80.

An Observation Is an Observation

Observation is one of the terms that you'll encounter if you read anything about statistics in this book or in the Excel online Help. An observation is just an observation. That sounds circular, but bear with me. Suppose that you're constructing a data set that shows daily high temperatures in your neighborhood. When you go out and observe that the temperature some fine July afternoon is 87° F, that measurement (87°) is your first observation. If you go out and observe that the high temperature the next day is 88° F, that measurement is your second observation.

Another way to define the term *observation* is like this: Whenever you actually assign a value to one of your random variables, you create an observation. For example, if you're building a data set of daily high temperatures in your neighborhood, every time that you go out and assign a new temperature value (87° one day, 88° the next day, and so on), you're creating an observation.

A Sample Is a Subset of Values

A *sample* is a collection of observations from a population. For example, if you create a data set that records the daily high temperature in your neighborhood, your little collection of observations is a sample.

In comparison, a sample is not a population. A *population* includes all the possible observations. In the case of collecting your neighborhood's high temperatures, the population includes all the daily high temperatures — since the beginning of the neighborhood's existence.

Inferential Statistics Are Cool but Complicated

As I note earlier in this chapter, some statistics are readily understood. For example, calculating the largest value in a set of numbers is most definitely a statistical measurement, but there's no mystery behind what you're doing. Determining the largest value in a data set is an example of descriptive statistics, and for the most part, we mere mathematical mortals can wrap our heads around such statistics.

The same can't be said for the second main branch of statistics: *inferential statistics.* Inferential statistics are based on a very useful but not at all intuitively obvious idea. If you look at a sample of values from a population and the sample is representative and large enough, you can draw conclusions about the entire population based on characteristics of the sample.

For example, for every presidential election in the United States, the major television networks (usually contrary to their earlier promises) predict the winner after only a relatively small number of votes have been calculated or counted. How do they do this? Well, they sample the population. Specifically, they stand outside polling places and ask exiting voters how they voted. If you ask a large sample of voters whether they voted for one guy or the other guy, you can make an inference about how all the voters voted. And then you can predict who has won the election.

Inferential statistics, although very powerful, possess two qualities that I need to mention:

>> **Accuracy issues:** When you make a statistical inference, you can never be 100 percent sure that your inference is correct. The possibility always exists that your sample isn't representative or that your sample doesn't return enough precision to estimate the population value.

This is partly what happened with the 2000 presidential election in the United States. Initially, some of the major news networks predicted that Al Gore had won based on exit polls. Then based on other exit polls, they predicted that

George W. Bush had won. Then, perhaps finally realizing that maybe their statistics weren't good enough given the closeness of the race, or perhaps just based on their own embarrassment about bobbling the ball, they stopped predicting the race. In retrospect, their trouble with calling the race wasn't surprising because the number of votes for the two candidates was *extremely* close.

>> **Steep learning curve:** Inferential statistics quickly gets pretty complicated. When you work with inferential statistics, you immediately start encountering terms such as *probability distribution functions,* all sorts of crazy (in some cases) parameters, and lots of Greek symbols.

WARNING

As a practical matter, if you haven't at least taken a statistics class — and probably more than one statistics class — you'll find it very hard to move into inferential statistics in a big way. You probably can, with a single statistics class and perhaps the information in this book, work with inferential statistics based on normal distributions and uniform distributions. However, working with inferential statistics and applying those inferential statistics to other probability distributions becomes very tricky. At least, that's my observation.

Probability Distributions Aren't Always Confusing

One of the statistical terms that you'll encounter a little bit in this book — and a whole bunch if you dig into the Excel Help file — is *probability distribution.* This phrase sounds pretty tricky, and in some cases, maybe it is. But you can actually understand intuitively what a probability distribution is with a couple of useful examples.

One common distribution that you hear about in statistics classes, for example, is a T distribution. A *T distribution* is essentially a normal distribution except with heavier, fatter tails. There are also distributions that are skewed (have the hump tilted) one way or the other. Each of these probability distributions, however, has a probability distribution function that describes the probability distribution chart.

In the next two sections, I look at two probability distributions: uniform distribution and normal distribution.

Uniform distribution

One common probability distribution function is a uniform distribution. In a *uniform distribution,* every event has the same probability of occurrence. As a simple example, suppose that you roll a six-sided die. Assuming that the die is fair, you have an equal chance of rolling any of the values: 1, 2, 3, 4, 5, or 6. If you roll the die 60,000 times, what you would expect to see (given the large number of observations) is that you'll probably roll a 1 about 10,000 times. Similarly, you'll probably also roll a 2, 3, 4, 5, or 6 about 10,000 times each. Oh sure, you can count on some variance between what you expect (10,000 occurrences of each side of the six-sided die) and what you actually experience. But your actual observations would pretty well map to your expectations.

The unique thing about this distribution is that everything is pretty darn level. You could say that the probability or the chance of rolling any one of the six sides of the die is even, or *uniform.* This is how uniform distribution gets its name. Every event has the same probability of occurrence. Figure 14-1 shows a uniform distribution that I generated by simulating 60,000 dice rolls. (How did I simulate those rolls? By entering the formula =RANDBETWEEN(1,6) and then filling that formula into 60,000 cells.) As you can see, the uniform distribution is essentially a horizontal line.

FIGURE 14-1: A uniform distribution generated by 60,000 dice rolls.

Normal distribution

Another common type of probability distribution is the *normal distribution,* also known as a *bell curve* or a *Gaussian distribution.*

A normal distribution occurs naturally in many situations. For example, intelligence quotients (IQs) are distributed normally. If you take a large set of people, test their IQs, and then plot those IQs on a chart, you get a normal distribution. One characteristic of a normal distribution is that most of the values in the population are centered around the mean. Another characteristic of a normal distribution is that the mean, the mode, and the median all equal each other. Figure 14-2 shows a normal distribution.

FIGURE 14-2: A normal distribution.

Do you kind of see now where this probability distribution business is going? A probability distribution just describes a chart that, in essence, plots probabilities.

REMEMBER

A probability distribution function is just a function, or equation, that describes the line of the distribution. As you might guess, not every probability distribution looks like a normal distribution or a uniform distribution.

Parameters Aren't So Complicated

After you grasp the concept that a probability distribution is essentially an equation or formula that describes the line in a probability distribution chart, you're ready to understand that a *parameter* is an input to the probability distribution. In other words, the formula or function or equation that describes a probability distribution curve needs inputs, and those inputs are called parameters.

Some probability distribution functions need only a single parameter. For example, to work with a uniform distribution, all you really need is the number of values in the data set. A six-sided die, for example, has only six possibilities. Because you know that only six possibilities exist, you can calculate that any possibility has a 1 in 6 chance of occurring.

REMEMBER

A normal distribution uses two parameters: the mean and the standard deviation.

Other probability distribution functions use other parameters.

Skewness and Kurtosis Describe a Probability Distribution's Shape

A couple of other useful statistical terms to know are skewness and kurtosis. *Skewness* quantifies the lack of symmetry in a probability distribution. In a perfectly symmetrical distribution, like the normal distribution (refer to Figure 14-2), the skewness equals zero. If a probability distribution leans to the right or the left, however, the skewness equals some value other than zero, and the value quantifies the lack of symmetry.

Kurtosis quantifies the heaviness of the tails in a distribution. In a normal distribution, kurtosis equals zero. In other words, zero is the measurement for a tail that looks like a tail in a normal distribution. The *tail* is the thing that reaches out to the left or right. However, if a tail in a distribution is heavier than in a normal distribution, the kurtosis is a positive number. If the tails in a distribution are skinnier than in a normal distribution, the kurtosis is a negative number.

Confidence Intervals Seem Complicated at First, but Are Useful

Probabilities often confuse people, and perhaps this happens most during the U.S. presidential elections. Pundits talk in all sorts of confusing ways about one candidate's chances of winning (often in ways confusing to even the pundits themselves).

Say, for example, some talking head on television says, "The results of a recent poll show that candidate Stem Winder would receive 51 percent of the vote were the election held today; the margin of error was +/- 3 percent with a confidence level of 95 percent."

Okay, this sounds like a mouthful, but break it down and things get a little clearer. What the survey really means is this: The pollsters took a sample of the U.S. population and asked them whom they would vote for today, and 51 percent of the sample said they would vote for Mr. Winder.

Now here's where this gets interesting. Largely because of the size of the sample, the pollsters can do some fancy math and infer that there's sort of a 95 percent chance (more on this later) that the real percentage of people who would vote "Winder" in the entire population is between 48 and 54 percent. Note that "margin of error" is basically just another way to describe the confidence interval.

Something important to understand about confidence levels is that they're linked with the margin of error. If the pollsters in the preceding example had wanted a range of values with a confidence level of 99 percent, the margin of error they calculated would be larger.

To put it another way, perhaps a 95 percent chance (sort of) exists that the real percentage of people in the whole population who would vote "Winder" is between 48 and 54 percent, but a 99 percent chance (again, sort of) exists that the real percentage of people with that answer is between 45 and 57 percent. The wider your range of possible values, the more confidence you have that the real data point falls within your range. Conversely, the more confident you want to be that the real data point is included in your range, the wider you have to make your range.

This is why a bit of a pet peeve of mine is that news organizations reporting on polls will often report the margin of error, but not the confidence level, for a poll. Without knowing the confidence level that the pollster used to calculate the margin of error, the information on margin of error is pretty meaningless.

Another important thing to understand about confidence levels is that the bigger you make your sample size, the smaller your margin of error will be using the same confidence level. If you sample two people on the sidewalk by asking them whom they plan to vote for, and one says "the challenger" and one says "the incumbent," you can't then assert with much confidence that when the whole country votes it will be a perfect 50-50 split. Data from this sample would have an enormous margin of error, unless you use an incredibly low confidence level for your calculations.

However, if you go out and randomly sample 5,000 people by asking whom they're voting for, you have some pretty solid ground to stand on when making a prediction about who's likely to win the presidential race. Put another way, a sample of 5,000 people leads to a much smaller margin of error than a sample of two, assuming that, for both samples, you want the same level of confidence for your range.

At this point, I should make a slight correction: When I said that what the confidence interval means is that a 95 percent chance exists that the real number falls within this range, that's not quite accurate, although it was easier to use as an explanation when first describing the basic concept of a confidence interval. What an interval with 95 percent confidence really means, *technically*, is that if, hypothetically, you were to take different samples from the same population over and over and over again, and then you calculated the confidence interval for those samples in the exact same way for each new sample, about 95 percent of the time the confidence intervals you calculated from the samples would include the real number (because your data from each sample will be slightly different each time, and therefore the interval you calculate will be slightly different as well). So when I say phrases like "95 percent chance" or "99 percent chance," that's what I really mean. (I need to include this clarification so that my old statistics professors don't start shaking their heads in shame if they read this book.)

My final point is this: Predicting election results is far from the only useful thing you can do with confidence intervals. As just one example, say that you had some Google Analytics data on two different web ads you're running to promote your small business, and you want to know which ad is more effective. You can use the confidence interval formula to figure out how long your ads need to run before Google has collected enough data for you to know which ad is really better. (In other words, the formula tells you how big your sample size needs to be to overcome the margin of error.)

IN THIS CHAPTER

» Calculating the future value and present value of an investment

» Determining a loan's payments, principal, and interest

» Calculating the required interest rate for a loan

» Figuring out the internal rate of return for an investment

» Learning various ways to calculate depreciation

Chapter **15**

Ten Ways to Analyze Financial Data

All kinds of people use Excel, including scientists, engineers, mathematicians, statisticians, and pollsters. But if you could somehow survey all the world's Excel users, I bet the typical user would have something to do with the financial industry. Whether they're accountants or adjusters, bankers or borrowers, or money managers or money lenders, financial types rely on Excel every day to analyze budgets, loans, investments, and other monetary minutiae.

But it's not just the financial pros who count on Excel (sometimes literally). Financial amateurs can also use Excel to analyze mortgages, car payments, college funds, savings accounts, and other workaday finances.

Whether you make a living working with money or for money, this chapter gives you ten useful techniques for analyzing financial data using Excel.

Calculating Future Value

If you have $1,000 and plan to invest it at 5 percent interest, compounded annually for ten years, the amount you'll receive at the end of ten years is called the *future value* of $1,000. You can use the Excel FV function to calculate the amount you'll receive.

Here's the syntax of the FV function:

```
FV(rate, nper, pmt[, pv][, type])
```

The *rate* argument is the interest rate of the investment; *nper* is the term of the investment; *pmt* is the amount of each regular deposit into the investment; the optional *pv* argument is your initial investment; and the optional *type* argument is a number indicating when deposits are due (0 or blank for end of period; 1 for beginning of period).

For example, to calculate the future value of $1,000 when it's invested at 5 percent annual interest for 10 years, you use the following formula:

```
=FV(.05, 10, 0, -1000)
```

REMEMBER

When you're working with FV, cash outflows are considered negative amounts, so you need to enter the *pmt* and *pv* arguments as negative numbers.

If you plan on depositing an extra $100 per year in that same investment, the formula changes to this:

```
=FV(.05, 10, 100, -1000)
```

When calculating a future value, be careful of the values you use for the *rate* and *nper* arguments. If you're not making regular deposits or you are making a single deposit annually, you can use the annual interest rate for the *rate* argument and the number of years in the investment for the *nper* argument.

For more frequent deposits, you need to adjust the *rate* and *nper* values accordingly. As a general rule, divide the annual interest rate by the number of deposits per year, and multiply the term of the investment by the number of deposits per year. For example, with monthly deposits, divide the annual interest rate by 12 and multiply the term by 12.

For an example, suppose that with the earlier investment, you want to deposit $15 per month. Here's the revised formula to handle monthly deposits:

```
=FV(.05 / 12, 10 * 12, 15, -1000)
```

Calculating Present Value

Investors use the concept of *present value* to recognize the time value of money. Because an investor can receive interest, $1,000 today is worth less than $1,000 ten years from today. For example, $1,000 invested today at 10 percent interest per year, compounded annually, would return $2,593.74. Therefore, the present value of $2,593.74 at 10 percent, compounded annually, for 10 years is $1,000. Or, worded differently, $1,000 today is worth $2,593.74 ten years from today.

To find the present value, you can use the Excel PV function, which takes five arguments:

```
PV(rate, nper, pmt[, fv][, type])
```

The *rate* argument is the interest rate; *nper* is the number of periods in the term; *pmt* is the amount of each payment; the optional *fv* argument is the future value you're trying to find the present value of; and the optional *type* argument is a number indicating when payments are made (0 or blank for end of period; 1 for beginning of period).

For example, the following formula calculates the present value of $2,593.74, the final value of an investment that returns 10 percent interest, compounded annually, for 10 years:

```
=PV(0.1, 10, 0, 2593.74)
```

REMEMBER

When you're working with the PV function, negative numbers are cash outflows and positive numbers are cash inflows. Enter a negative number when making a payment; enter a positive number when receiving cash.

Present value also applies to loans and mortgages. The money you receive when you take out a loan is the present value of the loan. When calculating present value, be careful what you enter in the *rate* and *nper* arguments. You must divide the annual interest rate by the number of payments per year. For example, if payments are monthly, you should divide the annual interest rate by 12. You must also multiply the term by the number of payments. For example, if payments are monthly, multiply the term by 12.

For example, if you'll be making monthly $15 deposits to the preceding investment, here's the formula to calculate the revised present value of the investment:

```
=PV(0.1 / 12, 10 * 12, 15, 2593.74)
```

Determining Loan Payments

When borrowing money, whether for a mortgage, car financing, a student loan, or something else, the most basic analysis is to calculate the regular payment you must make to repay the loan. You use the Excel PMT function to determine the payment.

The PMT function takes three required arguments and two optional ones:

```
PMT(rate, nper, pv[, fv][, type])
```

The required arguments are *rate*, the fixed rate of interest over the term of the loan; *nper*, the number of payments over the term of the loan; and *pv*, the loan principal. The two optional arguments are *fv*, the future value of the loan, which is usually an end-of-loan balloon payment; and *type*, the type of payment: 0 (the default) for end-of-period payments or 1 for beginning-of-period payments.

REMEMBER

A balloon payment covers any unpaid principal that remains at the end of a loan.

The following example calculates the monthly payment on a 3-percent, 25-year $200,000 mortgage:

```
=PMT(0.03 / 12, 25 * 12, 200000)
```

Note that the result of this formula is −948.42. Why the minus sign? The PMT function returns a negative value because a loan payment is money that you pay out.

As shown in the preceding formula, if the interest rate is annual, you can divide it by 12 to get the monthly rate; if the term is expressed in years, you can multiply it by 12 to get the number of months in the term.

With many loans, the payments take care of only a portion of the principal, with the remainder due as an end-of-loan balloon payment. This payment is the future value of the loan, so you enter it into the PMT function as the *fv* argument. You might think that the *pv* argument should therefore be the partial principal — that is, the original loan principal minus the balloon amount — because the loan term is designed to pay off only the partial principal. Nope. In a balloon loan, you also pay interest on the balloon part of the principal. Therefore, the PMT function's *pv* argument must be the entire principal, with the balloon portion as the (negative) *fv* argument.

Calculating a Loan Payment's Principal and Interest

It's one thing to know the total amount for a regular loan payment, but breaking down a loan payment into its principal and interest components is often handy. The principal part is the amount of the loan payment that goes toward paying down the original loan amount, whereas the rest of the payment is the interest you're shelling out to the lender.

To calculate loan payment principal and interest, you can use the PPMT and IPMT functions, respectively. As the loan progresses, the value of PPMT increases while the value of IPMT decreases, but the sum of the two is constant in each period and is equal to the loan payment.

Both functions take the same six arguments:

```
PPMT(rate, per, nper, pv[, fv][, type])
IPMT(rate, per, nper, pv[, fv][, type])
```

The four required arguments are *rate*, the fixed rate of interest over the loan term; *per*, the number of the payment period; *nper*, the number of payments over the term of the loan; and *pv*, the loan principal. The two optional arguments are *fv*, the future value of the loan; and *type*, the type of payment: 0 for end of period or 1 for beginning of period.

For example, the following two formulas calculate the principal and interest portions of the first monthly payment on a --percent, 25-year $200,000 mortgage:

```
=PPMT(0.03 / 12, 1, 25 * 12, 200000)
=IPMT(0.03 / 12, 1, 25 * 12, 200000)
```

Calculating Cumulative Loan Principal and Interest

To calculate how much principal or interest has accumulated between two periods of a loan, use the CUMPRINC or the CUMIPMT function, respectively. Both functions require the same six arguments:

```
CUMPRINC(rate, nper, pv, start_period, end_period, type])
CUMIPMT(rate, nper, pv, start_period, end_period, type])
```

Here, *rate* is the fixed rate of interest over the term of the loan; *nper* is the number of payments over the term of the loan; *pv* is the loan principal; *start_period* is the first period to include in the calculation; *end_period* is the last period to include in the calculation; and *type* is the type of payment: 0 for end of period or 1 for beginning of period.

For example, to find the cumulative principal or interest in the first year of a loan, set *start_period* to 1 and *end_period* to 12, as shown here:

```
CUMPRINC(0.03 / 12, 25 * 12, 200000, 1, 12, 0)
CUMIPMT(0.03 / 12, 25 * 12, 200000, 1, 12, 0)
```

For the second year, you'd set *start_period* to 13 and *end_period* to 24, and so on.

Finding the Required Interest Rate

If you know how much you want to borrow, how long a term you want, and what payments you can afford, you can calculate what interest rate will satisfy these parameters using the Excel RATE function. For example, you can use this calculation to put off borrowing money if current interest rates are higher than the value you calculate.

The RATE function takes the following arguments:

```
RATE(nper, pmt, pv[, fv][, type][, guess])
```

The three required arguments are *nper*, the number of payments over the term of the loan; *pmt*, the periodic payment; and *pv*, the loan principal. RATE can also take three optional arguments: *fv*, the future value of the loan (the end-of-loan balloon payment); *type*, the type of payment (0 for end of period or 1 for beginning of period); and *guess*, a percentage value that Excel uses as a starting point for calculating the interest rate.

TIP

If you want an annual interest rate, you must divide the term by 12 if it is currently expressed in months. Conversely, if you have a monthly payment and you want an annual interest rate, you must multiply the payment by 12.

RATE uses an iterative process in which Excel starts with an initial guess value and attempts to refine each subsequent result to obtain the answer. If you omit *guess*, Excel uses a default value of 10 percent. If after 20 tries Excel can't come up with a value, it returns a #NUM! error. If that happens, you should enter a *guess* value and try again.

On a related note, if you know the principal, the interest rate, and the payment, you can calculate the length of the loan by using the NPER function:

```
NPER(rate, pmt, pv[, fv][, type])
```

The NPER function's three required arguments are *rate*, the fixed rate of interest; *pmt*, the loan payment; and *pv*, the loan principal. The two optional arguments are *fv*, the future value of the loan, and *type*, the type of payment (0 or 1).

Determining the Internal Rate of Return

The *internal rate of return* is related to the net present value, which is the sum of a series of net cash flows, each of which has been discounted to the present using a fixed discount rate. The internal rate of return can be defined as the discount rate required to get a net present value of $0.

You can use the Excel IRR function to calculate the internal rate of return on an investment. The investment's cash flows don't have to be equal, but they must occur at regular intervals. IRR tells you the interest rate you receive on the investment. Here's the syntax:

```
IRR(values[, guess])
```

The *values* argument is required and represents the range of cash flows over the term of the investment. It must contain at least one positive and one negative value. The *guess* argument is optional and specifies an initial estimate for the Excel iterative calculation of the internal rate of return (the default is 0.1). If after 20 tries Excel can't calculate a value, it returns a #NUM! error. If you see that error, enter a value for the *guess* argument and try again.

For example, given a series of cash flows in the range B3:G3, here's a formula that returns the internal rate of return using an initial guess of 0.11:

```
=IRR(B3:G3, 0.11)
```

TIP

You can use the NPV function to calculate the net present value of future cash flows. If all the cash flows are the same, you can use PV to calculate the present value. But when you have a series of varying cash flows, use NPV, which requires two arguments: *rate*, the discount rate over the term of the asset or investment, and *values*, the range of cash flows.

Calculating Straight-Line Depreciation

The *straight-line* method of depreciation allocates depreciation evenly over the useful life of an asset. Salvage value is the value of an asset after its useful life has expired. To calculate straight-line depreciation, you take the cost of the asset, subtract any salvage value, and then divide by the useful life of the asset. The result is the amount of depreciation allocated to each period.

To calculate straight-line depreciation, you can use the Excel SLN function:

```
SLN(cost, salvage, life)
```

SLN takes three arguments: *cost*, the initial cost of the asset; *salvage*, the salvage value of the asset; and *life*, the life of the asset in periods. If you purchase an asset mid-year, you can calculate depreciation in months instead of years.

For example, if an equipment purchase was $8,500, the equipment's salvage value is $500, and the equipment's useful life is four years, the following formula returns the annual straight-line depreciation:

```
=SLN(8500, 500, 4)
```

The *carrying value* is the cost of an asset minus the total depreciation taken to date. For example, the depreciation for an asset with a cost of $8,500, a salvage value of $500, and a useful life of four years would be allocated as follows:

Year	Annual Depreciation Expense	Accumulated Depreciation	Carrying Value
Beginning of Year 1			$8,500
End of Year 1	$2,000	$2,000	$6,500
End of Year 2	$2,000	$4,000	$4,500
End of Year 3	$2,000	$6,000	$2,500
End of Year 4	$2,000	$8,000	$500

Returning the Fixed-Declining Balance Depreciation

When calculating depreciation, accountants try to match the cost of an asset with the revenue it produces. Some assets produce more in earlier years than in later years. For those assets, accountants use accelerated methods of depreciation, which take more depreciation in the earlier years than in the later years. *Fixed-declining balance* is an accelerated method of depreciation.

To calculate fixed-declining balance depreciation, you can use the Excel DB function:

```
DB(cost, salvage, life, period[, month])
```

The DB function takes five arguments: `cost`, the cost of the asset; `salvage`, the salvage value; `life`, the useful life; `period`, the period for which you're calculating depreciation; and the optional `month`, the number of months in the first year. If you leave `month` blank, Excel uses a default value of 12.

For example, if an equipment purchase was $8,500, the equipment's salvage value is $500, and the equipment's useful life is four years, the following formula returns the depreciation amount for the first year:

```
=DB(8500, 500, 4, 1)
```

The fixed-declining balance method of depreciation depreciates an asset with a cost of $8,500, a salvage value of $500, and a useful life of four years, as follows:

Year	Annual Depreciation Expense	Accumulated Depreciation	Carrying Value
Beginning of Year 1			$8,500
End of Year 1	$4,318	$4,318	$4,182
End of Year 2	$2,124	$6,442	$2,058
End of Year 3	$1,045	$7,488	$1,012
End of Year 4	$512*	$8,000	$500

Amount adjusted for rounding error.

Determining the Double-Declining Balance Depreciation

Double-declining balance is an accelerated depreciation method that takes the rate you would apply by using straight-line depreciation, doubles it, and then applies the doubled rate to the carrying value of the asset.

To determine the double-declining balance depreciation, you can use the Excel DDB function

```
DDB(cost, salvage, life, period[, factor])
```

The DDB function takes five arguments: *cost*, the cost of the asset; *salvage*, the salvage value; *life*, the useful life; *period*, the period for which you're calculating depreciation; and the optional *factor*, the rate at which the balance declines. The default value for *factor* is 2, but to use a value other than twice the straight-line rate, you can enter the factor you want to use, such as 1.5 for a rate of 150 percent.

For example, if an equipment purchase was $8,500, the equipment's salvage value is $500, and the equipment's useful life is four years, the following formula returns the depreciation amount for the first year:

```
=DDB(8500, 500, 4, 1, 2)
```

The double-declining balance method of depreciation depreciates an asset with a cost of $8,500, a salvage value of $1,500, and a useful life of four years, as follows:

Year	Annual Depreciation Expense	Accumulated Depreciation	Carrying Value
Beginning of Year			$8,500
End of Year 1	$4,250	$4,250	$4,250
End of Year 2	$2,125	$6,375	$2,125
End of Year 3	$625*	$7,000	$1,500
End of Year 4	$0*	$7,500	$1,500

*The DDB function does not depreciate the asset below the salvage value.

Chapter **16**

Ten Ways to Raise Your PivotTable Game

E xcel comes with so many powerful data-analysis tools and features that you might be wondering why you need to learn yet another: the PivotTable. The short answer is that the PivotTable is a useful weapon to add to your data-analysis arsenal. The long answer is that PivotTables are worth learning because they come with not just one or two but a long list of benefits.

Let me count the ways: PivotTables are easy to build and maintain; they perform large and complex calculations amazingly fast; you can quickly and easily update them to account for new data; PivotTables are dynamic, so components can be easily moved, filtered, and added to; and, finally, PivotTables can use most of the formatting options that you can apply to regular Excel ranges and cells.

Oh, wait, there's one more: PivotTables are fully customizable, so you can build each report the way you want. That customizability is on full display in this chapter, which covers ten techniques that will turn you into a PivotTable pro.

Turn the PivotTable Fields Task Pane On and Off

By default, when you click inside the PivotTable, Excel displays the PivotTable Fields task pane and then hides the PivotTable Fields task pane again when you click outside the PivotTable report.

Nothing wrong with that on the face of it. However, if you want to work with the commands in the Ribbon's PivotTable Tools contextual tab, you need to have at least one cell in the PivotTable report selected. But selecting any PivotTable cell means that you also have the PivotTable Fields task pane taking up precious screen real estate.

Fortunately, Excel also enables you to turn the PivotTable Fields task pane off and on by hand, which gives you more room to display your PivotTable report. You can then turn the PivotTable Fields task pane back on when you need to add, move, or delete fields.

To toggle the PivotTable Fields task pane off and on, follow these steps (all two of them!):

1. **Click inside the PivotTable.**
2. **Choose Analyze ⇨ Show ⇨ Field List.**

TIP

A quick way to hide the PivotTable Fields task pane is to click the Close button in the upper-right corner of the pane.

Change the PivotTable Fields Task Pane Layout

By default, the PivotTable Fields task pane is divided into two sections: the Fields section lists the data source's available fields and appears at the top of the pane, and the Areas section contains the PivotTable areas — Filters, Columns, Rows, and Values — and appears at the bottom of the pane. You can customize this layout to suit the way you work. Here are the possibilities:

>> **Fields Section and Areas Section Stacked:** This is the default layout.

>> **Field Section and Areas Section Side-By-Side:** Puts the Fields section on the left and the Areas section on the right. Use this layout if your source data comes with a large number of fields.

>> **Fields Section Only:** Hides the Areas section. Use this layout when you add fields to the PivotTable by right-clicking the field name and then clicking the area where you want the field added (instead of dragging fields to the Areas section). By hiding the Areas section, you get more room to display the fields.

>> **Areas Section Only (2 by 2):** Hides the Fields section and arranges the areas in two rows and two columns. Use this layout if you've finished adding fields to the PivotTable and you want to concentrate on moving fields between the areas and filtering the fields.

>> **Areas Section Only (1 by 4):** Hides the Fields section and displays the areas in a single column. Use this layout if you no longer need the Fields section. Also, this layout gives each area a wider display, which is useful if some of your fields have ridiculously long names.

Here are the steps to follow to change the PivotTable Fields task pane layout:

1. **Click any cell inside the PivotTable.**

2. **Click Tools.**

The Tools button is the one with the gear icon, as pointed out in Figure 16-1.

Excel displays the PivotTable Fields task pane tools.

3. **Click the layout you want to use.**

Excel changes the PivotTable Fields task pane layout based on your selection.

TIP

While you have the PivotTable Fields task pane tools displayed, note that you can also sort the field list. The default is Sort in Data Source Order, which means that Excel displays the fields in the same order as they appear in the data source. If you prefer to sort the fields alphabetically, click Sort A to Z.

Tools

FIGURE 16-1:
Click Tools to see
the PivotTable
Fields task pane
layout options.

Display the Details Behind PivotTable Data

The main advantage to using PivotTables is that they give you an easy method for summarizing large quantities of data into a succinct report for data analysis. In short, PivotTables show you the forest instead of the trees. However, sometimes you need to see some of those trees. For example, if you're studying the results of a marketing campaign, your PivotTable may show you the total number of earbuds sold as a result of a 1 Free With 10 promotion (see Figure 16-2). However, what if you want to see the details underlying that number? If your source data contains hundreds or thousands of records, you need to filter the data in some way to see just the records you want.

Advertisement	(All)		
Sum of Quantity	Column Labels		
Row Labels	1 Free with 10	Extra Discount	Grand Total
Earbuds	792	647	1439
HDMI cable	814	894	1708
Smartphone case	638	706	1344
USB car charger	1705	1655	3360
Grand Total	3949	3902	7851

FIGURE 16-2:
You've sold 792
earbuds, but
what are the
details behind
this number?

Fortunately, Excel gives you an easier way to see records you want by enabling you to directly view the details that underlie a specific data value. This is called *drilling down* to the details. When you drill down into a specific data value in a PivotTable,

Excel returns to the source data, extracts the records that comprise the data value, and then displays the records in a new worksheet. For a PivotTable based on a range or table, this extraction takes but a second or two, depending on how many records the source data contains.

To drill down into the details underlying a PivotTable data point, use either of the following methods:

>> Right-click the data value for which you want to view the underlying details and then click Show Details.

>> Double-click the data value.

Excel displays the underlying data in a new worksheet. For example, Figure 16-3 shows the details behind the 792 earbuds sold with the 1 Free with 10 promotion shown previously in Figure 16-2.

	A	B	C	D	E	F
1	Date	Product	Quantity	Net $	Promotion	Advertisement
2	8/21/2019	Earbuds	44	341.88	1 Free with 10	Search
3	8/20/2019	Earbuds	33	256.41	1 Free with 10	Social media
4	8/19/2019	Earbuds	77	598.29	1 Free with 10	Blog network
5	7/21/2019	Earbuds	132	1025.64	1 Free with 10	Search
6	7/20/2019	Earbuds	55	427.35	1 Free with 10	Social media
7	7/19/2019	Earbuds	99	769.23	1 Free with 10	Blog network
8	6/23/2019	Earbuds	121	940.17	1 Free with 10	Search
9	6/22/2019	Earbuds	66	512.82	1 Free with 10	Social media
10	6/21/2019	Earbuds	22	170.94	1 Free with 10	Blog network
11	6/16/2019	Earbuds	33	256.41	1 Free with 10	Blog network
12	6/15/2019	Earbuds	22	170.94	1 Free with 10	Blog network
13	6/14/2019	Earbuds	22	170.94	1 Free with 10	Blog network
14	6/5/2019	Earbuds	55	388.5	1 Free with 10	Blog network
15	6/13/2019	Earbuds	11	85.47	1 Free with 10	Blog network

When you attempt to drill down to a data value's underlying details, Excel may display the error message Cannot change this part of a PivotTable report. This error means that the feature that normally enables you to drill down has been turned off. To turn this feature back on, click any cell inside the PivotTable and then click Analyze ⇨ PivotTable ⇨ Options to display the PivotTable Options dialog box. Click the Data tab, select the Enable Show Details check box, and then click OK.

The opposite situation occurs when you distribute the workbook containing the PivotTable and you don't want other users drilling down and cluttering the workbook with detail worksheets. In this case, click Analyze ⇨ PivotTable ⇨ Options, click the Data tab, deselect Enable Show Details, and then click OK.

Sometimes you may want to see all of a PivotTable's underlying source data. If the source data is a range or table in another worksheet, you can see the underlying data by displaying that worksheet. If the source data is not so readily available, however, Excel gives you a quick way to view all the underlying data. Right-click the PivotTable's Grand Total cell (that is, the cell in the bottom-right corner of the PivotTable) and then click Show Details. (You can also double-click that cell.) Excel displays all of the PivotTable's underlying data in a new worksheet.

Apply a PivotTable Style

One of the nice things about a PivotTable is that it resides on a regular Excel worksheet, which means that you can apply formatting options such as alignments and fonts to portions of the PivotTable. This works well, particularly if you have custom formatting requirements. For example, you may have in-house style guidelines that you need to follow. Unfortunately, applying formatting can be time consuming, particularly if you're applying a number of different formatting options. And the total formatting time can become onerous if you need to apply different formatting options to different parts of the PivotTable. You can greatly reduce the time you spend formatting your PivotTables if you apply a style instead.

A *style* is a collection of formatting options — fonts, borders, and background colors — that Excel defines for different areas of a PivotTable. For example, a style might use bold, white text on a black background for labels and grand totals, and white text on a dark blue background for items and data. Defining all these formats manually might take half an hour to an hour. But with the style feature, you choose the one you want to use for the PivotTable as a whole, and Excel applies the individual formatting options automatically.

Excel defines more than 80 styles, divided into three categories: Light, Medium, and Dark. The Light category includes Pivot Style Light 16, the default formatting applied to PivotTable reports you create; and None, which removes all formatting from the PivotTable. You can also create your own style formats, as described in the next section, "Create a Custom PivotTable Style."

Here are the steps to follow to apply a style to a PivotTable:

1. **Click any cell within the PivotTable you want to format.**

2. **Click the Design tab.**

3. **In the PivotTable Styles group, click the More button.**

   The style gallery appears.

4. **Click the style you want to apply.**

   Excel applies the style.

Create a Custom PivotTable Style

You may find that none of the predefined PivotTable styles gives you the exact look that you want. In that case, you can define that look yourself by creating a custom PivotTable style from scratch.

Excel offers you tremendous flexibility when you create custom PivotTable styles. You can format 25 separate PivotTable elements. These elements include the entire table, the page field labels and values, the first column, the header row, the Grand Total row, and the Grand Total column. You can also define *stripes*, which are separate formats applied to alternating rows or columns. For example, the First Row Stripe applies formatting to rows 1, 3, 5, and so on; the Second Row Stripe applies formatting to rows 2, 4, 6, and so on. Stripes can make a long or wide report easier to read.

Having control over so many elements enables you to create a custom style to suit your needs. For example, you might need your PivotTable to match your corporate colors. Similarly, if the PivotTable will appear as part of a larger report, you might need the PivotTable formatting to match the theme used in the larger report.

The only downside to creating a custom PivotTable style is that you must do so from scratch because Excel doesn't enable you to customize an existing style. Boo, Excel! So if you need to define formatting for all 25 PivotTable elements, creating a custom style can be time consuming.

If you're still up for it, however, here are the steps to plow through to create your very own PivotTable style:

1. **Click the Design tab.**

2. **In the PivotTable Styles group, click More.**

   The style gallery appears.

3. **Click New PivotTable Style.**

   The New PivotTable style dialog box appears, as shown in Figure 16-4.

4. **Type a name for your custom style.**

5. **Use the Table Element list to select the PivotTable feature you want to format.**

6. **Click Format.**

   The Format Cells dialog box appears.

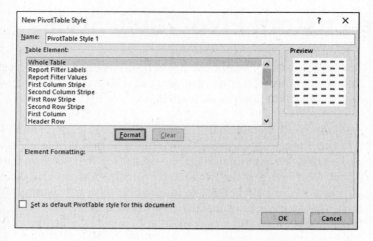

FIGURE 16-4:
The new
PivotTable Style
dialog box.

7. **Use the options in the Font tab to format the element's text.**

   You can choose a font, a font style (such as bold or italic), and a font size. You can also choose an underline, a color, and a strikethrough effect.

8. **Use the options in the Border tab to format the element's border.**

   You can choose a border style, color, and location (such as the left edge, top edge, or both).

9. **Use the options in the Fill tab to format the element's background color.**

   You can choose a solid color or a pattern. You can also click the Fill Effects buttons to specify a gradient that changes from one color to another.

10. **Click OK.**

    Excel returns you to the New PivotTable Style dialog box.

11. **Repeat Steps 5 through 10 to format other table elements.**

    Handily, the New PivotTable Style dialog box includes a Preview section that shows you what the style will look like when it's applied to a PivotTable. If you're particularly proud of your new style, you might want to use it for all your PivotTables. Why not? To tell Excel to use your new style as the default for any future PivotTable you forge, select the Set as Default PivotTable Style for This Document check box.

12. **When you're all done at last, click OK.**

    Excel saves the custom PivotTable style.

Weirdly, after you close the New PivotTable Style dialog box, Excel doesn't apply the new style to the current PivotTable. Dumb! To apply the style yourself, select any cell within the PivotTable, click Design, click the More button in the PivotTable Styles group to open the style gallery, and then click your style in the Custom section that now appears at the top of the gallery.

If you need to make changes to your custom style, open the style gallery, right-click your custom style, and then click Modify. Use the Modify PivotTable style dialog box to make your changes, and then click OK.

If you find that you need to create another custom style that's similar to an existing custom style, don't bother creating the new style from scratch. Instead, open the style gallery, right-click the existing custom style, and then click Duplicate. In the Modify PivotTable style dialog box, adjust the style name and formatting, and then click OK.

If you no longer need a custom style, you should delete it to reduce clutter in the style gallery. Click the Design tab, open the PivotTable Styles gallery, right-click the custom style you no longer need, and then click Delete. When Excel asks you to confirm, click OK.

Preserve PivotTable Formatting

Excel has a nasty habit of sometimes not preserving your custom formatting when you refresh or rebuild the PivotTable. For example, if you applied a bold font to some labels, those labels might revert to regular text after a refresh. Excel has a feature called Preserve Formatting that enables you to preserve such formatting during a refresh; you can retain your custom formatting by activating it.

The Preserve Formatting feature is always activated in default PivotTables. However, another user could have deactivated this feature. For example, you may be working with a PivotTable created by another person and he or she may have deactivated the Preserve Formatting feature.

Note, however, that when you refresh or rebuild a PivotTable, Excel reapplies the report's current style formatting. If you haven't specified a style, Excel reapplies the default PivotTable style (named Pivot Style Light 16); if you have specified a style — as described in the earlier section "Apply a PivotTable Style" — Excel reapplies that style.

Here are the steps to follow to configure a PivotTable to preserve formatting:

1. **Click any cell within the PivotTable that you want to work with.**

2. **Choose Analyze ⇨ PivotTable ⇨ Options.**

   The PivotTable Options dialog box appears with the Layout & Format tab displayed.

3. **Deselect the Autofit Column Widths on Update check box.**

   Deselecting this option prevents Excel from automatically formatting things such as column widths when you pivot fields.

4. **Select the Preserve Cell Formatting on Update check box.**

5. **Click OK.**

   Excel preserves your custom formatting each time you refresh the PivotTable.

Rename the PivotTable

When you create the first PivotTable in a workbook, Excel gives it the uninspiring name PivotTable1. Subsequent PivotTables are named sequentially (and just as uninspiringly): PivotTable2, PivotTable3, and so on. However, Excel also repeats these names when you build new PivotTables based on different data sources. If your workbook contains a number of PivotTables, you can make them easier to distinguish by giving each one a unique and descriptive name. Here's how:

1. **Click any cell within the PivotTable that you want to work with.**

2. **Click Analyze ⇨ PivotTable.**

3. **Use the PivotTable Name text box to type the new name for the PivotTable.**

   The maximum length for a PivotTable name is 255 characters.

4. **Click outside the text box.**

   Excel renames the PivotTable.

Turn Off Grand Totals

A default PivotTable that has at least one row field contains an extra row at the bottom of the table. This row is labeled Grand Total and includes the total of the values associated with the row field items. However, the value in the Grand Total row may not actually be a sum. For example, if the summary calculation is Average, the Grand Total row includes the average of the values associated with the row field items.

Similarly, a PivotTable that has at least one column field contains an extra column at the far right of the table. This column is also labeled "Grand Total" and includes the total of the values associated with the column field items. If the PivotTable contains both a row and a column field, the Grand Total row also has the sums for each column item, and the Grand Total column also has the sums for each row item.

Besides taking up space in the PivotTable, these grand totals are often not necessary for data analysis. For example, suppose you want to examine quarterly sales for your salespeople to see which amounts are over a certain value for bonus purposes. Because your only concern is the individual summary values for each employee, the grand totals are useless. In such a case, you can tell Excel not to display the grand totals by following these steps:

1. **Click any cell within the PivotTable that you want to work with.**

2. **Click Design ⇨ Grand Totals.**

Excel displays a menu of options for displaying the grand totals.

3. **Click the option you prefer.**

The menu contains four items:

- **Off for Rows and Columns:** Turns off the grand totals for both the rows and the columns.

- **On for Rows and Columns:** Turns on the grand totals for both the rows and the columns.

- **On for Rows Only:** Turns off the grand totals for just the columns.

- **On for Columns Only:** Turns off the grand totals for just the rows.

Excel puts the selected grand total option into effect.

The field headers that appear in the report are another often-bothersome PivotTable feature. These headers include Sort & Filter buttons, but if you don't use those buttons, the field headers just clutter the PivotTable. To turn off the field headers, click inside the PivotTable and then choose Analyze ⇨ Show ⇨ Field Headers.

Reduce the Size of PivotTable Workbooks

PivotTables often result in large workbooks because Excel must keep track of a great deal of extra information to keep the PivotTable performance acceptable. For example, to ensure that the recalculation involved in pivoting happens quickly and efficiently, Excel maintains a copy of the source data in a special memory area called the *pivot cache.*

If you build a PivotTable from data that resides in a different workbook or in an external data source, Excel stores the source data in the pivot cache. This greatly reduces the time Excel takes to refresh and recalculate the PivotTable. The downside is that it can increase both the size of the workbook and the amount of time Excel takes to save the workbook. If your workbook has become too large or it takes too long to save, follow these steps to tell Excel not to save the source data in the pivot cache:

1. **Click any cell in the PivotTable.**

2. **Click Analyze ⇨ PivotTable ⇨ Options.**

   The PivotTable Options dialog box appears.

3. **Click the Data tab.**

4. **Deselect the Save Source Data with File check box.**

5. **Click OK.**

   Excel no longer saves the external source data in the pivot cache.

Use a PivotTable Value in a Formula

You might need to use a PivotTable value in a worksheet formula. You normally reference a cell in a formula by using the cell's address. However, this won't work with PivotTables because the addresses of the report values change as you pivot, filter, group, and refresh the PivotTable.

To ensure accurate PivotTable references, use Excel's GETPIVOTDATA function. This function uses the data field, PivotTable location, and one or more (row or column) field/item pairs that specify the exact value you want to use. This way, no matter what the PivotTable layout is, as long as the value remains visible in the report, your formula reference remains accurate.

Here's the syntax of the GETPIVOTDATA function:

```
GETPIVOTDATA(data_field, pivot_table, [, field1, item1][, ...]
```

The two required fields are `data_field`, which is the name of the field you're using in the PivotTable's Values area, and `pivot_table`, which specifies the cell address of the upper-left corner of the PivotTable. The rest of the arguments come in pairs: a field name and an item in that field.

For example, here's a GETPIVOTDATA formula that returns the PivotTable value where the Product field item is Earbuds and the Promotion field item is 1 Free with 10:

```
=GETPIVOTDATA("Quantity", $A$3, "Product", "Earbuds",
    "Promotion", "1 Free with 10")
```

Figure 16-5 shows this formula in action.

FIGURE 16-5: The GETPIVOTDATA function doing its thing.

GETPIVOTDATA is a bit complicated, so let me put your mind at ease right away by saying you'll almost never have to peck out this function and all its arguments by hand. Instead, Excel conveniently handles everything for you when you click the PivotTable value you want to use in your formula. Phew!

Appendix

Glossary of Data Analysis and Excel Terms

absolute reference: A cell address used in a formula that Excel doesn't adjust if you copy the formula to some new location. To create an absolute cell reference, you precede the column letter and row number with a dollar sign ($).

Access: A database program developed and sold by Microsoft. Use Access to build and work with large, sophisticated, relational databases; you can easily export information from Access databases to Excel. Just choose the Access Microsoft Office menu's Export command.

add-in: Software that adds one or more features to Excel. ***See also*** *Analysis ToolPak; Solver*.

Analysis ToolPak: An Excel add-in with which you perform statistical analysis.

arithmetic operators: The standard operators that you use in Excel formulas. To add numbers, use the addition (+) operator. To subtract numbers, use the subtraction (–) operator. To multiply numbers, use the multiplication (*) operator. To divide numbers, use the division (/) operator. You can also perform exponential operations by using the exponential operator (^). ***See*** *operator precedence*.

ascending order: A sorting option that alphabetizes labels and arranges values in smallest-value-to-largest-value order. ***See also*** *chronological order; descending order*.

ASCII text file: A type of text file that in essence is just straight text and nothing else. ***See also*** *delimited text file; importing*.

AutoFilter: An Excel tool (available from the Data tab's Filter command) that helps you produce a new table that's a subset of your original table. For example, in the case of a grocery list table, you could use AutoFilter to create a subset that shows only those items that you'll purchase at a particular store, in specified quantities, or that exceed a certain price.

automatic subtotals: Formulas that Excel adds to a worksheet automatically. Excel sets up automatic subtotals based on data groupings in a selected field.

average: Typically, the arithmetic mean for a set of values. Excel supplies several averaging functions. ***See also*** *median; mode*.

best-fit trendline: A straight line through a chart's data points where the differences between the chart points that reside above the line and those that reside below the line cancel each other out. ***See also*** *trend analysis*.

binomial distributions: Used to calculate probabilities in situations in which you have a limited number of independent trials, or tests, that can either succeed or fail. Success or failure of any one trial is independent of other trials.

Boolean expression: *See* *logical expression*.

break-even analysis: A worksheet model that calculates the number of units a product or business must sell to recoup all costs (or, to put it another way, to reach a profit of $0).

calculated field: Used to insert a new row or column into a PivotTable and then fill the new row or column with a formula.

calculated item: An amount shown in a PivotTable that you create by calculating a formula. Frankly, adding a calculated item usually doesn't make any sense. But, hey, strange things happen all the time, right?

changing cell: A worksheet cell that Excel modifies in an attempt to find a solution to a problem. Also called a *variable cell*.

chart legend: Identifies the data series that you plot in your chart.

chart type: Includes column, bar, line, pie, XY, surface, and so on.

chronological order: A sorting option that arranges labels or values in chronological order such as Monday, Tuesday, Wednesday, and so on. *See also* *ascending order*; *descending order*.

coefficient of determination: A measure of how well a trendline fits the data.

color scales: A data visualization feature that compares the relative values in a range by applying shading to each cell, where the color reflects each cell's value.

combinations: Given a data set, the number of ways that a subset of that data can be grouped, without repeats, where the order isn't important (that is, each subset is unique). *See also* *permutations*.

comma-separated values: A type of delimited text file in which each record appears on a line of text and each field is separated by a comma.

comparison operator: A mathematical operator used in a logical expression. For example, the > comparison operator makes *greater than* comparisons, and the = operator makes *equal to* comparisons. *See also* *logical expressions*.

conditional formatting: A special format that Excel applies only to cells that satisfy one or more criteria.

consolidating: Combining the data from multiple worksheets — called the *source ranges* — into a single summary report — the *destination range*.

constraint: A condition that a cell in a data model must satisfy before Solver accepts a solution.

correlation: A measure of the relationship between two sets of data.

counting: Used for useful statistical functions for counting cells within a worksheet or list. Excel provides four counting functions: COUNT, COUNTA, COUNTBLANK, and COUNTIF. Excel also provides two useful functions for counting permutations and combinations: PERMUT and COMBIN.

criteria: Conditions that specify which subset of data you want to extract from a table or database.

criteria range: A worksheet range that contains copies of a table's header as well as one or more logical expressions that define a filter for the table.

cross-tabulation: An analysis technique that summarizes data in two or more ways. For example, if you run a business and summarize sales information both by customer and by product, that's a cross-tabulation because you tabulate the information in two ways. *See also* PivotTable.

CSV: *See comma-separated values.*

custom calculation: A formula that you define yourself to produce PivotTable values that wouldn't otherwise appear in the report if you used only the source data and Excel's predefined summary calculations.

data analysis: The application of tools and techniques to organize, study, reach conclusions and sometimes also make predictions about a specific collection of information.

database functions: A special set of functions for quick statistical analysis of information stored in Excel tables.

database query: *See query.*

delimited text file: A type of text file. Delimited text files use special characters, called *delimiters,* to separate fields of information in the report. For example, such files commonly use the Tab character to delimit. *See also* ASCII text file; importing.

dependent variable: In regression analysis, the variable that changes with respect to the independent variable.

descending order: A sorting order that arranges labels in reverse alphabetical order and values in largest-value-to-smallest-value order. *See also* ascending order; chronological order.

descriptive statistics: Describe the values in a set. For example, if you sum a set of values, that sum is a descriptive statistic. If you find the largest value or the smallest value in a set of numbers, that's also a descriptive statistic.

dirty: Describes data that's disorganized, inconsistent, or incorrect.

drilling down: In a PivotTable, displaying the data source details behind a calculated value.

exponential trend: A trend that rises or falls at an increasing rate.

exporting: In the context of databases, moving information to another application. If you tell your accounting system to export a list of vendors that Excel can later read, for example, you're exporting. Many business applications, by the way, do easily export data to Excel. ***See also*** *importing.*

external data: Data that resides outside the active Excel workbook in a another workbook, a file, a database, a server, or a website.

field: In a table or database, a category or type of information. In an Excel table, each column represents a field.

field settings: Determine what Excel does with a field when it's cross-tabulated in the PivotTable. ***See also*** *cross-tabulation; PivotTable.*

filter: A condition that Excel applies to a table that defines a subset of the table's records.

fixed-width: A type of text file in which each item uses a set amount of space.

formulas: Calculation instructions entered into worksheet cells. Essentially, this business about formulas going into workbook cells is the heart of Excel. Even if an Excel workbook did nothing else, it would still be an extremely valuable tool. In fact, the first spreadsheet programs did little more than calculate cell formulas. ***See also*** *text labels; value.*

frequency distribution: Organizes the values in a data set into numeric ranges called *bins* and then tells you the number of observations that fall within each bin.

function: A prebuilt formula that you can use to more simply calculate some amount, such as an average or standard deviation.

function arguments: Needed in most functions; also called *inputs.* All database functions need arguments, which you include inside parentheses. If a function needs more than one argument, you separate arguments by using commas. ***See also*** *database functions.*

future value: The amount that money invested now will be worth at a specified time in the future given an interest rate and regular deposits.

header row: A top row of field names in your table range.

histogram: A chart that shows a frequency distribution.

icon set: A data visualization feature that adds a particular icon to each cell in the range, with that icon telling you something about the cell's value relative to the rest of the range.

importing: In the context of databases, grabbing information from some other application. Excel rather easily imports information from popular databases (such as Microsoft Access), other spreadsheets (such as Lotus 1-2-3), and from text files. ***See also*** *exporting.*

independent variable: In regression analysis, the variable based on which the dependent variable changes.

inferential statistics: Based on a very useful, intuitively obvious idea that if you look at a sample of values from a population, and if the sample is representative and large enough, you can draw conclusions about the population based on characteristics of the sample.

iteration: A formula optimization technique that tries multiple interim solutions in an attempt to converge on the true solution.

kurtosis: A measure of the tails in a distribution of values. *See also* *skewness.*

linear trend: A trend in which the dependent variable is related to the independent variable by some constant amount.

linear regression: Regression analysis in which the best-fit trendline is a straight line.

list: *See* *table.*

logarithmic trend: A trend in which the data rises or falls very quickly at the beginning, but then slows down and levels off over time.

logical expression: Describe a comparison that you want to make. To construct a logical expression, you use a comparison operator and then a value used for the comparison.

mean: *See* *average.*

median: The middle value in a set of values. Half the values fall below the median, and half the values fall above the median. *See also* *average; mode.*

Microsoft Access: *See* *Access.*

Microsoft Query: *See* *Query.*

mode: The most common value in a set. *See also* *average; median.*

moving average: Smooths a data series by averaging the series values over a specified number of preceding periods.

nonlinear regression: Regression analysis in which the best-fit trendline is a curve.

normal distribution: The infamous bell curve. Also known as a *Gaussian distribution.*

objective cell: In an optimization process, the cell that contains the formula you want to optimize. Also called the *target cell.* *See also* *changing cell; constraint.*

observation: An item from a data set. Suppose that you're constructing a data set that shows daily high temperatures in your neighborhood. When you go out and *observe* that the temperature some fine July afternoon is 87°F, that measurement is your observation.

Open Database Connectivity (ODBC): A database standard that enables a program to connect to and manipulate a data source.

one-input data table: A data table that varies only one of the formula's input cells.

operator precedence: Standard rules that determine the order of arithmetic operations in a formula. For example, exponential operations are performed first. Multiplication and division operations are performed second. Addition and subtraction operations are performed third. To override these standard rules, use parentheses. *See also* *formulas.*

optimization modeling: A problem-solving technique in which you look for the optimum value of an objective function while explicitly recognizing constraints.

outer field: In a PivotTable, the field "farthest" from the value area: the leftmost field if you have two fields in the row area; the topmost field if you have two fields in the column area. The other field is called the *inner field* because it's "closest" to the value area.

outlier: A value that's much higher or lower than the other values in the same data set.

parameter: An input to a probability distribution function.

percentile: The percentage of items in a sample that are at the same level or a lower level than a given value. *See also rank.*

permutations: Given a data set, the number of ways that a subset of that data can be grouped, in any order, without repeats. *See also combinations.*

pivot cache: An area of memory that Excel uses to store a PivotTable's source data.

PivotChart: A cross-tabulation that appears in a chart. *See also cross-tabulation.*

pivoting: Moving a field from one area to another in a PivotTable.

PivotTable: Perhaps the most powerful analytical tool that Excel provides. Use the PivotTable command to cross-tabulate data stored in Excel lists. *See also cross-tabulation.*

polynomial trend: A trend with a best-fit line of multiple curves derived using an equation that uses multiple powers of x.

population: The complete set of observations for some phenomenon. *See also sample.*

power trend: A trend in which the data increases or decreases steadily.

present value: The amount that some future value is worth now given an investment's interest rate and regular deposits.

primary key: In sorting, the field first used to sort records. *See also secondary key; sort;* and, if you're really interested, *tertiary key.*

probability distribution: A chart that plots probabilities. *See also normal distribution; uniform distribution.*

probability distribution function: An equation that describes the line of the probability distribution. *See also probability distribution.*

query: A database feature that specifies how you want to extract, sort, and filter data to use in a worksheet.

Query Wizard: A tool that comes with Excel and enables you to query a database and then place the results into an Excel workbook.

R²: *See* *coefficient of determination.*

rank: The position of an item in a data set relative to the other items. *See also* *percentile.*

raw data: Data that has not been manipulated or analyzed in any way.

record: A collection of related fields in a table. In Excel, each record goes into a separate row.

refreshing pivot data: Updating the information shown in a PivotTable or pivot chart to reflect changes in the underlying data. You can click the Refresh data tool provided by the PivotTable toolbar button to refresh.

regression analysis: Plotting pairs of independent and dependent variables in an XY chart and then finding a linear or exponential equation that best describes the plotted data.

regression equation: A mathematical equation that specifies the exact relationship between the dependent variable and the independent variable.

relational database: Essentially, a collection of tables or lists. *See also* *table; list.*

relative reference: A cell reference used in a formula that Excel adjusts if you copy the formula to a new cell location. *See also* *absolute reference.*

running total: The cumulative sum of the values that appear in a given set of data.

sample: A collection of observations from a population.

scatter plot: An XY chart that visually compares pairs of values. A scatter plot is often a good first step when you want to perform regression analysis. *See also* *regression analysis.*

scenario: A data-analysis technique that stores multiple input values for a worksheet model and enables you to apply those values quickly.

secondary key: In sorting, the second field used to sort records. The secondary key comes into play only when the primary keys of records have the same value. *See also* *primary key; sort.*

skewness: A measure of the symmetry of a distribution of values. *See also* *kurtosis.*

solve order: The order in which calculated item formulas should be solved. *See also* *calculated item.*

Solver: An Excel add-in with which you perform optimization modeling. *See also* *optimization modeling.*

Solver variables: The variables in an optimization modeling problem. *See* *optimization modeling.*

sort: To arrange list records in some particular order, such as alphabetically by last name. Excel includes easy-to-use tools for doing this, by the way.

standard deviation: Describes dispersion about the data set's mean. You can think of a standard deviation as an average deviation from the mean. ***See also*** *average; variance.*

summary calculation: The calculation that Excel uses to populate the PivotTable data area.

table: A collection of related data stored in a row-and-column format, where each row represents a single item of data and each column represents a single type or category of data.

tertiary key: In sorting, the third field used to sort records. The tertiary key comes into play only when the primary and secondary keys of records have the same value. ***See also*** *primary key; secondary key; sort.*

text file: A file that's all text. Many programs export text files, by the way, because other programs (including Excel) often easily import text files.

text functions: Used to manipulate text strings in ways that enable you to easily rearrange and manipulate the data that you import into an Excel workbook. Typically, these babies are extremely useful tools for scrubbing or cleaning the data that you want to analyze later.

text labels: Includes letters and numbers that you enter into worksheet cells but that you don't want to use in calculations. For example, your name, a budget expense description, and a telephone number are all examples of text labels. None of these pieces of information gets used in calculations.

top/bottom rule: A conditional formatting rule in which Excel applies a conditional format to those items that are at the top or bottom of a range of values.

trend analysis: Data analysis that identifies the overall direction over time of the values in a data set.

trendline: A line through a chart's data points that visualizes the overall trend of the data.

two-input data table: A data table that varies two of the formula's input cells.

uniform distribution: Having the same probability of occurrence in every event. One common probability distribution function is a uniform distribution.

value: Some bit of data that you enter into a workbook cell and may want to later use in a calculation. For example, the actual amount that you budget for some expense would always be a number or value. ***See also*** *formulas; text labels; workbook.*

variance: Describes dispersion about the data set's mean. The variance is the square of the standard deviation. ***See also*** *average; standard deviation.*

web query: Grabbing data from a table that's stored in a web page. Excel provides a very slick tool for doing this, by the way.

weighted average: A version of the average calculation that takes into account the relative importance of each value in a data set.

what-if analysis: A worksheet data model designed to help you analyze hypothetical scenarios.

x-values: The independent values in a regression analysis.

XML: Extensible Markup Language, a standard that enables the management and sharing of structured data using simple text files.

y-intercept: In a trend line, the value of *y* at the point where the trend line crosses the y-axis.

y-values: The dependent values in a regression analysis.

z-value: In statistics, describes the distance between a value and the mean in terms of standard deviations. (How often does one get to include a legitimate *Z* entry in a glossary! Not often, but here I do.) *See also average; standard deviation.*

Index

GRG Nonlinear, 48

grouped frequency distributions, creating, 232–233

grouping
  date values, 148
  numeric values, 147–148
  PivotTable values, 147–149
  related data, 24–26
  text values, 148–149
  time values, 148

Grouping dialog box, 147–148

GROWTH function, 211–213

H

header row, 312

headers, 55

highlighting
  cells, 10–11
  cells based on formulas, 19–20
  top/bottom values in ranges, 13–14

histogram, 250, 312

Histogram dialog box, 251–252

I

icon sets
  analyzing cell values with, 16–17
  defined, 312

icons, explained, 3–4

IF function, 19

Import Data dialog box, 78, 81, 82, 86, 94

importing. *See also* exporting
  data from Access tables, 78–79
  data from web pages, 83–85
  data from Word tables, 79–80
  defined, 312
  delimited text files, 81–82
  external data, 78–87
  fixed-width text files, 82–83
  text files, 80
  XML files, 85–87

independent variable, 312

Index calculation, 164–166

index summary calculations, 164–166

indicators icon sets, 17

inferences, 237

inferential statistics
  about, 237, 253
  calculating correlation, 264–265
  calculating covariance, 265–266
  defined, 312
  determining regression, 261–263
  performing f-tests, 268–269
  performing z-tests, 259–261
  sampling data, 254–256
  tips for, 277–278
  using ANOVA tools, 267–268
  using t-test tools, 256–259

inner field, 158

input range, 250

Insert Calculated Field dialog box, 171–172, 175, 176

Insert Calculated Item dialog box, 173–174, 175, 176

Insert Chart dialog box, 182, 189

Insert Slicers dialog box, 153

inserting
  columns in Excel tables, 58
  fields for custom calculations, 171–172
  items for custom calculations, 173–174
  rows in Excel tables, 58

interest, calculating, 289

internal rate of return, determining, 291

Internet resources
  book updates, 4
  Cheat Sheet, 4
  sample workbooks, 4

interval, of moving average, 243

IPMT function, 289

IRR function, 291

iterations, 37, 313

values. *See also* formulas; text labels; workbooks
- defined, 316
- duplicate, 12
- filtering in PivotTables, 149–154
- grouping in PivotTables, 147–149
- PivotTable, 306–307
- retrieving from tables, 121–122
- samples as subsets of, 276–277

Var calculation, 157
VAR function, 130
VARA function, 130
variable cells, 44
variance. *See also* average; standard deviation
- calculating, 233–234
- defined, 316

Varp calculation, 157
VARP function, 130
VAR.P function, 233–234
VARPA function, 130
VAR.S function, 233–234

W

Warning icon, 4
Web API, 84
web pages
- as external data, 76
- importing data from, 83–85

web query, 316
websites
- book updates, 4
- Cheat Sheet, 4
- sample workbooks, 4

weighted average, 165, 316
what-if analysis. *See also* data tables
- defined, 317
- performing, 9

Word tables
- as external data, 76
- importing data from, 79–80

workbooks
- about, 97–98
- calculating, 36
- copying worksheet data, 101
- deleting cell contents, 100
- deleting columns, 98
- deleting range contents, 100
- deleting rows, 99
- editing, 97–102
- formatting numeric values, 100–101
- moving worksheet data, 101
- PivotTable, 306
- replacing data in fields, 102
- resizing columns, 99
- resizing rows, 99–100
- sample, 4

worksheets
- consolidating data from multiple, 26–29
- copying data, 101
- grouping, 24–26
- moving data, 101
- moving PivotCharts to other, 185–186

X

XML files
- defined, 317
- as external data, 76
- importing, 85–87

x-values, 317

Y

y-intercept, 317
y-values, 317

Z

z-Test: Two Sample for Means dialog box, 259–260
z-tests, performing, 259–261
z-value, 317. *See also* average; standard deviation

Author Bio

Paul McFedries is the president of Logophilia Limited, a technical writing company, and has worked with computers large and small since 1975. While now primarily a writer, Paul has worked as a programmer, consultant, database developer, and website developer. Paul has written more than 90 books that have sold over four million copies worldwide. Paul is also the proprietor of Word Spy (wordspy.com), a website that has been tracking recently coined words and phrases since 1995. Paul invites everyone to drop by his personal website at mcfedries.com, or to follow him on Twitter (@paulmcf and @wordspy).

Dedication

To Karen and Chase, who make life fun.

Acknowledgements

If we're ever at the same cocktail party and you overhear me saying something like "I wrote a book," I hereby give you permission to wag your finger at me and say "Tsk, tsk." Why the scolding? Because although I did write this book's text and take its screenshots, those represent only a part of what constitutes a book. The rest of it is brought to you by the dedication and professionalism of Wiley's editing, graphics, and production teams, who toiled long and hard to turn my text and images into an actual book.

I offer my heartfelt thanks to everyone at Wiley who made this book possible, but I'd like to extend some special thank-yous to the folks I worked with directly: Executive Editor Steve Hayes, Project Manager and Copy Editor Susan Christophersen, and Technical Editor Guy Hart-Davies. I'd also like to give a big shout-out to my agent, Carole Jelen, for helping to make this project possible.

Publisher's Acknowledgments

Executive Editor: Steve Hayes

Project Manager and Copy Editor: Susan Christophersen

Technical Editor: Russ Mullen

Sr. Editorial Assistant: Cherie Case

Production Editor: Magesh Elangovan

Cover Image: © brijith vijayan / iStockphoto